Mobile Marketing

FOR

DUMMIES®

by Michael Becker and John Arnold

D1402506

WILEY

Wiley Publishing, Inc.

Mobile Marketing For Dummies®

Published by
Wiley Publishing, Inc.
111 River Street
Hoboken, NJ 07030-5774

www.wiley.com

Copyright © 2010 by Wiley Publishing, Inc., Indianapolis, Indiana

Published by Wiley Publishing, Inc., Indianapolis, Indiana

Published simultaneously in Canada

No part of this publication may be reproduced, stored in a retrieval system or transmitted in any form or by any means, electronic, mechanical, photocopying, recording, scanning or otherwise, except as permitted under Sections 107 or 108 of the 1976 United States Copyright Act, without either the prior written permission of the Publisher, or authorization through payment of the appropriate per-copy fee to the Copyright Clearance Center, 222 Rosewood Drive, Danvers, MA 01923, (978) 750-8400, fax (978) 646-8600. Requests to the Publisher for permission should be addressed to the Permissions Department, John Wiley & Sons, Inc., 111 River Street, Hoboken, NJ 07030, (201) 748-6011, fax (201) 748-6008, or online at http:// www.wiley.com/go/permissions.

Trademarks: Wiley, the Wiley Publishing logo, For Dummies, the Dummies Man logo, A Reference for the Rest of Us!, The Dummies Way, Dummies Daily, The Fun and Easy Way, Dummies.com, Making Everything Easier, and related trade dress are trademarks or registered trademarks of John Wiley & Sons, Inc. and/ or its affiliates in the United States and other countries, and may not be used without written permission. All other trademarks are the property of their respective owners. Wiley Publishing, Inc., is not associated with any product or vendor mentioned in this book.

For general information on our other products and services, please contact our Customer Care Department within the U.S. at 877-762-2974, outside the U.S. at 317-572-3993, or fax 317-572-4002.

For technical support, please visit www.wiley.com/techsupport.

Wiley also publishes its books in a variety of electronic formats. Some content that appears in print may not be available in electronic books.

Library of Congress Control Number: 2010935570

ISBN: 978-0-470-61668-0

Manufactured in the United States of America

10 9 8 7 6 5 4 3 2 1

WILEY

About the Authors

Michael Becker is the North American managing director for the Mobile Marketing Association and a leader in the mobile marketing industry, assuming the roles of industry entrepreneur, volunteer, and academic. He is also the founder and vice president of strategy at iLoop Mobile, an industry-leading mobile marketing solutions provider.

Michael served on the MMA Global Board of Directors (2008, director at large; 2009, global board vice chair) and served on the MMA North American board of directors (2004, 2005, 2007, 2008, and 2009). He founded and co-chaired both the award-winning MMA Academic Outreach Committee and the *MMA International Journal of Mobile Marketing*. He is also a member of the Direct Marketing Association's annual programming advisory and mobile councils.

In addition to his industry and volunteer roles, Michael is a contributing author to *Mobile Internet For Dummies*, *Social Media Marketing For Dummies*, *Reinventing Interactive and Direct Marketing*, is a co-author of *Web Marketing All-in-One Desk Reference For Dummies*, and this book, *Mobile Marketing For Dummies*. He has authored more than 60 articles on mobile marketing and is an accomplished public speaker on the topic.

In his spare time, Michael is pursuing his doctorate on the topic of mobile-enhanced customer managed interactions and vendor relationship management at Golden Gate University. Michael was awarded the MMA Individual Achievement Award in 2007 and the Direct Marketing Educational Foundation Rising Stars Award in 2009 for contributions to the mobile and direct marketing industries.

John Arnold is a leading marketing expert, author, and speaker specializing in marketing advice for small businesses, franchises, associations, and organizations. John writes the "Marketing Tools & Technologies" column for *Entrepreneur Magazine* and he is the author of several marketing books, including *Web Marketing All-in-One Desk Reference For Dummies*, *E-Mail Marketing For Dummies*, and this book, *Mobile Marketing For Dummies*.

John is also a highly regarded marketing technology trainer who knows how to deliver solid takeaways that people can implement in their business or organization right away. His no-hype and highly practical approach cuts through the clutter as he explains the most useful marketing strategies, technologies, and tactics with clarity, artful simplicity, and meaningful application.

To inquire about John being a marketing speaker, trainer, or consultant for your small business, franchise, association, or organization, visit www.johnarnold.com.

Dedication

Michael Becker: I dedicate this book to my family. They keep me focused on what is important. I also dedicate it to all those looking to establish and nurture a flourishing, intimate, and integrative relationship through and with the new and exciting medium of mobile.

John Arnold: I dedicate this book to the individual entrepreneurs who love the spirit of free enterprise and who live to share their personal passions with their customers and their communities, and to the One who causes all things to work together for good.

Authors' Acknowledgments

Michael Becker: I would first like to thank my family. Their encouragement and support as I pursue my dreams is invaluable to me.

I would also like to thank John Arnold. Without John's encouragement, focus, expertise, direct contributions, time management and editing skills, this book would have never seen the light of day. John is simply amazing.

Thanks to the outstanding team at Wiley Publishing, including Steve Hayes, Leah Cameron, and Linda Morris, and to Jennifer Hatherley for filling the role of technical editor for the manuscript.

Finally, I send thanks to everyone at iLoop Mobile, the Mobile Marketing Association, the Direct Marketing Association, the Internet Advertising Bureau, my partners and competitors, and all my colleagues within the mobile marketing industry. Your encouragement, support, and fellowship contributes to the advancement of this wonderful industry — mobile marketing.

John Arnold would first like to thank my wife and kids for encouraging me while working on multiple projects at a time. You guys are the best family anyone could hope for.

Next, I would like to thank Michael Becker for his passion for mobile marketing and for sharing his knowledge not only in this book, but in the hundreds of speaking engagements, consultations, meetings, articles, whitepapers, text books, and conversations he contributes to annually.

Thanks to Matt Wagner for running an ideal literary agency. None of my books would have been possible without his experience and guidance.

Special thanks to the super team of professionals at Wiley Publishing. I'd like to thank Steve Hayes for his patience in dealing with contracts. I would also like to thank Leah Cameron and Linda Morris for editing the manuscript, asking tough questions, and for patiently understanding our definition of the word *deadline*. Thanks also to our technical editor, Jennifer Hatherley.

Contributing Authors

When we started this project, we decided early on that no book about mobile marketing should be written by a single author because too many things are rapidly changing and emerging for one person to know everything.

To complete this book, we relied on the contributions of numerous leaders in the marketing industry. Each of them has shared their unique prospective and personal mobile marketing expertise.

The following contributors were instrumental in the development and authority of the material in this book. Our thanks and admiration goes out to each of them because they added a great deal of experience and value to the pages by writing and submitting many ideas, examples, and details that we may have otherwise overlooked. They are listed in alphabetical order.

Douglas Busk, executive vice president, mobile strategy and business development, Whoop: Doug holds more than a decade of mobile marketing and product development expertise. From leading text messaging at Verizon Wireless to advising the 2008 Barack Obama presidential campaign on its landmark mobile marketing efforts, if it can be done in wireless, Doug has done it. A dedicated proponent of not only the industry's powerful marketing capabilities, but its charitable possibilities as well, Doug helped lead the industry in the creation of non-profit giving via text messaging to benefit those impacted by Hurricane Katrina. In his "free" time, Doug has been an active participant in multiple industry groups, including the Mobile Marketing Association, dotMOBI, CTIA, and others. He is currently based in Atlanta, where he leads business development and mobile strategy for Whoop (www.whoop.com), which supplies a design platform for the creation of smartphone applications.

James Citron, president and CEO of Mogreet: James is the visionary behind the mobile industry's leading platform for the delivery of mobile video. When he isn't waxing poetic about mobile video, MMS, or the iPad, James is running one of the leading mobile marketing companies in the country. James has spent the last 10 years in the mobile industry, as both an analyst advising on telecommunications mergers and acquisitions and as an operator launching mobile products and businesses in more than twenty countries. Mr. Citron is a graduate of Princeton University. His Twitter name is @jamescitron.

Ben Gaddis, director, mobile and emerging media, T3: Ben Gaddis is director of mobile and emerging media strategy at T3, where he leads the agency's mobile offering and develops emerging applications and media strategies for T3's clients. With almost ten years of experience focused on technology in advertising, Ben has developed mobile strategies and programs for AT&T, Frito-Lay, Nokia, and American Airlines.

Eric Holmen, senior vice president, business development and marketing, The Marketing Arm, Wireless Practice: Eric lost, destroyed, or wore out more mobile phones last year than most of us will ever own. While president of the mobile marketing company SmartReply, he acquired a mobile ad network and launched a mobile payment system for retail, while building one of the largest mobile marketing companies in North America. At The Marketing Arm, Eric brings a big vision of mobile as the new reality of multi-channel marketing and advertising for the Fortune 100 set. "This kind of job means you gotta know your devices, carriers, benefits, and potential, which means carrying around a lot of mobile devices." His pedigree includes Catalina Marketing and Sears, and is a grad of M.I.T. and the University of Redlands. He has three unwired kids and an Ironman wife. On weekends, you'll find him busily dropping phones over the side of his sailboat into the Pacific waters off southern California (where he peacefully gets zero bars).

Gabe Karp, executive vice president and general counsel of ePrize, LLC: Gabe oversees the legal services, fulfillment, and human resources teams at ePrize. He has overseen more than 5,000 interactive promotional campaigns in 36 countries with no legal challenges. These campaigns include online and mobile-based loyalty programs, prize drawings, instant win games, skill based contests, and so on. Gabe is a respected authority and frequent speaker and writer on legal issues surrounding interactive promotions, including mobile marketing, user-generated content, social networking, and emerging technologies. He assisted in revising Puerto Rico's sweepstakes regulations adopted in 2009, has consulted the Federal Trade Commission regarding CAN-SPAM regulations, and helped legislators and regulators from several states draft and enforce legislation in those jurisdictions applicable to the interactive promotion industry.

Jeannette Kocsis, senior vice president of digital marketing for Harte-Hanks, Inc.: Jeannette is a digital marketing expert, having started with search engine optimization in 1997, owned and operated an e-commerce site, and, in 1999, owned a community Web site with more than 100,000 regular monthly visitors. Today, Jeannette is senior vice president of digital marketing for Harte-Hanks, Inc. Working at the Agency Inside Harte-Hanks, she oversees strategy and media across all vertical markets and is responsible for bringing new trends like mobile and social into client strategies. Jeannette is a frequent speaker on mobile and social media, and she is published on a regular basis. Jeannette was named to the Mobile Women to Watch for 2010 list by *Mobile Marketer*. At the time of this writing, Jeannette has a variety of mobile devices, including an iPhone, an iTouch, and a Blackberry (for work). Jeannette lives in the Hudson Valley of New York State, with her family and their Great Dane.

Christian Loredo, mobile guru: Christian eats, sleeps, and breathes mobile! He has had experience with both large companies and small, wireless carriers and startups. Christian enjoys watching the mobile world develop and advance, helping companies mobilize their mission statements, and trying to stay a couple steps ahead of consumer experiences for enhancing their interactions with mobile devices, applications, and brands. Christian also is passionate about extreme sports and is an expert snowboarder, mountain biker, and is amped about his latest sport, kite-surfing! His dream is to go heli-skiing, and show all his friends (especially those who couldn't make it!) how incredible it is . . . as they're all dialed in via mobile! Text CML to 44265 for his personal contact info.

Erin (Mack) McKelvey, senior vice president of marketing, Millennial Media: Erin (Mack) McKelvey leads all areas of Millennial Media's corporate and product marketing, external communications, and industry relations. She also serves as the company spokesperson. Mack has more than thirteen years of business-to-business and consumer marketing and communications experience in the entertainment and mobile industries. She is an active member of the Mobile Advertising and the Women in Wireless Committees within the Mobile Marketing Association (MMA), and is an active member of the Mobile Advertising and the Networks and Exchanges Committees within the Interactive Advertising Bureau (IAB). Mack is a frequent industry speaker, and she was recently named one of the 2010 Mobile Women to Watch, by *Mobile Marketer*. She has also served as an awards judge and as an advisory board member to numerous industry conferences and events.

Kerry Nagle, vice president of campaign operations, Millennial Media: Kerry Nagle joined Millennial Media as one of its founding members. With an extensive background in advertising, including online, remarketing, and performance analysis, she leads the advertiser and publisher-side analytics and process teams. Kerry is responsible for delivering a large number of key company priorities including campaign execution, ROI maximization, and inventory monetization. She has been integral in executing first-to-market products, determining the viability of new products and their relevance to the mobile marketplace and advertisers. Currently, Kerry is an active member of the IAB and MMA. Driving best practices, Kerry is committed to sustaining innovation through Millennial Media and the mobile advertising industry.

Jeffrey J Russell, mobile product manager: Jeff loves to create and deliver mobile products for the U.S. and emerging markets. Many of these products are mature consumer and mobile platform products for large U.S. and international companies such as Microsoft, Apple, VeriSign, Sprint, Verizon Wireless, Vodaphone, and AT&T. Some of the more interesting products have been off-beat. Jeff created mobile product that used Japanese-style anime to teach Japanese/urban English. The concept and artwork was put on display at the Visionarium in Santa Maria da Feira, Portugal. In Cebu, Philippines, he created a three-screen social network product tying a commercial Web site, mobile voting, and television programming together. Jeff's life goal list is still huge and it includes ice diving under the Antarctica ice shelf, traversing the length of the Congo, and climbing some flat-topped mountains in Venezuela. Jeff continues to pull life and mobile inspiration from his son, Greyson.

Publisher's Acknowledgments

We're proud of this book; please send us your comments at http://dummies.custhelp.com. For other comments, please contact our Customer Care Department within the U.S. at 877-762-2974, outside the U.S. at 317-572-3993, or fax 317-572-4002.

Some of the people who helped bring this book to market include the following:

Acquisitions and Editorial

Project Editor: Linda Morris

Acquisitions Editor: Steven Hayes

Copy Editor: Linda Morris

Technical Editor: Jennifer Hatherley

Editorial Manager: Jodi Jensen

Editorial Assistant: Amanda Graham

Sr. Editorial Assistant: Cherie Case

Cartoons: Rich Tennant
(www.the5thwave.com)

Composition Services

Project Coordinator: Katherine Crocker

Layout and Graphics: Kelly Kijovsky, Christine Williams

Proofreaders: Melissa Cossell, Penny Stuart

Indexer: Ty Koontz

Publishing and Editorial for Technology Dummies

    Richard Swadley, Vice President and Executive Group Publisher

    Andy Cummings, Vice President and Publisher

    Mary Bednarek, Executive Acquisitions Director

    Mary C. Corder, Editorial Director

Publishing for Consumer Dummies

    Diane Graves Steele, Vice President and Publisher

Composition Services

    Debbie Stailey, Director of Composition Services

Contents at a Glance

Table of Contents

Part II: Executing Direct Mobile Marketing Campaigns... 77

Chapter 4: Getting Ready for a Text Messaging Campaign 79

Chapter 5: Executing Common Text Messaging Campaigns 105

Introduction

Marketers are always looking to make their communications more personal, more targeted, and more relevant. Mobile is arguably the most personal, targeted, and relevant marketing channel available.

Mobile devices provide individuals with almost instant access to friends and family, location-based information, productivity tools, entertainment, and all the benefits of accessing the Internet from almost anywhere. If you're responsible for marketing a business or organization, making sure your marketing campaigns find their way on to mobile devices is one of the most important jobs you have.

This book shows you how to create and run engaging mobile marketing campaigns using today's mobile technology. We explain the opportunities and strategies you need to reach mobile consumers and get them to engage. We show you how to deliver mobile messages including SMS, MMS, and mobile e-mail.

Because your prospects and customers have to opt in for you to deliver mobile messages to them, this book explains how to build a quality mobile opt-in list full of subscribers who reward your mobile marketing efforts. We also show you how to create great mobile Internet sites, mobile applications, advertising campaigns, and social media interactions.

This book also shows you how to take advantage of voice by creating voice campaigns and how to enable your customers to make purchases on their phones through mobile commerce and point-of-sale campaigns.

Mobile marketers are subject to many legal requirements and industry guidelines, and many mobile marketing campaigns require carrier approval. This book shows you how to adhere to professional standards, follow the rules, and get through the processes involved in setting up your campaigns.

Mobile marketing has the ability to provide you with all kinds of great data on your customers and prospects, including their location data, so we include tips and ideas for using mobile tracking reports and analytics to improve your strategy and increase your sales.

Mobile technology is emerging and developing all the time, and new ways of marketing are adapting all the time too. The best time to start marketing through the mobile channel is today. Get ready, get set, go for it!

About This Book

Mobile Marketing For Dummies is written to answer your questions about mobile marketing and to give you tips and ideas for executing the various steps involved in a successful mobile marketing campaign.

This book isn't written to impress technically savvy pocket-protector types. It's for marketers and business owners who have to make the most of every minute of every day. We include lots of bulleted text with concise descriptions and ideas for implementing each topic immediately.

The content in each chapter stands alone, so you don't have to read all the chapters in order. You can use this book like an entire series of books on the subject of mobile marketing. You can scan through the Table of Contents and read about a single topic to refresh your memory or to get a few ideas before beginning a task, or you can read an entire chapter or a series of chapters to gain understanding and gather ideas for executing one or more parts of an entire mobile marketing campaign.

Sidebars are included in this book as interesting additional tidbits or to give anecdotal examples of the tips and ideas in the book. You don't have to read them to benefit from this book.

Conventions Used in This Book

To make this book easier to scan and internalize, we use the following conventions:

- ✔ Words in *italics* are used to point out industry terminology or words that have special definitions in the book.

- ✔ Words in **bold** represent the keyword or the main idea in bulleted lists.

- ✔ Web addresses and snippets of programming code appear in a different font, as in www.MobileMarketingForDummies.com.

- ✔ Placeholder text in code is in italic, as in <a href="http://www.*yourwebsite*.com/page.html#anchorname>, where *yourwebsite* should be replaced with the actual name of your Web site.

Foolish Assumptions

It's hard to imagine that anyone has managed to stay completely away from mobile phones. However, to get the most out of this book, we assume that you already

- ✔ Are familiar with the basic functions of a mobile phone
- ✔ Are responsible for (or are soon to be responsible for) marketing in a business or an organization
- ✔ Know how to use a computer and a mouse
- ✔ Have a Web site or a physical location (or you soon will)
- ✔ Have a product or service that people need or have an idea for a product or service that people need

How This Book Is Organized

Mobile Marketing For Dummies is divided into five parts according to the different types of mobile marketing campaigns you can create and deploy.

Part 1: Getting Up to Speed on Mobile Marketing

Part I explains where mobile marketing fits into a marketing mix and describes the benefits and limitations of mobile devices as marketing tools. We give you insight into the consumer landscape including tips for understanding laws and industry regulations as well as advice for developing a mobile marketing strategy and choosing partners to help you execute on your plans.

Part II: Executing Direct Mobile Marketing Campaigns

Part II helps you to build a solid foundation for sending text messages, multimedia messages, and mobile e-mails. We show you how to obtain a common short code, gain opt-in subscribers to your messaging campaigns, and promote your business with messages. We explain how to set up a variety of campaigns and tips for designing e-mails for mobile screens.

Part III: Mobile Media, Publishing, and Advertising

Part III explains how to go about building mobile Internet sites, mobile applications, and advertising campaigns. Part III also shows you the power of mobile when applied to social media and voice campaigns. We tell you how to use layout and design elements to make your mobile sites effective on mobile devices and we show you how to develop and distribute mobile applications. We explain how to make money through mobile advertising and the importance of making your social media content accessible on mobile devices. Part III also shows you how to enable marketing campaigns using a mobile phone's most used and yet often overlooked feature — voice. After all, it's still a phone, no matter how many other bells and whistles it has!

Part IV: Mobile Commerce and Analytics

Part IV is where your mobile marketing strategy finds an enduring future. We explain how to enable monetary transactions through mobile devices such as mobile Internet purchases, point-of-sale scanners, and mobile wallets. We also show you how to use mobile marketing analytics to track your campaigns and determine whether your strategy is working.

Part V: The Part of Tens

In Part V, we include two chapters that list ten important bite-sized summaries of mobile marketing information. The first list contains ten ways to reach consumers on mobile devices today. The second list covers ten mobile marketing resources you should become familiar with so your mobile marketing can advance and grow, along with new advancements in technology and industry best practices. In addition, we include a Glossary to collect the definitions of mobile marketing terms into one convenient resource.

Icons Used in This Book

When you are scanning through the contents of this book looking for tips, reminders, and ideas, you can look for the following icons in the margin to help you find important information fast:

This icon signifies a tip, idea, shortcut, or strategy that can save you time or trouble.

 This icon signifies information that you should remember and file away in your brain for later reference.

 This icon signifies important details that might cause your strategy to stumble or come to a halt if left unaddressed.

 This icon signifies information that is technical in nature. It's for geeks only, and you can skip it if you don't fit that description.

Where to Go from Here

If you aren't familiar with mobile marketing or if you don't know a lot about mobile devices, you might want to start with Part I and read each chapter in order. If you are an experienced and tech-savvy marketer with a good idea of which direction you want to take your mobile marketing, you can scan through each part's Table of Contents and read the chapters or topics in any order.

Either way, it's time to get started with building your business and deepening your customer interactions with mobile marketing!

Part I

Getting Up to Speed on Mobile Marketing

The 5th Wave   By Rich Tennant

"This model comes with a particularly useful function – a simulated static button for breaking out of long winded conversations."

In this part . . .

Almost everything you can do with traditional marketing can be adapted to work on mobile devices. However, marketing through mobile channels isn't always simple. Mobile device standards and best practices are still emerging and consumer behavior and laws are rapidly shifting. Adapting your marketing for mobile is an ongoing task.

Chapter 1 gives you an overview of mobile marketing so that you see the big picture and can identify the possibilities of mobile marketing. This chapter also allows you to easily skip to the other parts of this book that deal with topics in more detail.

Chapter 2 helps you come up with your mobile marketing strategy and shows you how to estimate your mobile marketing reach so you can approach mobile marketing with goal achievement in mind.

Chapter 3 covers the laws, industry regulations, and best practices you need to know in order to keep your mobile marketing campaigns compliant and consumer-friendly.

Chapter 1

Unveiling the Possibilities of Mobile Marketing

In This Chapter

▶ Discovering mobile marketing and its key elements

▶ Exploring the myriad of mobile devices and networks

▶ Finding out about the three forms of mobile marketing

▶ Reviewing the many capabilities of mobile devices

*W*e've become a mobile society, worldwide. People around the world are on the go, and nearly everyone has a mobile phone or a mobile device of some kind to help them connect with people, information, and businesses from anywhere. Sure, people are still making and receiving phone calls with their mobile phones, but increasingly, they're also texting, searching the Web, downloading applications, consuming content, responding to ads, spending money, and generating value for themselves and marketers, not just with phones but a wide range of devices as explained below.

The mobile device is increasingly becoming a cornerstone of our mobilized society. In fact, for many people around the globe, a mobile device has become their primary communication and commerce tool. Whenever our world changes, so must the practice of marketing. This book is all about showing you how to embrace this change. We show you how to embrace the emerging practice of mobile marketing and engage your customers through and with the mobile devices they use.

In this chapter, we get you started. We provide you with a detailed definition of mobile marketing and review its key elements. And because the mobile device is the cornerstone of any mobile marketing practice, we review in detail the three categories of mobile devices, the networks that enable them, and the eight mobile media paths that are the backbone of mobile marketing. When you're done reading this chapter, you'll have the foundation you need to understand everything else you find in this book.

Marketers are gravitating to mobile

In June 2010, the Mobile Marketing Association (www.mmaglobal.com), along with *Chief Marketer, Advertising Database Express,* and Kinesis Survey Technologies released a study titled, "Second Annual View from Madison Avenue." According to this study, total U.S. media in 2010 expenditures (the money that marketers allocate to engage their customers through media channels like television, radio, newspapers, outdoor signage and other media channels including mobile) will total about $128 billion. The MMA report estimates that mobile media will account for 1.8%, or $2.3 billion, of this total spending. By 2011, the MMA report estimates that total mobile media spending in the U.S. will grow to $5.5 billion, or 4.0% of the $135 billion that will be spent on media in the U.S. This is a 124% increase! Remember, these are just the U.S. media numbers. Mobile marketing is growing all over the world in every market sector. Moreover, as you find through the rest of this book, mobile marketing is not just about media spending but also about engaging your audience in all sorts of ways to deliver value. The impact of mobile marketing is simply staggering.

Defining Mobile Marketing

Mobile marketing, according to the Mobile Marketing Association (www.mmaglobal.com), is "a set of practices that enable organizations to communicate and engage with their audience in an interactive and relevant manner through any mobile device or network." That definition contains just 26 words, but it packs in a lot of meaningful terminology.

In the following sections, and through this entire book, we discuss what these 26 words really mean and how they can be used to engage your customer in a manner that generates meaningful results that are mutually beneficial for both you, your business, your customers, and potential customers — essentially, everyone!

Examining the five elements of mobile marketing

Take a look at that definition again and then check out the following bullet points, which pull out and refine the five key elements of the definition of mobile marketing:

✔ **Organizations:** Organizations are commercial entities — brands, agencies, marketers, non-profits, enterprises (including individuals), and so on — with products, services, and offerings they wish to deliver to the market. In other words, organizations are you and your companies. Mobile marketing works for any type of business.

✔ **Practices:** Practices consist of the many faces and facets of marketing activities, institutional processes, industry player partnerships, standards making, advertising and media placing and buying, direct response managing, promotional engagements, relationship management, customer services, loyalty management, and social media stewardship. In other words, *practices* include all the things that you want to oversee and do to engage your customers. All types of marketing practices can be applied to mobile marketing.

✔ **Engagement:** This is the process by which you and your customers interact in a two-way (push and pull) dialogue to build awareness, conduct transactions, support, and nurture each other. Mobile marketing is one of the most engaging forms of marketing because it's done through and with such a personal device.

✔ **Relevancy:** Mobile interactions can provide information (for example, a user's location, the time of day, activity, and so on). You can use this information to understand the context of your customer's current environment in order to tailor and to create an appropriate experience that is closely linked (dare I say relevant) to his current context. For example, if someone in New York is doing a search on the mobile Internet for pizza, you want to show them listings for pizza shops nearby and not send them to Lima, Ohio, to get their pizza. Mobile marketing is highly relevant.

✔ **Mobile devices and networks:** These terms refer to any wireless-enabled device regardless of form factor or network. Although certain types of devices have their limitations, you can execute some type of marketing campaign on every type of mobile device.

Identifying mobile consumers

Take a moment to think about the impact that the Internet and the personal computer have had on our society and the world. Yet, as of this writing only 25% of the global population uses the Internet, and there are only about 1 billion personal computers.

Now consider the potential impact of mobile devices. Worldwide, 4.6 billion people subscribe to mobile services, and that number will likely increase to 5.5 billion by the end of 2010. Given that there are 6.8 billion people around the world, we're talking about nearly everyone on the planet. (About 2 billion or so people still don't have a mobile device, but you can sure do a lot of marketing with the other 5 billion!)

In the United States, comScore (www.comscore.com) reports that around 234 million people subscribe to mobile phone services. In fact, the mobile phone is becoming their primary phone. According to the Centers for Disease Control, nearly 25% of the U.S. population has shut off their landline phones and are mobile-only. (Another 15% of the U.S. has a landline phone, but really don't use it.) In addition, many of these people have multiple mobile devices. There are more than 280 million mobile subscriptions in the U.S. (including wireless cards for computers, e-readers, and so on).

The reach of the mobile device is staggering. Nearly everyone on the planet can be engaged with a mobile device. In developing countries, it may be the only way to engage someone digitally.

Your customer is mobile and you should be too. Consumers send trillions of text messages around the world each year, view and download billions of mobile Web pages and applications, and increasingly use their mobile devices not just for personal communication, but also for leisure, entertainment, work, and shopping.

A number of factors play a role in a consumer effectively responding to mobile programs, including her age, gender, ethnicity, location, the type of phone or mobile device she has, her employment levels, education, and more. We can't go into all the details here, but take it from us: mobile media is not a channel just for the youth of the world; nearly everyone is using one or more of the various mobile media paths discussed throughout this book in one way, shape, or form. In fact, according to a Microsoft Advertising Mobile Consumer Usage study, the mobile device is the third-most-used media, coming just behind television and computers.

Exploring the types of mobile devices

When most people think about mobile marketing, the first thing that comes to their mind is a mobile phone. It's easy to look at a mobile phone and think, "It's just a phone," and minimize all the rich capabilities that today's mobile phones have. It's also easy to disregard the other mobile devices (like the Apple iPad or iTouch, PlayStation Portable game terminals, e-books, and GPS devices) that people carry with them as not being pertinent for mobile marketing.

The device in your hand isn't really just a phone anymore. Sure, you can make voice calls with it, but that function is just the tip of the iceberg. Today's mobile devices are also newspapers, maps, cameras, radios, stores, game consoles, video music players, calculators, calendars, address books, stereos, TVs, movie theaters, and concert halls.

For the purposes of mobile marketing, and the content of this book, you should be familiar with three categories of devices:

✓ **The feature phone:** The feature phone (see Figure 1-1) is the most common phone out in the market. As of June 2010, about 75% of the phones carried in the U.S. are feature phones. These phones run a real-time operating system (RTOS), which is a *closed operating system* — one in which you can't make modifications such as adding functionality to a mobile browser or changing the user experience on the phone. There are two common RTOSs: a home-grown Nucleus OS created by the mobile phone's manufacturer, and Qualcomm's Brew (which is predominantly used by Verizon Wireless in the United States). Understanding the capability of the feature phone is important to you because it means you will be limited to engaging these consumers with SMS, MMS, voice, and limited mobile Internet.

✔ **The smartphone:** The smartphone (see Figure 1-2) is a mobile device that integrates mobile phone capabilities with the more common features typically associated with a personal computer, including Internet, applications, e-mail, entertainment, and rich media services. Moreover, smartphones increasingly include location, motion and related sensors, touchscreens, and full keyboards. Smartphones are categorized by the operating system they use. The top smartphone operating systems (OS) are the Apple iPhone, Google Android, Microsoft Windows Phone, Research in Motion BlackBerry, HP Palm, Samsung Baba, Nokia Symbian, and Linux-based operating systems such as the MeeGo, which is used in Nokia high-end phones. Smartphones account for approximately 25% of the U.S. market today. Nielsen expects that by the end of 2011, nearly 50% of consumers will be carrying a smartphone. More and more people will have smartphones and be able to surf the Internet, use e-mail, and download applications, but even by the end of 2011, a significant portion of consumers will still be carrying feature phones, so you'll want to cater to their needs and phone capabilities too.

Keep in mind that it's really easy to get caught up in the hype of a particular manufacturer's marketing. For example, for all the attention it attracts, the iPhone accounts for only 5% of the U.S. market. (See Table 1-1.)

Figure 1-1:
Feature phones are the most common type of phone today.

Figure 1-2:
Smart-
phones
represent
around
25% of the
market and
actually
have more
features
than feature
phones.

✔ **Connected device:** The connected device category is the industry catch-all term for all non-phone, mobile-enabled devices. In other words, it's a device that leverages mobile networks, but is primarily not a phone. This includes tablet computers (Apple iPad, Cisco Cius, HP Slate), e-readers (Amazon Kindle, Barnes and Noble Nook), portable gaming devices (PlayStation Portable), and so on.

Table 1-1	Smartphone Device Penetration in the United States (comScore, 2010)		
	Percentage of Smart Phone Market	*Percentage of Total Market*	*Users (in Millions)*
Research in Motion BlackBerry	42	8	9
Apple	25	5	11
Microsoft	15	3	7
Palm	5	1	2
Google	9	2	4

Throughout this book, we interchangeably use the terms *mobile phone, mobile device,* and *phone.* Keep in mind that we're covering all the device categories no matter what term we use.

Getting to know mobile networks: The basics

The basic premise of mobile marketing is that you're engaging the consumer over *mobile networks.* There are three basic mobile networks:

- ✔ **Mobile carrier network:** The mobile carrier network (also referred to as the operator network) consists of a series of radio towers (so-called *cell towers*) that transmit and receive radio signals that talk with a mobile device. All kinds of technologies and acronyms go into making all this work: CMDA, TDMA, GSM, LTE, EDGE, and so on, but you really don't need to know anything about these. You'll also hear terms like *2G, 3G,* and *4G,* with the higher numbers referring to faster data speeds over the network. A 4G network is pretty close to broadband Internet speeds over mobile carrier networks (for example, its speed enables things like real-time, interactive video conferencing and social media). Again, you don't need to know much about this, other than to understand that 4G is just starting to get released in the United States and only about 30%–40% of consumers use 3G now. Most consumers are on 2G. This means that a lot of 2G text messaging goes on with very little 4G real-time video streaming. This makes more sense when you read the rest of this book and understand all that you can do with mobile marketing.

- ✔ **Wi-Fi and WiMAX:** *Wi-Fi,* or wireless fidelity, more commonly referred to as a wireless local area network, is a wireless network powered by a small terminal connected to an Internet connection. You see them most often in homes, coffee shops, airports — actually, you see and hear about them all over the place. WiMAX is a Wi-Fi network on steroids. A WiMAX network is a Wi-Fi network that is broadcast over miles rather than a few hundred feet like Wi-Fi. Why should you care about this? Most new phones, that is, smartphones and connected devices, by definition can connect to Wi-Fi and WiMAX networks to access the Internet. In fact, if you try to download really large files, like applications or videos, on devices like the iPhone, the mobile carrier may require you to either switch to a Wi-Fi network or connect to a personal computer to download the content because they'd prefer to restrict these larger data files from being downloaded over the carrier network. A huge amount of mobile marketing (ad serving, application downloading, and mobile Internet browsing) happens over these networks.

- ✔ **Local frequency:** Finally, a number of low frequency channels can be used to exchange data and interact with the mobile device, like Bluetooth, radio frequency identification (RFID), and Near Field Communication (NFC). *Bluetooth* is a low-bandwidth radio spectrum that has a reach of about 1 to 109 yards, depending on the power of the device. RFID and NFC systems are similar in concept to Bluetooth in that they're both short-range communication systems, but they have unique identification and commerce capabilities.

Getting Your Bearings on the Three Forms of Mobile Marketing

Here are three basic approaches you should consider when integrating mobile marketing into your marketing strategy (you can read more about actually creating your strategy in Chapter 2):

✔ Direct mobile marketing

✔ Mobile-enabled traditional and digital media marketing

✔ Mobile-enabled products and services

The next sections give you an overview of all three approaches so you can decide which approach is going to fit your business best.

Direct mobile marketing

One of the really special things about mobile marketing is that it provides you with the opportunity to interact directly with a person — not a household address, or a post office, or a television network — because mobile devices are personal to a single person.

Direct mobile marketing involves sending messages directly to a consumer or receiving messages directly from a consumer. The mobile channel provides you with two basic forms of direct mobile messages to engage your customer, and there's really no middle man:

✔ **Marketer-initiated communication:** This occurs when the marketer starts the engagement with the consumer — for example, sends a message, places a call, or pushes an application alert. It is sometimes referred to as *push marketing*.

✔ **Consumer-initiated communication:** This occurs when the consumer starts the engagement with the marketer — for example, visits a mobile Web site, places a call, downloads an application, and so on. It is sometimes referred to as *pull marketing*.

Mobile marketing is an extremely effective direct marketing practice. Marketers consistently see response rates of 8–14% to their initiated communication (compared to less than 1% for most direct marketing channels).

With all forms of direct mobile marketing, you must first get a consumer's explicit permission prior to sending him a text message, making a call, or initiating a communication. Because you need permission, you can't engage in direct mobile marketing without combining your campaigns with other forms of marketing to gain the permission in the first place. You can read about gaining permission in Chapters 3 and 4.

Mobile-enabled traditional and digital media marketing

Mobile-enabled traditional and digital media mobile marketing refers to the practice of mobile-enhancing your traditional and new-media programs (TV, radio, print, outdoor media, Internet, e-mail, voice, and so on) and inviting individual members of your audience to pull out a phone or connected device and respond to your mobile call to action, as shown in Figure 1-3.

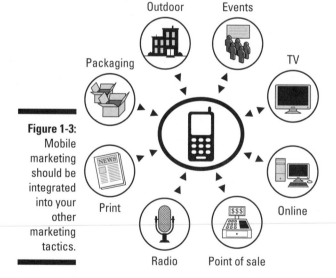

Figure 1-3: Mobile marketing should be integrated into your other marketing tactics.

On television, for example, your call to action may ask viewers to text a keyword to a short code to cast a vote. Or, you may ask them to fill out a form on the Web or mobile Internet, including their mobile phone number, to participate in the program. See Chapter 2 for more on adding mobile marketing to your traditional marketing strategy.

Mobile-enabled products and services

Increasingly, companies are turning to mobile devices and networks to deliver their products and services. For example, banks have launched mobile Web sites and applications so that you can access your bank account to check your balance, transfer money, and find the nearest ATM. Media companies like CNN or ESPN use mobile media as a new media for delivering their content.

A lot of companies are integrating mobile services like text messaging as a way of enhancing the experience with their products. For example, Hasbro recently added text messaging to their last version of the game Clue. Players can receive text messages that influence the flow of the game while they're playing. We explain more about mobile-enabled products and services in Parts II and III of this book.

Getting the Most Out of Mobile Devices

Mobile devices today are increasingly chock-full of really exciting capabilities that you should know about. The capabilities described in the following sections help you determine the *user context,* which means knowing where someone is and what he's doing when he interacts with one of your marketing campaigns so that you can tailor your marketing engaging for optimal results.

Not every mobile device supports all the capabilities described in this section, and not every operating system allows you to access them. You can find out more about what most mobile devices are capable of by visiting the Web site for DeviceAtlas at www.deviceatlas.com.

Dialing and pressing

Dialing and pressing is all about using the voice channel of the mobile phone. You can encourage people to call a phone number by asking them to dial 1-800-XXX-XXXX to experience the sounds of the movie or call 408-XXX-XXXX to listen in on the game, for example.

You don't have to answer the calls yourself; you can use an *interactive voice response (IVR) system,* which is used to automate phone calls with customers and more commonly for customer support. With an IVR system, when someone calls you, the automated system picks up and asks the caller to make selections such as "Press 1 to receive a ringtone," "Press 2 to get your last five transactions," or "Press 3 to get the movie listings sent to your phone." You can read more later in this chapter about how IVR can humanize your approach. For more background on IVR, see Chapter 11.

Bar codes and other uses for the camera

Another way to leverage the camera phone is to have it interact with an installed or embedded application on the phone. In Japan, for example, phones have bar-code readers (or QR code readers) embedded in their operating systems. These readers allow users to scan certain types of bar codes called QR codes. QR codes, also called 2D bar codes, come in many varieties; we'll talk more about these in Chapter 5. When a consumer scans the code in a magazine, for example, the phone automatically recognizes the code and processes the command buried within the bar code. The buried command may instruct the phone to follow a series of instructions, such as: open a mobile Internet browser, go to the restaurant related to the bar code, and then display how many seats are available at the restaurant. The mobile Internet page may even include functions that allow the mobile subscriber to reserve a table.

Texting

Texting simply means sending and replying to text messages. You can place the call to action in traditional, new, and mobile media by saying something like "text *win* to 12345 to enter the sweepstakes." You can also obtain a mobile subscriber's opt-in via texting. (For more detail on opt-in management, see Chapter 3 for regulations, Chapter 4 for setting up your programs, or Chapter 5 for examples.)

Mobile marketing programs and any other programs that use text messaging (such as IVR, Internet, or mobile Internet) must use a common short code (CSC) to address and route the message traffic. For details on CSCs, read Chapter 4.

Snapping and scanning

The camera is a wonderful tool for interacting with your customers. You can instruct audience members to take a picture of a specific object or graphic and then instruct them to e-mail or text (via MMS) the picture to your mobile marketing program. When your program receives a picture, it processes the picture and then opts the mobile subscriber in to the program. The process is also enhanced with services like 2d bar codes. See Chapter 5 for more on these emerging technologies.

Two companies lead the pack in this field: SnapTell (www.snaptell.com), based in Palo Alto, California, and Los Angeles-based LinkMeMobile (www. linkmemobile.com).

Submitting

Another great way to invite someone into your mobile marketing program is to present her a form on an Internet page or a mobile Internet page, or in an installed application. A customer can opt in to receive text alerts.

Using star and pound

Two companies — Zoove (`www.zoove.com`) and Singletouch (`www.single touch.com`) — have developed two alternative opt-in channels using symbol keys on your phone for single-button interaction. If, for example, a mobile subscriber on the Sprint network presses **267 — that is, **AOL — and the Send/Talk button on his phone (typically, the green button), in return, an AOL promotional mobile Internet site is sent to his phone. We delve into this feature more in Chapter 5. Both services are still limited in their deployment across wireless carrier networks.

Finding the way with location

Location is a very powerful tool and one of the unique features of mobile marketing. When mobile subscribers are out and about, they *usually* know where they are, but their phones *always* know. Location information can make your programs more contextually relevant to a user's location.

You can identify a mobile subscriber's location in several ways:

- **User-provided information:** The consumer can provide the ZIP code, address, or phone number of his current location. (If he provides a landline number, you can look up the address in a publicly accessible database.)

- **CellID triangulation:** Every cellular tower is in a fixed location (big steel towers tend not to move around a lot), and each tower has an identification number, commonly referred to as CellID (cellular tower ID). If you know the IDs of the towers that a mobile phone has in range, you can triangulate the mobile subscriber's location with reasonable accuracy. (This system is how Google Maps works.) High-end phones such as the iPhone, BlackBerry, and Nokia- and Microsoft-powered smartphones can tell your application the CellIDs of the towers they're connected to. Then your mobile application provider can look up the towers' Global Positioning System (GPS) coordinates in publicly accessible databases such as OpenCellID (`www.opencellid.org`).

- ✓ **GPS:** The Global Positioning System relies on a constellation of satellites surrounding the planet. The location of a mobile phone equipped with GPS can be determined down to a few yards anywhere on the planet. If the wireless carrier and phone permit this function, an application provider can access the phone's GPS data to enhance the application you're offering.

- ✓ **A-GPS:** Some phones are equipped with Assisted GPS (A-GPS), which combines GPS, CellID, and other enhanced network capabilities to refine the location of the mobile subscriber.

- ✓ **Local access points:** Low-bandwidth transmitter/receivers, such as Bluetooth and Wi-Fi, can be used to approximate a mobile subscriber's location because the access-point transmitters are in fixed locations. When a mobile phone connects to an access point, you can approximate the mobile subscriber's location.

- ✓ **Fem2Cells:** The emerging minitower cellphone technology called Fem2Cells has no practical marketing use today, but I'm noting it here because some applications should be available soon, given all the creative minds out there.

With location, you can create context-sensitive experiences. When a consumer opts in to your mobile marketing campaign, you can send a location-relevant coupon, not just some generic discount for a store halfway around the country from where the consumer is currently located, or you can serve up advertising that's relevant to a nearby establishment.

Many companies such as Yahoo! use search terms and proximity access point data to determine a user's location. The main purpose of this type of location detection is serving location-relevant advertising.

Although location-enabled services are great ideas, we still have some time to wait before location services are ready for use by the average consumer.

Many marketers try to build location services in which the location is the primary value proposition. Location by itself has little value, however; location is an enabling feature that gives value to other services, such as mapping, search, and advertising.

Ticketing and identification with NFC and RFID

Although the technologies are far from mainstream at this point, some phones are being equipped with RFID and NFC chips. These let you do a lot of really cool things, like device tracking and contactless payment.

In Germany, for example, NFC-enabled phones are used to purchase train tickets. A user simply swipes the phone past an NFC reader, and the reader charges her linked billing account (a credit card) for the purchase of the ticket.

No commercialized version of RFID has been developed yet. But RFID chips can be used to identify you and can even personalize signs as you walk by. (Did you see the scene in *Minority Report* in which Tom Cruise walks by a sign and the sign talks to him? That's what we're talking about.)

Discovering Available Mobile Paths and Capabilities

Marketing paths are the combination of the tools, technologies, and media we use to communicate our messages and reach consumers. For example, advertising on a billboard is often referred to as outdoor advertising, which is one type of marketing path. When it comes to mobile, many different types of marketing paths can be used to reach consumers (see Figure 1-4).

The next sections give you an overview of the different paths so that you are familiar with all the ways you can engage consumers with your messages through mobile marketing.

Although each of the mobile paths can work all by themselves, they are more effective when combined together. For example, a text message can deliver a mobile Web site link, which when clicked may include a phone number link. When that phone number link is clicked, it places a call. The call may present a prompt for the user to say or press 1. When the 1 key is pressed, an application or content download may begin. Granted, this string of linkages would present a terrible user experience, but hopefully it demonstrates that all the paths can work together.

Defining text messaging (SMS)

Short message service (SMS), commonly referred to as *text messaging* or just *text,* is an incredibly versatile path to nearly all mobile phones on the planet. An SMS is a 160-character alphanumeric digital message that can be sent to and from a mobile phone — that is, it consists of letters (A, B, C, D, a, b, c, d . . .) and numbers (1, 2, 3, 4, !, @, #, $ . . .) that can be exchanged among mobile phones.

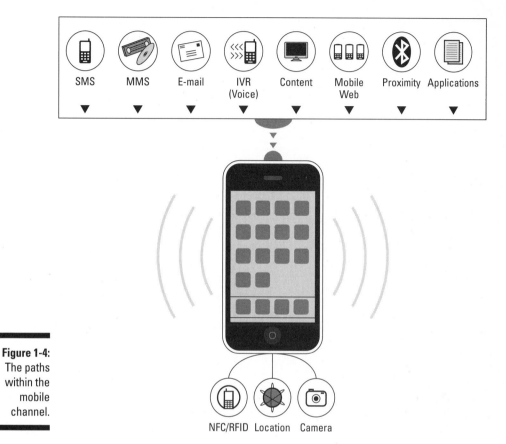

Figure 1-4:
The paths
within the
mobile
channel.

Keep in mind the 160-character limit includes spaces. You'll need to get creative with abbreviations to get the most out of your message. There are some pretty standard word abbreviations common in popular culture that you can think about using; just be sure to know your audience to determine their adoption level of these abbreviations. Not everybody will LOL (laugh out loud) if they don't understand the message.

Text messaging is an extremely popular service that caught on in the United States via TV shows that asked people to text in to cast votes or win prizes. From these basic roots, text messaging has blossomed into a rich interactive medium. In the United States, billions of text messages are sent every day. In fact, text messaging has become the primary mobile communications medium. Collectively, we're sending more than 2 billion text messages a day in the United States alone!

More than just a person-to-person channel, text messaging is now the cornerstone of mobile marketing. In addition to offering voting services, you can launch trivia programs, provide search capability, send information and text alerts, trigger interactive calls, deliver content, operate coupon programs (see Figure 1-5), and even charge people for content and services consumed on the phone (such as ringtones and television subscriptions).

Figure 1-5:
Text messaging coupons are a popular form of promotion.

See Chapters 4 and 5 for details on what you can do with SMS in the context of mobile marketing.

Text messaging may also be used as a billing medium for content to be consumed on the phone (such as games, applications, ringtones, and images) as well as for charitable donations billed to the mobile subscriber's phone bill. When used in this context, text messaging is referred to as Premium SMS, or PSMS. See Chapter 13 for more on this topic.

Leading text messaging application providers include iLoop Mobile (www. iloopmobile.com), Waterfall Mobile (www.waterfallmobile.com), Vibes Media (www.vibes.com), Velti (www.velti.com), 2ergo (www.2ergo.com), Mobile Interactive Group (www.migcan.com), and others.

Making it rich with multimedia messaging (MMS)

Multimedia Messaging Service (MMS) is sometimes referred to as *picture messaging* or *video messaging* to help differentiate it from SMS, which is text-only messaging. MMS is delivered almost the same way as text messaging, but can include multimedia objects (images, audio, video, or rich text), often in a slideshow format, meaning that the multimedia objectives are sequenced and played per the publisher's established script and timing. Because MMS supports more than text — and because a picture is worth a thousand words — with MMS, you can

✔ Tell a story with captivating images, sound and full motion video to delight, entertain, inform, and engage

✔ Embed links to mobile Web sites in the message to IVR call services, application storefronts, and more so that your viewers can get more information

✔ Offer compelling coupons with pictures, sound, and even video

You need to use a mobile marketing application provider that specializes in MMS to power your MMS programs. We show you a number of ways to use MMS in Chapter 6.

Mobilizing your e-mail

An e-mail message can be originated and delivered from any standard e-mail system or through mobile carrier networks. E-mail can be an effective means of delivering messages to a mobile phone or mobile-enabled terminal. Messages are accessed on the phone via the mobile Internet browser or via an e-mail application installed on the phone.

Mobile e-mail is most popular on a class of mobile phones referred to as *smartphones,* including Research In Motion's BlackBerry, Apple's iPhone, and phones running Google's Android software or Symbian and/or Microsoft mobile operating systems. E-mail is rarely used specifically with mobile marketing in mind; controlling the user experience is difficult, and many technical hurdles and legal land mines still need to be overcome. See Chapter 7 for more details on mobile e-mail marketing.

Leading companies that specialize in e-mail marketing services include Constant Contact (www.constantcontact.com), mobileStorm (www.mobilestorm.com), CheetahMail (www.cheetahmail.com), Trumpia (www.trumpia.com), and Silverpop (www.silverpop.com).

Humanizing your message with voice

The *voice path* refers to your phone's standard telephone capability — the means by which you make and receive phone calls, in addition to talking with a live person. Another option? Remember the tip we gave you earlier in this chapter? Use an interactive voice response (IVR) system commonly used in automated customer support. When you call most businesses today, you reach an automated prompt that tells you to say or press 1 to get this, or to say or press 2 to get that.

IVR can be a power mechanism for marketing activities beyond support. An example of using voice for mobile marketing is streaming audio via the voice channel. National Public Radio (NPR) uses the voice channel to stream live and recorded radio broadcasts via the voice channel of mobile phones. You can dial a toll-free number and listen to an NPR show. Alternatively, you can send a text message or click a link on a mobile Web site, and suddenly your phone rings. When you pick up, you hear the live or recorded broadcast piping through the phone. For more on engaging your customers with voice, see Chapter 11.

Be sure to leave enough time to beta test your IVR program; nothing will frustrate your customers more than feeling like they are locked into talking to a computer without getting the answers they need. IVR done well is mobile efficiency at work; IVR done badly is a great way to alienate your customers and possibly lose a few to frustration.

Leading IVR mobile services providers include Angel.com (`www.angel.com`), CommerceTel (`www.commercetel.com`), and SmartReply (`www.smart reply.com`).

Reaching people on the mobile Internet

The term *mobile Internet* is used primarily to refer to browsing Web sites on a mobile device. The Internet connection on a mobile device, however, can also be used to power the data connection for applications (see Chapter 9). For the purposes of this book, when we refer to the mobile Internet, we're referring primarily to mobile browsing.

With the mobile Internet, you can create rich and compelling mobile experiences filled with text, colors, and images. You don't need to create an entire Web site for a mobile campaign, though. You can create a *microsite* or *landing page* — a smaller version of a mobile Internet site. The difference between a microsite and a mobile Internet site is that the mobile Internet site is designed to be persistent — to hang around for a while — whereas a microsite or landing page tends to be designed for a specific marketing promotion. A site of this sort may hang around for a few months, but at the end of the promotion, the marketer turns it off. Also, unlike persistent mobile sites, microsites tend to have very few pages, with content limited strictly to the promotion. Figure 1-6 shows some examples of promotional microsites.

Figure 1-6:
Mobile
Internet
microsites
can be used
for time-
sensitive
programs.

Leading mobile Internet service providers include iLoop Mobile (www. iloopmobile.com), Starcut (www.starcut.com), MAXX Wireless (www.maxxwireless.tv), Netbiscuits (www.netbiscuits.com), Velti (www.velti.com), Madmobile (www.madmobile.com), July Systems (www.julysystems.com), iconmobile (www.iconmobile.com), Wapple (www.wapple.net), 2ergo (www.2ergo.com), Mobile Interactive Group (www.migcan.com), Siteminis (www.siteminis.com), UNITY Mobile (www. unitymobile.com), and others.

 When looking for a service provider to design your mobile site or microsite, look for one that knows and understands the challenges involved with the browsing interface on a mobile phone, including up-and-down scrolling, bread-crumb-based navigation, and the difficulty of adding visual interest without using mobile browser killers like Adobe Flash artwork (leading method of distributing video on traditional Web sites) or badly formatted video.

Engaging consumers with applications and downloads

Installed applications such as games, social networking, news and weather, navigation, banking, entertainment, messaging (SMS, MMS, e-mail, instant messaging, or picture messaging), audio and video players, and browsers may be preinstalled on the mobile phone by the manufacturer or wireless carrier. Alternatively, they may be installed by mobile subscribers who download them via the mobile Internet; embedded links in received text messages; from an application store; or a process called *side loading,* in which the phone is connected to a computer and the applications are sent from the computer to the phone.

Applications can provide a rich interactive experience beyond the limitations of the mobile browser. Special applications can be installed on a phone to serve streaming video (TV) and audio (radio), social networking services, and a wide range of other services.

Not all phones support installable applications, and some wireless carriers don't allow these applications to connect to the Internet after they've been installed. However, as more people adopt smartphones, this will change. Applications are a huge and growing part of the mobile marketing marketplace.

Mobile applications (often just called *apps*) are growing in number exponentially. With this trend comes competition. If you want consumers to download your app, make sure it has lots of usable functionality and lots of relevance to your consumer's needs. App development can be costly, so do your homework on consumers' interest in an app first. With thousands of apps to choose from, many apps are developed at great expense and then ignored by consumers because they didn't offer anything consumers couldn't live without.

Making connections through proximity paths: Bluetooth and Wi-Fi

The proximity paths, Bluetooth and Wi-Fi, may be used to engage consumers in what is referred to as *proximity marketing*, or the localized distribution of content to a mobile device. The *Bluetooth path* refers to the use of the Bluetooth communication channel on the phone.

That little blue icon on your phone represents Bluetooth capability. If you use Bluetooth, you probably use it to pair your phone with a peripheral device such as a wireless headset or hands-free car kit. You also may use it to sync your phone with your laptop computer or to send pictures from your phone to your printer. Wi-Fi is the channel that connects your phone to the Internet via a Wi-Fi access point.

In addition to working with peripheral devices, both Bluetooth and Wi-Fi can be used for mobile marketing — a practice called *Bluecasting*. A marketer places Bluetooth access points and a Bluetooth transmitter in a public area (such as a mall, airport lounge, bus stop, or movie theater) or at a live event. When a consumer walks by the access point, if his phone is set to receive Bluetooth requests automatically, his phone beeps, and he's asked to accept a pairing request from the Bluetooth access point. If he accepts the request, the Bluetooth access point sends an image, ringtone, game, or other communication to his phone.

Leading Bluecasting providers include BLIP Systems (www.blipsystems.com), Ace Marketing (www.acemarketing.net), AURA (www.aura.net.au/), Proximity Media (www.proximitymedia.com), and others.

Make sure you are clear with your Bluecasting permission statements. Pushing content to consumers' phones without the consumers' solicitation or consent is a modern-day discourtesy sometimes termed *Bluejacking.* Make sure you look into standards and the code of ethics here to ensure you are helping your customers, not annoying them. Also, never, never, ever engage in *Bluesnarfing,* which is the unauthorized access of information from a wireless device through a Bluetooth connection. Bluesnarfing is illegal in many countries due to privacy issues involved with unauthorized access to personal information such as contacts and calendars.

All hands on deck: Manning your portals

As you research different ways to engage your customer through and with the mobile channel, you may come across the terms *on-deck* or *off-deck* or *carrier portal.* *On-deck* and *carrier portal* refer to the same thing: They are the default mobile Web and application portals set by the carrier on mobile phones running on their networks. The carrier portal is prime real estate to engage consumers; for example, more applications are still downloaded from the carrier portals combined than from popular application stores like Apple iTunes.

Apple iTunes, or any non-carrier applications like iTunes or Getjar (www. getjar.com), illustrates the concept of off-deck. *Off-deck* refers to any non-carrier–controlled mobile presence. Increasingly, as consumers adopt smartphones, download applications in the billions, and are more and more mobile, more traffic will move off the carrier deck and into the hands of the market.

Advertising on the small screen

Although not necessarily a stand-alone path or channel, mobile advertising is also an effective means of engaging prospective customers. Mobile advertising is the practice of placing a paid sponsor or promotional messaging within one of the various mobile media paths listed previously. With mobile advertising, you can

- ✔ Build your brand
- ✔ Acquire new customers and generate sales
- ✔ Monetize your mobile media paths and portals

You can accomplish so much with mobile advertising. See Chapter 8 for more details. Leading players include AdMob, recently acquired by Google (www.admob.com), Millennial Media (www.millennialmedia.com), Crisp Wireless (www.crispwireless.com), JumpTap (www.jumptap.com),

Smaato (www.smaato.com), Microsoft Advertising (http://advertising.microsoft.com), and others.

Having a hard time with consumers catching on to your brand's mobile presence? Go where you know the mobile users are — place mobile advertising on related mobile sites and apps that you know your consumers frequent. Use these popular sites to crowd source for you.

Cashing in on mobile commerce

Mobile commerce, as defined by the Mobile Marketing Association (www.mmaglobal.com), is the one- or two-way exchange of value facilitated by a mobile consumer electronic device (for example, a mobile handset) enabled by wireless technologies and communication networks. This may sound a bit complicated, but it's really not. It means that billions of dollars are exchanged every day from transactions occurring via the mobile media paths we discuss in this chapter. People buy content (applications, ringtones, and images), purchase physical goods and services, make donations, and even buy virtual goods (like virtual furniture for their online house or clothes for their game avatar). For more on mobile commerce, see Chapter 13.

Chapter 2

Mapping Out Your Mobile Marketing Strategy

*D*eveloping a mobile marketing strategy can be fairly straightforward; however, the task does involve reviewing a lot of data and sifting through marketing objective, technology, and channel details that are unique to mobile marketing. You then need to integrate these details with your overall multichannel marketing strategy. Developing and executing an effective mobile marketing strategy takes time, attention, and a keen understanding of every aspect of your market, your business, and even other businesses that provide the mobile services and connections you need.

You can make the processes as detailed and complex (or as simple) as you like, but keep in mind that developing a strategy is an iterative, try, learn, try again process. Take comfort, however, in the fact that firms both large and small throughout the world have developed and executed on mobile marketing strategies to generate results and return on their investments. You can do it, too!

This chapter outlines the process for mapping out your mobile marketing strategy. We explain how to formulate your objectives and identify key players in the mobile marketing industry that you need to interact with for your strategy to work. We show you how to calculate the costs of mobile marketing and how to evaluate your reach so you can start to define your audience and the potential size of your audience.

Adding a Mobile Strategy to Your Marketing Plan

Marketing, at its core, is about communication and engagement. As a marketer, it's your job to communicate and engage your customer; that is, impart information and news about your products, services, and related activities to your audience (customers, clients, partners, and society at large) so that they can know what your organization does and how to engage with your offers.

Mobile marketing is basically a very powerful way of enabling communication and engagement with your prospects and customers in all sorts of interactive and productive ways.

When you're planning to employ mobile marketing, you should first start with your high-level goals and objectives before you jump into tactics and execution details. You should start by thinking about how you'll weave mobile marketing into your entire marketing plan. In other words, you'll want to keep your overall goals in mind (company and product branding, customer acquisition, retention and relationship management, support/care, social media engagement) as you assemble the parts of your plan. Your overall goals may include one or more of the following:

- ✔ **Increasing brand awareness and recall (*branding*):** Increase the number of potential customers that know about you, the number of news stories or blog posts written about you, click-through rates on a mobile Web site, consumer brand recall of your marketing, or your advertising programs and brand.

- ✔ **Generating leads and identifying new prospects (*acquisition*):** The objective here is to fill up the opt-in database so that you have qualified, interested people to market to in the future.

- ✔ **Acquiring new customers (*acquisition*):** Generate initial transactions from first-time buyers, drive first-time attendance to events or traffic to retail stores.

- ✔ **Increasing revenues and profits from existing customer base (*retention* and *relationship management*):** That is, generate repeat purchases from customers both for existing and new products at sustainable profit levels.

- ✔ **Enhancing existing customer loyalty and activity (*retention* and *relationship management*):** For example, increase loyalty point redemption, stimulate word-of-mouth activities, increase customer participation in programs, drive attendance to an event, store, Web site, and so on.

- ✔ **Improving resolution time for all customer inquiries/complaints (*customer support/care*):** Make people happier by addressing their questions, issues, and problems in a cost-effective, low-stress, timely manner.

✔ **Stimulating social media engagement world-of-mouth/viral marketing activities (*social media engagement*):** Get your audience talking positively about you, evangelizing your service with the market and offering support.

These are not simply *mobile marketing* objectives, but *marketing* objectives. Remember, mobile marketing is simply a tool to help you deliver value to your customer, to help you market and achieve your company's objectives.

The following sections explain the key resources you need to get your mobile marketing plan under way with your overall objectives in mind.

Harnessing information and experience

To build a successful mobile marketing plan, draw upon the following:

✔ **Industry experience:** Industry experience, both yours and your partner's, pertains to your specific industry, such as retail, to the overall mobile marketing industry, and to the way mobile marketing can be used in your industry. You can also accelerate your expertise and experiences by joining a trade association like the Mobile Marketing Association (www.mmaglobal.com) and an association that caters to your business (like Shop.org for retail).

✔ **Historical customer data, trends, and predictions:** Gather as much data as you can (research analyst reports, case studies both from your industry and others, your past customer transactions, and so on). You can find this data in your own company databases, in industry news articles, at industry trade associations, in industry analyst reports, on sites like Slideshare (www.slideshare.com), Marketing Charts (www.marketing charts.com), Pew Internet Research (www.pewinternet.com), and countless other sources. Data is everywhere. See the section, "Including Customer Analysis in Your Strategy" later in this chapter for more.

✔ **Competitive analysis:** Conduct a competitive analysis and evaluate the competition. Understand what they're doing, think about what they might do, and consider the way these actions will affect your response to them and the market. You must be a chess player, thinking several moves ahead. Great sources of competitive analysis include reviewing your competitor's Web site, reading their press releases, and listening to them speak at conferences.

✔ **Industry best practices and rules:** As noted in Chapter 3, make sure you understand the industry best practices and regulations.

Gathering all this information and experience takes time. Moreover, sifting through it all and generating insights that help you make decisions also takes time. So don't wait. Get started now and, over time, you'll become an expert!

Identifying seven key components of a mobile marketing plan

Your marketing objectives, and all the information you collect to support your plan, should be written down and included in a plan that provides a complete 360 degree view of your mobile marketing efforts. Your plan should cover the following seven key components:

- ✔ **Your target audience:** The plan should specifically call out who you want to reach — your prospects, customers, partners, society at large, and so on.

- ✔ **Your offerings:** The plan should detail exactly what you offer and the value your customers will get from the offers; in other words, how will your offers fulfill their needs, alleviate their pains, and meet their demands. In addition, you should think about how your offerings will change as your customer moves through the *journey* — a marketing concept that refers to the stages of customer engagement. See the next section, "Managing the Customer Journey."

- ✔ **Your quantified objectives:** You should detail what it is you want to accomplish, such as increase brand awareness, improve sales in a particular region by X percent, become the number one player in your market within Y years by holding Z percentage of the market share, and so on.

- ✔ **Resources:** Your plan should detail all the resources (people, partners, money, technology, services, and so on) you need to accomplish your objectives.

- ✔ **The communication efforts:** Your plan should be very specific as to what you want to say to the market, and the channels, including mobile, you use to communicate your message to the market. Also be specific about how this message and your communications will change through every stage of the customer lifecycle.

- ✔ **Delivery channels:** Your plan should detail how you plan to get your offerings out to the market.

- ✔ **Exchange:** Finally, your plan needs to be specific regarding how you'll conduct your business and exchange value with your audience.

Managing the customer journey

For your marketing to be successful, you must understand your customer's *journey.* The journey, in this sense, includes all the engagements you have with your customers from the time they first start thinking about taking an action, for example, buying a house, to the point they stop. To understand your customer's journey, you should consider both the customer lifecycle — that is, the stages of engagement with your customers — as well as the specific thought processes your customers take when they're considering buying a good or a service. When you understand this thought process, you can then find ways to augment this journey through mobile marketing practices using all the tools and techniques discussed throughout this book.

The customer *lifecycle* is a concept you can use to develop a broad understanding of how you interact with and engage your customers. In the lifecycle, shown in Figure 2-1, all customers go through a few "windows" of engagement as they interact with you:

- ✔ **Transaction window:** This marks the first time you communicate or engage with a customer regarding your product or service offerings. The objective in the transaction window is to "acquire" the customer — that is, have them buy something from you or use your product or service.

- ✔ **Relationship window:** After you've successfully acquired a customer, you have started a relationship with her. In the relationship window, you look to nurture the relationship and have her buy more from you over time.

- ✔ **Support and care window:** In the event that some aspect of your relationship or transaction with the customer isn't working — the customer doesn't understand your product, say, or your product breaks in shipping — your customer may contact you for help and support. When she does so, she's entered the support and care window. The objective in this window is to solve the customer's problem or answer her question in a satisfactory, cost-effective way so that the customer may re-enter the relationship window.

- ✔ **Evangelism window:** The evangelism window refers to using social media sites like Facebook (`www.facebook.com`), Twitter (`www.twitter.com`), or Foursquare (`www.foursquare.com`) to encourage your customers to share their positive experiences about your products and services with their personal networks.

Within this customer lifecycle, consider your interactions with customers at a more granular level; that is, as a series of interactions that may occur within any one of the above lifecycle windows. We call this exercise *customer journey analysis*. Performing a customer journey analysis is a good way for you to begin to understand your customer's behavior in great detail. It also helps you understand how mobile marketing can improve your customer's overall experience with you. The customer journey specifically refers to all the actions a customer takes from the initial stage of wanting to do something, such as buying a house, to the conclusion of the activity, that is, buying or not buying the house.

Angel Evan from Dark Matter (`www.the-dark-matter.com`), a leading mobile marketing strategic agency, has provided the example of a customer journey analysis shown in Figure 2-2. In this example, a customer moves through the process of buying a home. From a mobile prospective, note that different stages in the customer journey offer many possible points of mobile interaction. For example, when a customer decides to buy a home, she may start by visiting your Web site, where a link allows her to sign up for text messaging alerts about houses that meet her profile. (See Chapter 5 for more about text alerts.)

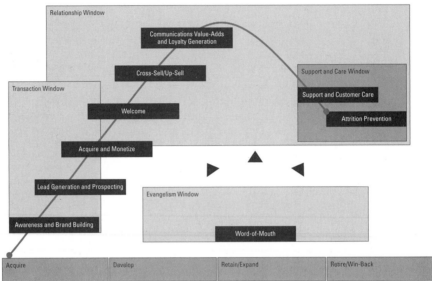

Figure 2-1:
The customer lifecycle.

Adapted from the Direct Marketing Association. Used by permission.

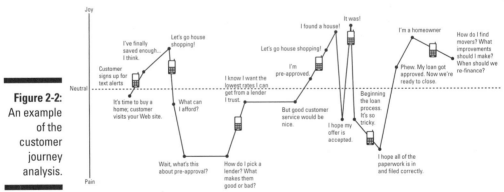

Figure 2-2:
An example of the customer journey analysis.

Courtesy of Dark Matter

Designing your mobile tools based on a variety of device features

Mobile devices today are more than simple telephones: They're rich computing platforms that come in various shapes and sizes, running off of a myriad of networks and on numerous operating systems that support a wide range of variant capabilities. In fact, as noted in Chapter 1, they may not even be phones.

Creating the best mobile experience for your customers starts with usability of the mobile experience you want to build. Your marketing plan needs to take into account the following challenges with mobile devices in order to be effective:

- ✔ The screens vary and are typically smaller than most computer screens.

- ✔ Navigation is limited on a mobile device. You're dealing with a different keyboard and no mouse, and up and down and side to side navigation varies. See Figure 2-3.

- ✔ Mobile devices have no or limited printer access.

- ✔ Bandwidth may be restricted, although this is becoming less of an issue with smartphones and the latest networks.

- ✔ Data connections often cost money (in some cases, a lot of money).

Figure 2-3:
The keyboard is limited on most phones, so don't ask users to type a lot.

Don't get discouraged. The positive features of newer smartphones outweigh the challenges. Your mobile marketing solution can still use rich methods of information exchange. Here are some of the things that mobile devices excel at:

- ✔ Taking, displaying, and exchanging pictures
- ✔ Taking, playing, and exchanging videos
- ✔ Recording, playing, and exchanging music
- ✔ Sending messages via SMS, MMS, or e-mail
- ✔ Telling you where they are (GPS-based features)
- ✔ Facilitating commerce (transaction ability built-in)
- ✔ Browsing the Internet
- ✔ Oh, yeah, and making calls, too

Choosing an approach for getting it done

There are the four basic approaches to choose from when executing a mobile marketing strategy or campaign:

- ✔ **Do-it-yourself:** With this approach, you go it alone: You develop your own strategies, create and execute your own programs, and build all your own technology. This takes a massive commitment and investment — think things through before taking on this approach.

- ✔ **Agency:** With an agency approach, you contract with one or more marketing agencies or specialized mobile agencies or service providers to handle everything for you.

- ✔ **Platform:** With the platform approach, you handle the strategic, creative, and tactical execution of programs yourself, and you use a mobile service provider's licensed software application or platform for your technology.

- ✔ **Hybrid:** With the hybrid approach, you choose elements of each of the two aforementioned approaches. For example, you may outsource creative work to a mobile service provider or agency and keep strategy for yourself, or license a platform for one part of a campaign.

Which approach you select depends on how much of the overall mobile marketing process you want to personally take on and what pieces you see as being critical to your company's competitive advantage and core business offerings.

Including Mobile Service Providers in Your Strategy

Mobile marketing isn't something you should plan to do all alone. In order to get your mobile marketing done, you need to include other service providers from the mobile marketing industry.

The companies that enable mobile marketing to happen on a technical and professional level are called *mobile service providers*. Mobile service providers are people, companies, business practices, and marketers all ready and willing to help you leverage the myriad of mobile paths so that you can engage your customers with compelling mobile and mobile marketing programs. Mobile service providers are a part of the entire *strategic mobile marketing ecosystem* (shown in Figure 2-4).

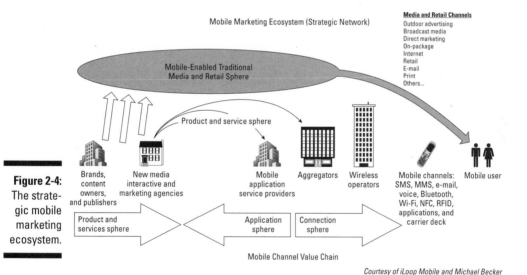

Figure 2-4: The strategic mobile marketing ecosystem.

Courtesy of iLoop Mobile and Michael Becker

In order to successfully launch a mobile marketing campaign, you should consider working with one or more of the following mobile service providers:

- **Traditional media providers:** When you use mobile to connect with customers, you have to follow certain rules and regulations designed to offer the consumer a certain amount of control. Traditional media providers are well versed on these regulations and guidelines and are good for those not willing or able to research the laws. Traditional media players include television, newspapers, magazines, radio stations, retail and point-of-sales displays, e-mail, Internet, billboard providers, and other out-of-home promotional media players. For example, most aspects of mobile marketing legally require consumers to explicitly opt-in to receive your messages. Unless your customers and prospects already know how to contact you and take the initiative themselves, you must obtain a mobile subscriber's consent via a medium other than mobile, as shown in Figure 2-5. You can read more about opt-in in Chapters 3 and 4.

✔ **Wireless carriers:** Wireless carriers (also commonly referred to as mobile operators, wireless networks, or wireless operators) provide the piping, towers, billing systems, support, outlets, and more so that you can engage your customers via the mobile channel. You may be surprised to discover that there are literally hundreds of wireless carriers around the world. The United States has about 50, but the market is dominated by the big four national carriers: AT&T Mobility, Sprint, T-Mobile, and Verizon Wireless. These four companies account for about 93 percent of all the mobile subscribers in the country.

✔ **Connection aggregators:** You aren't likely to work directly with a wireless carrier, unless you work for a very large brand. Instead, you will work with a connection aggregator. *Connection aggregators* are companies that contract with and, well, "aggregate," messaging (including SMS, MMS, content, and billing services) across multiple wireless carriers both locally and throughout the rest of the world. Aggregators are the bridge between you, the wireless carriers, and other service providers. You can work with one connection aggregator and gain access to literally hundreds of wireless carrier networks around the world. Aggregators help make the market more efficient because application providers and wireless carriers don't need to enter into hundreds or thousands of independent contracts to reach their customers. The majority of marketers do not need to work directly with wireless carriers or aggregators; instead, your application provider will take care of these relationships for you. The leading aggregators include Mobile Messenger (www.mobilemessenger.com), Syniverse (www.syniverse.com), OpenMarket (www.openmarket.com), mBlox (www.mblox.com), Sybase 365 (www.sybase.com), MX Telecom (www.mxtelecom.com), Ericsson (www.ericsson.com), Netsize (www.netsize.com), Clickatel (www.clickatel.com), and Motricity (www.motricity.com).

Many aggregators specialize in one or more countries, so if you're going global, you may need to work with a few aggregators and/or your application provider (see below) will.

For a thorough list of connection aggregators, visit the connection aggregator section at US Short Codes Administration at www.usshortcodes.com/csc_aggregators.html.

✔ **Application providers:** Application providers provide the software and support services necessary to deliver mobile marketing campaigns to your customers and prospects. These companies are called *application providers* because they provide the applications that power the customer experience. For example, if you're planning an SMS campaign, you need an SMS application to create and send the text messages. Table 2-1 shows a list of some of the most prominent application providers.

Figure 2-5:
A point of sales display promotion in a retail setting.

Table 2-1	Mobile Marketing Application Providers
Leading Application Providers	
Text messaging	iLoop Mobile (www.iloopmobile.com), Waterfall Mobile (www.waterfallmobile.com), Vibes (www.vibes.com), Impact Mobile (www.impactmobile.com), 2ergo (www.2ergo.com), Celtra (www.celtra.com), Velti (www.velti.com), mobileStorm, (www.mobilestorm.com), Ping Mobile (www.pingmobile.com), Telescope (www.telescope.tv), Textopoly (www.textopoly.com), and others.
Multimedia messaging (MMS)	Mogreet (www.mogreet.com) and CellySpace offered by Skycore (www.cellyspace.com).
E-mail	Constant Contact (www.constantcontact.com), ExactTarget (www.exacttarget.com), Harte-Hanks (www.harte-hanks.com), Trumpia (www.trumpia.com), CheetahMail (www.cheetahmail.com), Merkle (www.merkle.com), mobileStorm (www.mobilestorm.com) are just a few of many traditional e-mail providers. A few specialize in mobile push e-mail, like Research in Motion (www.researchinmotion.com), Good Technologies (www.good.com), and Eco Files (www.ecofilesmobile.com).

(continued)

Table 2-1 *(continued)*

	Leading Application Providers
Bluetooth	BLIP Systems (www.blipsystems.com), Ace Marketing (www.acemarketing.net), and Proximity Media (www.proximitymedia.com).
Voice and inte-grated response	CommerceTel (www.commercetel.com), SmartReply (www.smartreply.com), Jingle Networks (www.jinglenetworks.com), Angel.com (www.angel.com), and VoiceCorp (www.voice-corp.com).
Mobile Internet	iLoop Mobile (www.iloopmobile.com), Netbiscuits (www.netbiscuits.com), 2ergo (www.2ergo.com), Velti (www.velti.com), July Systems (www.julysystems.com), Iconmobile (www.iconmobile.com), dotMobi (www.dotmobi.mobi), and Mobile Interactive Group (www.migcan.com). Check out mobiThinking (www.mobithinking.com) for a great source of mobile Internet knowledge.
Installed applications	Nellymoser (www.nellymoser.com), July Systems (www.julysystems.com), UI Evolution (www.uievolution.com), Mobile Distillery (www.mobile-distillery.com), Digby (www.digby.com), Applicable Media (www.applicablemedia.com), Trailer Park (www.trailerpark.com), Teleca (www.teleca.com), Unity Mobile (www.unitymobile.com), Catchwind (www.catchwind.com), The Hyperfactory (www.hyperfactory.com) and Usablenet (www.usablenet.com). You can also build applications in-house.
Content distribu-tors and aggregators	SendMe (www.sendme.com), MyThum (www.mythum.com), Cellfish (www.cellfish.com), Snackable Media (www.snackablemedia.com), Flycell (www.flycell.com), Playphone (www.playphone.com), and Buongiorno (www.buongiorno.com).

If you're going to do a lot of mobile marketing across a wide range of mobile media paths, you may consider working with a mobile application and services platform provider (also referred to as *platform provider*). The platform provider is a company that combines multiple mobile marketing capabilities into one solution. Some of the leading platform providers include Velti (www.velti.com), 2ergo (www.2ergo.com), iLoop Mobile (www.iloopmobile.com), Tagga Media (www.tagga.com), MIG (www.migcan.com), and others.

✔ **Content owners and publishers:** *Content owners* are individuals and organizations that produce, hold the rights to, and sell content. For example, if you want to build a mobile application, you may need to get a license from a content owner or publisher to use its documents, presentations, images, audio, and other forms of static and rich, interactive, media. When a content owner controls the media channel that is used to deliver content to your customer, the content owner is considered a *publisher.* This is an important distinction when it comes to mobile advertising. Flip ahead to Chapter 10 for the details on mobile advertising.

✔ **Marketing and advertising agencies:** Marketing and advertising agencies are the companies that help organizations, content owners, and publishers market and promote their goods and services to customers. They provide marketing strategy, creative, branding, public relations, and other communication and marketing services to you and similar organizations. They help you develop and execute your overall marketing and specific mobile marketing programs.

✔ **Media providers:** Media providers give you access to traditional print, television, radio, outdoor media, packaging, point-of-sales, telephone, mobile, in-store, and other media where you can place a mobile call to action.

✔ **Enablers:** *Enablers* include trade associations, governments, standards bodies, and mobile device manufactures. Enablers are a critical, and often overlooked, part of the mobile marketing ecosystem. Including enablers helps you to stick to best-practices and avoid violating government regulations.

✔ **Registrars:** Registrars are the organizations that manage the numbers we use to send text messages and the domains for the Internet. Neustar (www.neustar.com) manages the Common Short Code registry in the United States (www.usshortcodes.com), whereas dotMobi (www.dotmobi.mobi/) is the top-level domain registrar for mobile Internet domains. (They also offer a number of developer tools and training programs.)

✔ **Governments:** Governments play a big part in the industry since they help define the laws that we all must adhere and help establish oversight for the industry. For more information on government regulations, see Chapter 3.

You should recognize that you may actually play many of the preceding roles during the course of executing a given strategy. Sometimes you're a customer; other times you're the marketer, content owner, brand, publisher, or even the application provider. This perspective helps you think about achieving your goals more broadly.

Understanding the Costs of Mobile Marketing

Mobile marketing has up-front and variable costs that you need to be aware of before you execute your strategy. Planning for the costs of executing your plan allows you to determine how much money you'll make or how much money you're willing to risk to achieve a particular goal. This section explains what costs you need to include in your plan.

Calculating upfront mobile marketing costs

Some costs for mobile marketing happen before you even begin a campaign. The following lists upfront costs and gives typical estimates so you can make sure to include them in your mobile marketing plan:

- ✔ **Strategy and resources:** You want to estimate the costs for your team, their training, and the development and maintenance of your strategy.

- ✔ **Mobile marking application fees:** These are the fees you pay to obtain the application logic that powers your mobile marketing programs. On average, depending on the functionality you license and the geography you're in, mobile marketing application fees range anywhere from $500–$15,000 per month.

   In addition to monthly fees, you should plan on paying initial account setup and training fees when you sign up with an application provider or connection aggregator. Fees may be higher if you're getting something very specialized. If you try to build the mobile marketing applications yourself, who knows? It could be quite expensive.

- ✔ **Connection aggregator fees:** These fees apply if you decide to go it alone and build out your own application logic. You need to bind your application to a connect aggregator, which costs you between $1,000 and $5,000 per month, depending on who you go with and the regions you want to cover. The connection aggregator fees are typically included in the mobile marketing application provider fees, which is another benefit of working with them. You can read more about connection aggregators above.

- ✔ **Common short code leases:** A common short code is a phone number that is only four to six digits long. If you're going to run any text messaging mobile marketing programs, you must lease a common short code. In the United States, short code leases cost anywhere from $500–$1,000 per month and they are billed quarterly. You may be able to rent a short code from your application provider or connection aggregator, but they'll probably charge you a similar fee. You can read more about short codes in Chapter 4.

Variable mobile marketing costs

Depending on who you're working with, you may be quoted a single number for your entire mobile marketing program, for example, $25,000 plus the traditional media and retail promotion fees, or you may get a breakdown of the costs. The following is a list of the variable costs in the typical mobile marketing program:

- ✔ **Program strategy development:** These can include all the activities needed to conceive of your campaign and lay out the plan.

- ✔ **Creative concept development:** These are all the design activities associated with your campaign.

- ✔ **Content licensing and creation:** These include licensing fees or design fees for any content you may use for the campaign, for example, images, ringtones, videos, news feeds, and so on.

- ✔ **Mobile marketing application:** These are the fees you pay for hosting and reporting on your campaign during the entire period of your campaign (that is, if you're not already licensing a platform or haven't built it yourself).

- ✔ **Tactical execution of program:** This includes creative, program certifications (as needed), technical implementation on mobile marketing application platform providers, legal costs (if you're running a sweepstakes program, for example), and any custom non-recurring software development that may be needed to tailor the application(s) to your specific campaign requirements.

- ✔ **Transactional items:** These include messaging traffic (SMS, MMS, e-mail), Internet and mobile Internet page views, advertising page views/click-throughs, content downloads, Interactive Voice Response (IVR) minutes, content royalties, images recognized, and so on.

- ✔ **Traditional media and retail channels:** These are the fees for promoting the program in any traditional media channels.

You can often reuse portions of your marketing strategy, marketing and campaign creative, and any custom software and content development for future programs. If you keep this in mind, you can save yourself quite a bit of money and time down the road.

Basing Your Strategy on Your Mobile Reach

Mobile reach refers to how many people you can possibly engage through a particular mobile pathway. For example, compare Internet users to mobile phone users.

The potential reach of the Internet is measured by the 1.4 billion people who have access to a computer and an Internet connection. Although the potential reach for mobile phones is three times greater than the potential reach of Internet users — there are 3.1 billion unique mobile users (4.6 billion mobile subscriptions) at the time of this writing — the sheer number of mobile users out there doesn't tell you everything you need to know about your reach. Several technical and behavioral factors limit mobile reach, and failing to consider them could mean one or more of your goals are actually impossible to achieve.

If you're looking for mass market reach, you need to use the mobile pathways that have the technical ability to engage the largest audience, such as text messaging, voice, mobile Internet, and some multimedia services. On the other hand, if you're looking to reach a small niche market, you need only to consider the reach in a small sub-segment of the market, such as iPhone users, for example. The following sections show you the factors that affect your reach so you can be sure your objectives match up with your potential reach.

Dealing with interoperability

Interoperability refers to whether a particular mobile path or capability, such as SMS or camera functions, can work across a mobile network and whether the particular capability is supported across the wide array of mobile enabled devices.

For example, SMS is supported on nearly 90% of all phones. Therefore, it is *interoperable* across nearly all major mobile operator networks. In contrast, Bluetooth is not installed on the majority of mobile devices. Its use as a marketing tool, while growing, is also hampered by differences in technical implementation and what is supported by a particular network or phone. For example, many BlackBerrys won't accept a content download initiated from a Bluetooth alert.

Interoperability is important, because in many cases you may not know what mobile carrier or network your audience is using and, especially for mass market marketing programs, you don't want to miss out on a big portion of the market because your program does not work on one or more mobile phones and devices or mobile carriers or networks your typical customer carries.

A world full of mobile users

By the end of 2010, early 2011, estimates suggest that there will be more than 5 billion mobile subscriptions and more than 10 billion mobile-enabled devices. Keep in mind that there are only about 6.8 billion people on the planet! In fact, we're seeing100 percent penetration for mobile phone use in most developed countries and rapid growth in all developing countries. Mobile is the most cost-effective and reliable means of communication to deploy in developing regions.

Standing up to standards

Standards consist of industry technical and business policies that have been established to ensure the reliability, repeatability, supportability and sustainability of a particular mobile channel, feature, or function you're looking to leverage. You need to work within two types of standards to build your mobile strategy:

- **Industry regulations and best practices:** Government regulations and industry best practices often lag behind what is technically possible. Chapter 3 provides detail on industry regulations and best practices.

- **Technology standards:** With certain mobile capabilities, like SMS, the technical standards are well understood, but with others, such as application development, they are not. Make sure you share a high-level view of your plans with your application providers to make sure the standards associated with the technology you leverage match the standards in your plan.

Adapting to mobile phone adoption

When you're developing mobile marketing programs, you should keep in mind that there are thousands of phones on the market, all with different capabilities. For example, if you build a mobile application, but your customers have phones that support only text messaging, your programs are sure to fail. Your provider can also help you understand the types of phones your target market uses. They can also help detect the phones your customers are using in real time as your customer interacts with your campaign, and they can then tailor the mobile experience to the unique capability of your customer's device.

Figure 2-6 shows a list of the top mobile phones in the United States as of December 2009.

Courtesy of comScore, Dec. 2010

Figure 2-6: The top 25 mobile handsets in use in the United States.

Before you decide to target people with a specific phone, you want to be sure your audience is broad enough to achieve your goals. For example, based on all the media attention, you may get the impression that everyone on the planet has an iPhone, or that they've replaced their iPhones with Google Androids, or similar smartphones. The reality is, however, that most people do not have smartphones.

The iPhone accounts for only 5% of the mobile phone market in the United States at the time of this writing, and its market share is significantly lower worldwide. If you bet your entire mobile marketing strategy on the fact that your customers have an iPhone, you miss 95% of the market. However, that 5% represents a niche market that can generate a lot of money for you and value for your customers, so you may want to target that audience specifically in your plan if the demographics of iPhone users make sense for your business.

The average consumer changes his phone about every 18–36 months, so assuming that every new phone released has some new capability, it will still take years for that capability to propagate through the market for it to even be considered a mass-market medium for marketers. Make sure your plans aren't ahead of the customer innovation adoption cycle.

Figuring on feature adoption

Just because someone has the hottest, most capable new phone in existence, with the fastest Internet connection, doesn't mean that he knows how to or chooses to use all its features. If you've ever had a Swiss Army knife, think about how often you use the micro-saw. It's a cool thing to have, but you rarely, if ever use it.

Mobile phones are the same way. As of this writing, the majority of phones, about 90%, support text messaging, but only 60% of mobile subscribers on average use it. Nearly 75% of phones support the mobile Internet, but only 20% – 30% of us, on average, use it (in the U.S.).

Mobile device feature adoption varies significantly by geographic region. In most developing markets, very little rich media is used; consumers primarily use text messaging.

The moral of the story is that you need to consider mobile feature adoption into your plans as well. You can build a mobile marketing program on the hottest capability, and your market may have the right phone, but it may still not engage in the program for any number of reasons.

Evaluating ecosystem efficiencies

Ecosystem efficiency is not always the most obvious factor to consider when it comes to mobile reach, but it is an important one. *Ecosystem efficiencies* refer to all the players within the value chain being responsible for and playing a part in the delivery of a mobile program and being able to efficiently perform their duties in an ongoing and sustainable fashion. By *sustainable,* we mean they can repeatedly and reliably deliver their services on time with high quality and can make payments on time to ensure each player can stay in business.

For mature programs like SMS, the market is relatively efficient, but for emerging capabilities, this is not always the case. In other words, if you're trying a new and emerging mobile capability, plan on something breaking and develop contingencies, with your partners, for how to handle it.

Profiling your customer

Certain consumer profile factors significantly affect consumers' interest and ability to participate in mobile marketing programs. These factors include age, gender, ethnicity, household income, education, and the types of phones they use, to name just a handful of factors. Young people tend to text message more than older people, but this is leveling out. Leading research firms like comScore (www.comscore.com), Nielsen (www.nielsen.com), Insight Express (www.insightexress.com) and Dynamic Logic (www.dynamic logic.com) can help you better understand the various ways to segment user profiles. See the next section for more details on this point. You can also find out some great consumer behavior and profiling research (for free) at Pew Internet (www.pewinternet.com).

Reaching for geography

Geography is a big mobile reach factor because not all mobile capabilities are uniformly available in each region around the world, nor will each mobile player be effective in every region around the world. Moreover, even if mobile capabilities are uniformly available, the execution process may be different, the business models may be different, the technical standards may be different, the laws may be different, and so on.

Take SMS, for example. Common short codes do not work across international borders. You need a different code for every country you want to conduct text messaging programs in. In some countries, you can lease a code. In others, you can only lease keywords (see Chapter 4 for more on SMS, common short codes, and keywords). They are also priced differently around the world. Luckily, however, the technology implementation is similar enough to generally be considered standard. Moreover, in developed countries like the United States, all the mobile media paths are increasingly being adopted by mobile consumers across various consumer profiles (refer to the section, "Profiling your customer," earlier in this chapter). However, in countries like Brazil, China, and Russia, SMS usage is high (70–80%), whereas mobile video usage is low (1%–4%), as is the usage of other rich media mobile media paths like mobile Internet and applications.

 Pay attention to the geography you want to run your programs in and work with you application providers and partners to ensure that you understand all the intricacies of each country you want to run a program in.

Determining the applicability of your strategy

Taking into account all the variables we discuss in the previous sections, we can rate the mass-market applicability of each mobile path. Table 2-2 scores each mobile channel at a macro level and how it rates against the mass-marketing applicability criteria.

Table 2-2   **Mobile Path Marketing Applicability Rating**

	Voice	SMS	MMS	E-mail	Mobile Internet	Proximity (Bluetooth and Wi-Fi)	Content	Applications
Interoperability	X	X	X		X			
Standards	X	X	X	X	X			
Device adoption	X	X	X		X			
Device feature adoption	X	X						
Ecosystem and player health	X	X	X	X				
Customer profile	X	X	X					
Geography	X	X	X		X			
	7/7	7/7	6/7	2/7	4/7	0/7	0/7	0/7

Figure 2-7 depicts channel marketing applicability visually and shows that voice, SMS, and mobile Internet channel are the most applicable for mass-market programs, whereas all other channels are appropriate for niche marketing programs or simple experimentation at this point.

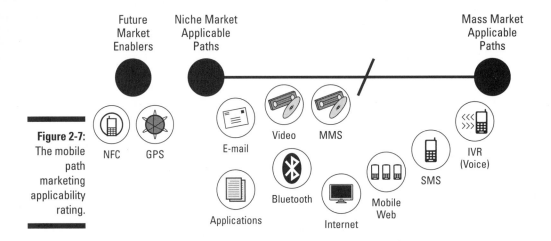

Figure 2-7: The mobile path marketing applicability rating.

 Just because a particular mobile path is not applicable for mass market use does not mean that you should ignore it. Some channels, like the mobile Internet and video, are perfect for niche markets — that is, markets where you can be fairly assured that consumers have mobile devices capable of accessing the mobile Internet, have data plans (they're paying their wireless carriers to be able to use data services like mobile Internet on their phones), and know how to use the features. For instance, business market segments, iPhone users, and high-end niche consumer markets are perfectly suited for rich mobile experience, whereas the anonymous mass-market is not. You should rely on voice and text messaging until you better understand what your target market has in its hands and whether it knows how to use it.

 Consider the mobile marketing mantra: *Global reach, regional relevance.* The mobile channel has become the world's most ubiquitous media channel, meaning that with mobile, your marketing programs can have global reach. However, what really matters for mobile marketing success is that you consider how all the factors discussed in this book differ within each region around the world. Every country and region around the world, even different regions within a country (like U.S. west coast versus east coast) has different consumer mobile adoption profiles. Even the processes and technologies for launching programs may differ. In other words, you must keep in mind that it is important for you to tailor your efforts in every region to run mobile marketing programs that are regionally relevant.

Including Customer Analysis in Your Strategy

The technical ability for your customers to engage in your mobile marketing campaign isn't the only consideration you have to think about when determining your reach. You also need to consider whether your customers are even willing to engage. For example, younger audiences may be more willing to engage with your marketing if you include a mobile game or ringtone download in your campaign. The key factors to evaluate customer preferences are

- Demographic data
- Psychographic data
- Preference data
- Behavioral data
- Situational context

The following sections show you which factors are most likely to affect your strategy so you can give them careful consideration when building a plan and setting goals.

Demographic factors that affect your strategy

Demographic factors consist of the data points that detail a population's inherent characteristics. Keeping track of demographic factors is very important because demographic factors are often the greatest determinants of behavior. For example, targeting African-American or Hispanic customers isn't about tracking their heritage or skin color. Rather, you need to know things like the fact that customers from these ethnic groups tend to index higher in the use of all mobile services over other ethnicities, or that the types of phones they use are different from other ethnicities. The following is a list of demographic factors to consider:

- **Age:** Birth date or age range (such as 14–24)
- **Gender:** Male or female
- **Race/ethnicity:** Caucasian, African-American, Asian, Hispanic, biracial, multicultural, and so on

- ✔ **Religion:** Catholic, Muslim, atheist, and so on

- ✔ **Marital status:** Single, married, divorced, domestic partnership, and so on

- ✔ **Number of children:** Zero, one, two, three, and so on

- ✔ **Level of education:** None, high school, some college, college graduate, doctorate, life experience, and so on

- ✔ **Occupation:** Too many options to list individually (isn't that great?)

- ✔ **Income:** Monetary range (such as $50,000–$75,000 per year)

- ✔ **Nationality:** American, French, British, Chinese, and so on

- ✔ **Geography:** Residence, place of work (if you're a road warrior, American Airlines, seat B17, for example), and so on

Psychographic factors that affect your strategy

Psychographic factors include the qualitative factors that measure aspects of a customer's life. They also influence a customer's willingness to participate in mobile marketing. You need to analyze the following factors to ensure that your promotional strategies appeal to the segments of the market you're targeting:

- ✔ **Lifestyle:** Frequent traveler, parent with young children, empty-nester, and so on

- ✔ **Attitudes:** Political and other views

- ✔ **Interests:** Hobbies and pastimes (such as music)

- ✔ **Purchasing motives:** Purchasing for self or as a gift, for entertainment, for utility, and so on

- ✔ **Frequency of product use:** Daily, weekly, as needed, and so on

Aligning your strategy to preferences

Preferences are data volunteered by customers regarding their likes and dislikes, such as favorite food or least favorite music. Preference criteria you should consider include

✔ Days of the week and times when the customer will allow you to message or call him

✔ How many times the customer will allow you to contact him within a particular time frame (perhaps ten times a month, but no more than three times a week, for example)

✔ The customer's preferred mode of communication (mobile, e-mail, voice, instant messaging, and so on)

✔ The customer's preferred mobile device

By collecting information on a person's preferences and using it appropriately, you'll have a much better chance of meeting that customer's needs.

Planning for situational context

Mobile is personal, and nothing is more personal than your customer's situational context. *Situational context* refers to someone's location and what's going on around him at the time. For example, is it hot or cold outside? Did his favorite sports team just win or lose? Is he moving? If so, at what speed? Is he on a hill, going up or down? Near home, or far away? Are friends nearby? Is he near his favorite restaurant? Is the stock market up or down? What is he reading, watching, or viewing? These questions are just the tip of the iceberg.

Increasingly, a number of mobile marketing solutions, with a customer's permission of course, are able to gather and use situational information, such as the customer's location, activity, the weather, and so on. With this info you can tailor the user interaction in real time to fit the context. Ask your application provider about this. Companies like Bookit (www.bookit.com) and iLoop Mobile (www.iloopmobile.com) with its SmartSMS service are able to support this.

If you'd like to find out more about the differences in mobile behavior between different customer segments, you should check out the Carlson Marketing article "Bringing Mobile Segmentation to Life: Applying Customer Strategy to Build Stronger Relationships via Mobile Devices," which can be downloaded for free at

```
http://carlsonmarketing.mediaroom.com/index.php?s=55&item=151
```

In the article, Doug Rozen, Jeff Anulewicz, and Tom Senn identify eight mobile usage personas (Cord Hoards, Strictly Speaking, Utoolitarian, Lifeliners, Mobile Moths, Duty Callers, Funccessorizers, and Mavericks) and map the level to which each persona uses the mobile capabilities of talking, messaging, browsing, and downloading. This article provides a useful framework you can use to categorize your customers and to think about the types of mobile media they may use.

Chapter 3

Complying with Industry Regulations and Best Practices

In This Chapter

▶ Developing a mobile marketing policy

▶ Meeting the requirements of wireless carriers

▶ Complying with laws and industry standards

Mobile marketing is governed by a combination of laws, of which many were drafted before much of today's technology existed, and new laws and regulations set by a combination of industry leaders, wireless carriers, and government agencies.

As with any industry, mobile marketing has its fair share of regulations and best practices that you need to follow. Doing so enables you to stay in compliance with the rules of the industry, protect the consumer, and help ensure the consumer has the best possible user experience.

Regulations refer to government mandated rules and laws that must be followed on both the state and federal levels in the Unites States or throughout a particular region or in other parts of the world. *Best practices* and *guidelines* are a compilation of accepted industry practices, wireless carrier policies, and regulatory guidance that have been agreed upon by representative members of a particular industry.

This chapter provides a road map for complying with the industry's best practices, guidelines, rules, *and* regulations so you can stay on the right side of the law and consumer preferences.

Creating Your Company's Mobile Marketing Policy

Every company engaging in mobile marketing should have its own mobile marketing policy to ensure compliance with laws, regulations, and other standards in the marketplace. Your *mobile marketing policy* is a written document that outlines your company's position on key regulatory issues in mobile marketing and how you expect your employees and partners to react to these issues.

The following sections walk you through the components of a thorough policy that will give you the security and confidence you need anytime you run a mobile marketing campaign.

Adopting a code of conduct

A *company code of conduct* is a collection of statements within a mobile marketing policy that clearly states what you believe to be right and wrong when it comes to mobile marketing and consumer engagement in general. Think of your code as all of the following rolled up into one:

- **A statement of your intent:** For example, "Our goal is to engage our customers through the mobile channel in a safe, easy, consumer-friendly way so that they ultimately will consider their mobile devices as a seamless and natural medium through which they can interact with our brand."

- **Your framework within which you engage consumers and protect their data:** For example, "We insure that consumers interact with our brand strictly on a voluntary basis and in a highly secure environment using state-of-the-art encryption and other security protocols to protect against inadvertent disclosure, misappropriation, and external attack."

- **Your treatise for complying with laws and regulations:** For example, "We commit ourselves to ensure that our mobile marketing programs are in compliance with current and future laws, regulations, and industry best practices. We will work with the governing bodies, our partners, and regulators to evaluate our program no less often than quarterly and will establish a communication policy to advise our employees, clients, and partners of any changes to our programs that are necessary to be in compliance with these regulations; moreover, we will promptly address any industry audits conducted by the mobile carriers, application store, or related parties."

The Mobile Marketing Association maintains a recommended code of conduct, shown in Figure 3-1, that can be downloaded at `www.mmaglobal.com/ codeofconduct.pdf`.

Technology laws in the 1890s?

The gap between advancing technologies and laws is nothing new. A not-so-recent article in the *Harvard Law Review*, Vol. IV., No. 5, pp. 195-196, commented on the challenges that new technologies present to society and the protection of individuals:

> "Recent inventions and business methods call attention to the next step which must be taken for the protection of the person, and for securing to the individual what Judge Cooley calls the right "to be let alone." . . . . [New technologies] have invaded the sacred precincts of private and domestic life. . . . and the question whether our law will recognize and protect the right to privacy in this and other respects must soon come before our courts for consideration."

This law review article was published in December of 1890, and the *new technologies* in proliferation were "instantaneous photographs and newspaper enterprises." The mobile marketing channel is full of new technology, but the impact on legal and regulatory issues is not new.

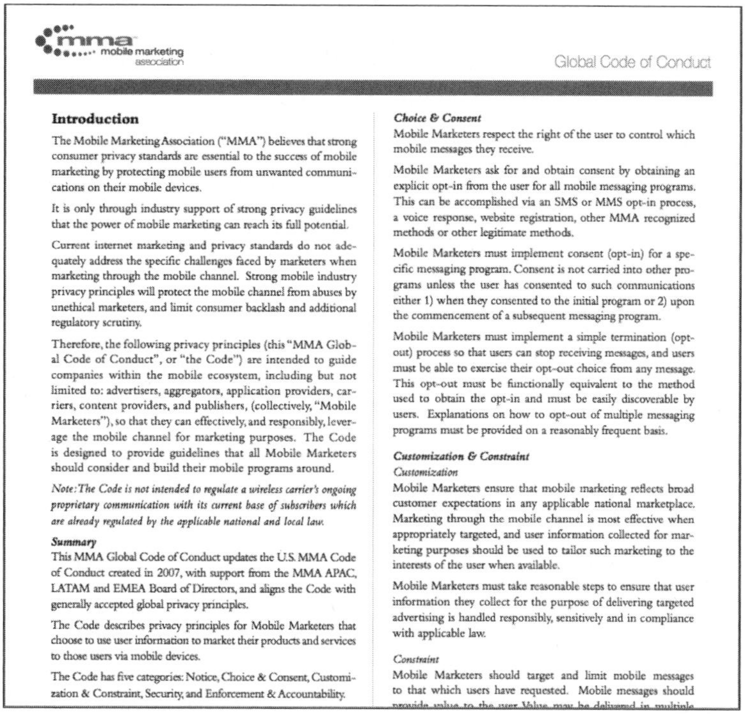

mma mobile marketing association

Global Code of Conduct

Introduction

The Mobile Marketing Association ("MMA") believes that strong consumer privacy standards are essential to the success of mobile marketing by protecting mobile users from unwanted communications on their mobile devices.

It is only through industry support of strong privacy guidelines that the power of mobile marketing can reach its full potential.

Current internet marketing and privacy standards do not adequately address the specific challenges faced by marketers when marketing through the mobile channel. Strong mobile industry privacy principles will protect the mobile channel from abuses by unethical marketers, and limit consumer backlash and additional regulatory scrutiny.

Therefore, the following privacy principles (this "MMA Global Code of Conduct", or "the Code") are intended to guide companies within the mobile ecosystem, including but not limited to: advertisers, aggregators, application providers, carriers, content providers, and publishers, (collectively, "Mobile Marketers"), so that they can effectively, and responsibly, leverage the mobile channel for marketing purposes. The Code is designed to provide guidelines that all Mobile Marketers should consider and build their mobile programs around.

Note: The Code is not intended to regulate a wireless carrier's ongoing proprietary communication with its current base of subscribers which are already regulated by the applicable national and local law.

Summary
This MMA Global Code of Conduct updates the U.S. MMA Code of Conduct created in 2007, with support from the MMA APAC, LATAM and EMEA Board of Directors, and aligns the Code with generally accepted global privacy principles.

The Code describes privacy principles for Mobile Marketers that choose to use user information to market their products and services to those users via mobile devices.

The Code has five categories: Notice, Choice & Consent, Customization & Constraint, Security, and Enforcement & Accountability.

Choice & Consent
Mobile Marketers respect the right of the user to control which mobile messages they receive.

Mobile Marketers ask for and obtain consent by obtaining an explicit opt-in from the user for all mobile messaging programs. This can be accomplished via an SMS or MMS opt-in process, a voice response, website registration, other MMA recognized methods or other legitimate methods.

Mobile Marketers must implement consent (opt-in) for a specific messaging program. Consent is not carried into other programs unless the user has consented to such communications either 1) when they consented to the initial program or 2) upon the commencement of a subsequent messaging program.

Mobile Marketers must implement a simple termination (opt-out) process so that users can stop receiving messages, and users must be able to exercise their opt-out choice from any message. This opt-out must be functionally equivalent to the method used to obtain the opt-in and must be easily discoverable by users. Explanations on how to opt-out of multiple messaging programs must be provided on a reasonably frequent basis.

Customization & Constraint
Customization
Mobile Marketers ensure that mobile marketing reflects broad customer expectations in any applicable national marketplace. Marketing through the mobile channel is most effective when appropriately targeted, and user information collected for marketing purposes should be used to tailor such marketing to the interests of the user when available.

Mobile Marketers must take reasonable steps to ensure that user information they collect for the purpose of delivering targeted advertising is handled responsibly, sensitively and in compliance with applicable law.

Constraint
Mobile Marketers should target and limit mobile messages to that which users have requested. Mobile messages should

Courtesy of the Mobile Marketing Association

Figure 3-1: The Mobile Marketing Association's Global Code of Conduct document.

Publishing your privacy policy

A privacy policy is absolutely critical if you want to collect information from consumers. Although privacy policies are not actually required in the U.S., consumers expect them when your business is engaged in electronic commerce and collecting consumer data. Not only does a privacy policy help to inform and please consumers, but you also save yourself a lot of legal headaches later if you can demonstrate your adherence to a publicly available privacy policy if someone complains about your privacy practices.

Your mobile marketing policy should clearly spell out how your company plans to

✔ Obtain permission when you want to engage someone in your mobile marketing programs.

✔ Keep a record of someone's permission after you obtain it.

You should take the security of consumers' information very seriously. If you don't, you may ruin any possible future relationship with a consumer at the very least. At worst, you could pay a severe fine and even end up in jail (especially in Europe, which has incredibly stringent consumer protection laws).

Typical privacy policies include five things:

✔ **A list of the categories of information collected:** This isn't just names, addresses, or phone numbers. Mobile devices also have the ability to collect less obvious information such as location data and behavioral data. Make sure you include all forms of information collection and tracking in your policy.

✔ **A list of the categories of third parties with whom data is shared:** As a best practice, you should not share personally identifiable consumer data with any third parties unless it's absolutely necessary to carry out a legitimate business practice. For example, if you're using a third party to administer digital coupon delivery to consumers, you need to share information about your consumers' mobile devices with that third party.

✔ **A description of the process (if any) by which consumers can review and request changes to their collected information:** A common method is to provide an e-mail or postal address for consumers to send requests for changing or deleting information you've collected about them.

✔ **A description of the process by which the operator notifies consumers of material changes to the operator's privacy policy:** An acceptable policy is simply to state in your policy that you may make material changes from time to time and that consumers should periodically check back for the most up-to-date terms. If you anticipate making significant changes to your privacy policy, you can send an e-mail to all those whose e-mail addresses you've collected pursuant to the policy to notify them of the change.

    ✔ **The effective date of the privacy policy:** Most privacy policies begin with "Last revised on [date]."

Having a privacy statement doesn't do much good if you don't follow it. In fact, not following a documented privacy policy can get you into more legal trouble than not having any policy at all. You should post your policy anywhere you collect consumer information, such as a Web site or through the mobile channel. Figure 3-2 shows an example from a Web site by ePrize, the world leader in interactive promotions. If you've never drafted a privacy policy before, don't start now. We strongly encourage you to seek the advice of a legal professional regarding the content of your policy and where to post it.

To find out more about privacy statements, go to `http://mmaglobal.com/privacy-policy`.

Figure 3-2:
Publish a link to your privacy policy wherever you collect information.

Terms of Use link may also be called Privacy Policy.

Courtesy of Siteminis

Stating your permission practices

The use of consumer information and most forms of outbound mobile communications require opt-in permission from the recipient before they are legal or permitted by mobile carriers. Your mobile marketing policy should include a statement of your permission practices so you can ensure that your information is usable and your messages will be deliverable and legal.

You must obtain prior opt-in permission from consumers before you can initiate engagement on their mobile devices. The following are examples of cases where opt-in permission is needed and examples of how opt-in might be applied in the interest of the best consumer discloser.

✔ To start, the marketing material you use to invite the consumer to engage in your mobile program must contain opt-in information about the cost of engagement. For example, adding *Std Txt&Data rates may apply* (which stands for *Standard text and data rates may apply*) as part of the legal information near the call to action to participate means that the consumer would be charged a fee by their carrier for all text messaging, multimedia messaging, and data — application downloads, Web site views, and so on — in accordance with the contract they've entered into with their mobile carrier. There are even more detailed versions of this language as detailed in the Mobile Marketing Association Consumer Best Practices (www.mmaglobal.com/bestpractices.pdf).

✔ Sending text messages on an ongoing basis. Your permission statement needs to outline the steps for obtaining prior permission. For example, your statement might require new customers to reply "yes" to all your text message prompts before they can receive future messages, as shown in Figure 3-3.

✔ Charging for content or services on a phone.

✔ Asking for donations through mobile devices. Your statement should detail the process for confirming present and future donations. For example, Figure 3-4 shows how making a $10 donation to support Haiti relief efforts requires the donor to reply "yes" to a confirmation message, even though the donation request was initiated by the prospective donor by sending a text message.

Figure 3-3:
Text messaging requires prior permission from recipients.

Figure 3-4: Mobile donations require a confirmation response from the donor.

✔ Tracking physical location. Some mobile applications can serve pertinent information to consumers based on their physical location. Before activating any location usage application, consumers must be prompted with the specific request for permission. Your statement should include a process for gaining permission, such as a check box or online form that asks users if they want to allow you to use their location. You request this permission in different ways depending on your venue:

• For a text messaging program, send a message that says, "Please reply *yes* to this message to share your location information."

• For a mobile application, a pop-up appears asking, "This application would like to use your current location." The pop-up includes two options to click: OK and Don't Allow.

• In the mobile Web context, include a link that states, "Please click this link to give permission to use your location."

Securing and managing consumer data

Personal information can take many forms, including a consumer's mobile phone number, address, health and financial data, current location, and behavioral data. In marketing, personal information is divided into two classes:

✔ **Personally identifiable information (PII):** PII is any and all information that can be used to identify a person.

✔ **Non-personally identifiable information (non-PII):** Non-PII is information collected through the course of the marketing process, such as clicks on a Web site, that can't immediately be linked to a specific person.

California's Online Privacy Protection Act

California is the only state that actually requires businesses collecting PII from California residents to have and post a privacy policy. The Online Privacy Protection Act has quite a few requirements, so if your business collects PII from residents, you should definitely consult with an attorney knowledgeable in this area.

Both PII and non-PII are collected in mobile marketing interactions. The information may simply be a person's phone number, as when someone text messages into a program, or it may include additional details such as age, name, and address. The information may be provided by the consumer during the course of his interaction with you or obtained later by combining data from multiple public and private data sources.

Regardless of how the information is collected, you *must* protect and safeguard all information that you collect during your interactions with consumers. You should collect only information that you really need. Frankly, why assume the liability of having it if you don't have to?

Your customer data is very valuable to your company, but keep in mind that it's even more valuable to identity thieves. These days, governments not only go after those who steal it. They also go after companies who allowed the data to be stolen.

Forty-five states, the District of Columbia, Puerto Rico, and the U. S. Virgin Islands have laws requiring notification of security breaches involving personal information. A number of these laws require that you store PII in encrypted format; the manner in which you store data could violate these laws even if you haven't had an actual breach.

As a general rule, if you include the following four steps in your mobile marketing policy and adhere to them, you'll usually be in compliance with data security laws:

- ✔ **Collect only data that you absolutely need:** If you collect your customers' Social Security numbers, but don't do anything with them, you've created unnecessary risk.

- ✔ **Limit internal access to customer data to only those people who absolutely need it:** Some businesses give everyone in their IT department access to all information out of convenience in case someone from IT has to fix something. But if you allow an employee who sets up e-mail accounts for new employees to have access to a customer's payment history, you've created unnecessary risk.

- ✔ **Store data in highly secure form:** Encryption has become standard of care.

- ✔ **As soon as you're done with a customer's data and have no further need for it, destroy it:** If you retain customers' data after they have closed their accounts, you've created unnecessary risk.

After you have a plan for storing your data, you should document your data management policy and make sure it spells out the logistics of all the concerns we mentioned previously. Your data management policy should answer questions such as, where is the data, how is it secured, who has access to it, what are the protocols for accessing, retaining, or deleting it, and so on.

If you hire a third party agency to manage the engagement and collect data, ensure an agreement is in place regarding the PII obtained and stored on your behalf. It should be managed, shared, and disposed of based on the security you require. It's wise not to make assumptions here; an agency might have a different viewpoint on this issue that is not in accordance with your policies.

Creating policies for special programs

Some mobile marketing campaigns have the potential to create unique legal and regulatory implications, so you need to address them individually in your mobile marketing policy. These special programs include

- ✔ **Winner data in prize promotions:** Talk with your attorney to make sure your policy addresses state and local laws in addition to national laws for contests and promotions. (You can read more about laws for contests and promotions a little later in this chapter in the section called, "Complying with sweepstakes rules.")

- ✔ **Incentives:** If you're using gifts, prizes, or other incentives to engage your customers, make sure your policy complies with local, state, and federal laws. These laws can be extremely complicated; consult your attorney or a specialist firm like ePrize (www.eprize.com).

- ✔ **Social media:** If your business has a social media presence, give some thought to whether your policies or procedures should treat those who interact through their mobile devices differently from those who access through laptops or desktops. For example, if you want to use mobile social media technology to utilize consumers' location data, you may run into legal issues with publically posting the physical location of individuals. Allowing the general public to know where specific individuals are (or that they aren't home right now) can present safety and privacy concerns.

Special program policies are often specific to your business, industry, or local jurisdiction. Get help from your attorney before you address them in your policy or in practice.

Complying with Trade Association Guidelines

Following industry guidelines is always important. Luckily, even though the mobile marketing industry is young, we have some great practices to follow. From the early days of the industry, industry leaders quickly realized that if they didn't regulate themselves in a responsible, consumer-friendly manner, governments would do it for them in a way that may stymie innovation and their ability to deliver customer value. (Don't get us wrong: Laws are good and we have to protect the customer, but self-regulation should take the lead.)

As a result, a number of influential trade organizations and documented best practices, guidelines, and policies have sprung up. You need to follow these guidelines if you want to be effective marketing through mobile channels. The following sections show you what you need to know.

Getting to know the influencers

There are a number of trade associations whose guidelines and best practices are well respected when it comes to mobile marketing. It's a good idea to become familiar with each association and their guidelines:

- ✔ **The Mobile Marketing Association (MMA):** The MMA is the leading worldwide trade organization whose members include agencies, advertisers, hand-held device manufacturers, carriers and operators, retailers, software providers and service providers, as well as any company focused on the potential of marketing through and with mobile devices. The MMA has established several standards and updates them often with notice to their members. For example, the MMA recently published Global Mobile Advertising Guidelines and highlighted the fact on their Web site, shown in Figure 3-5. The MMA's Consumer Best Practices Guidelines (www.mmaglobal.com/bestpractices.pdf) is a good place to start learning about accepted industry practices, wireless carrier policies, and regulatory guidelines that have been agreed on by representative member companies from all parts of the industry. Check back at their Web site every six months or so for updates.

Figure 3-5:
The Mobile
Marketing
Association
advertises
policy
updates to
members.

✔ **The Direct Marketing Association (DMA):** The DMA is a leading trade organization in both the United States and the United Kingdom that focuses on direct marketing practices, including mobile marketing. In 2009, the DMA included a mobile marketing section in its Guidelines for Ethical Business Practice guidelines (`www.dmaresponsibility.org/Guidelines/`), which are designed to help you execute your mobile marketing programs properly.

✔ **CTIA — The Wireless Association:** The CTIA is an international non-profit membership organization that has represented the wireless communications industry. Its membership includes wireless carriers and their suppliers, as well as providers and manufacturers of wireless data services and products. Participating wireless carriers, in conjunction with CTIA, have voluntarily adopted the Wireless Carrier Content Classification & Internet Access Control Guidelines. The Guidelines were developed along with an industry-approved Classification Criteria. This is another critical resource you should consult if you want to market to consumers through the mobile channel.

✔ **Interactive Advertising Bureau (IAB):** The IAB is an organization that includes more than 375 leading media and technology companies who are responsible for selling 86% of the online advertising in the United States. Among the IAB's core objectives are sharing best practices and educating industry members in responsible marketing methods to help fend off adverse governmental legislation and regulation. The IAB mobile committee produces best practices and mobile advertising guidelines, which are available at `www.iab.net/iab_products_and_industry_services/1421/1488/mobileplatform`.

✔ **Groupe Speciale Mobile Association (GSMA):** The GSMA is a global association spanning 219 countries and uniting nearly 800 of the world's mobile operators, as well as more than 200 companies in the broader mobile ecosystem, including handset makers, software companies, equipment providers, Internet companies, and media and entertainment organizations. This organization is focused on innovating, incubating, and creating new opportunities for its membership and the growth of the mobile communications industry. Information on the GSMS is available at www.gsmworld.com/.

In addition to the five most influential trade associations, an increasing number of guidelines and best practices are set by installed application providers. These guidelines aren't set by an association, but rather are set by the application stores. For example, the Apple store requires that any iPhone application that offers location-based services must notify and obtain consent from an individual before his location data is collected, transmitted, or otherwise used by the application. Make sure you are aware of any and all individual provider guidelines before going through the trouble of building an application, Web site, or other program involving a partner.

Embracing industry self-regulation

Many of the industry association guidelines are self-regulated. It's a good idea to be involved in the process and not just become a passive bystander. Join and support the organizations that form and publish these guidelines.

Also, keep in mind that industry regulations are not law, but many of the regulations are set according to known consumer behaviors and issues that attracted government involvement in the past. If you don't follow them, you might not only risk being kicked out of an association or being denied access, but you might also risk consumer backlash, lawsuits, or even getting the attention of lawmakers who enact new legislation to keep you and others from doing similar things. Police yourself, rather than having someone do it for you.

In many instances, abiding by industry guidelines is not optional. For example, in the U.S., the wireless carriers won't work with anyone who doesn't adhere to the MMA Consumer Best Practice Guidelines. If you're running a mobile marketing campaign that violates their guidelines, the wireless carriers shut down your program by deactivating your short code. In some situations, companies won't even do business with you if you're not a member of or certified by a particular trade organization.

Complying with U.S. Government Regulations

The U.S. government and individual states have managed to pass a few laws specifying what you can and cannot do with mobile marketing. The following sections highlight key laws, statues, and regulatory activities that intersect with mobile marketing. As with all legal analysis, consult with your attorney before setting your company policies or taking any action with legal implications.

Steering clear of mobile spam

Mobile spam is unsolicited, unwanted communications in the form of e-mail, text messages, multimedia messages, and so on. As you might imagine by looking at your e-mail inbox or junk folder, spam is one of the more heavily regulated activities. Different laws apply, depending on the specific technology used to send communications. Most communication practices fall under at least one of four federal statutes:

- ✔ **CAN-SPAM:** CAN-SPAM is a U.S. federal statute that regulates the senders of commercial electronic mail. Electronic mail messages regulated under CAN-SPAM include e-mail and other electronic messages sent through social networking sites, but do not include text messages. (Text messages are governed by the TCPA discussed in the following bullet point.) In order to comply with CAN-SPAM, check the current law at ftc.gov/spam. If you violate any of the CAN-SPAM laws, the U.S. Federal Trade Commission (FTC) can prosecute you.

  In addition to FTC involvement in spam, the Federal Communications Commission (FCC) has imposed a ban on sending unwanted commercial e-mail messages to wireless devices if the e-mail address receiving the e-mail includes a wireless domain e-mail address listed at www.fcc. gov/cgb/policy/DomainNameDownload.html. This is a special rule designed to prohibit marketers from sending commercial e-mail to mobile devices.

- ✔ **Telephone Consumer Protection Act (TCPA):** The TCPA was passed by Congress in 1991 — long before SMS technology existed. The TCPA generally applies to telephone solicitations and other calls made to phone numbers, including wireless numbers. The FCC has noted that the law encompasses both voice calls and text calls to wireless numbers, including SMS messages. One of the things the TCPA prohibits is the use of auto-dialers — computers that dial phone numbers — without prior express consent from the owner of the mobile number or account. Without getting into all the legal mumbo jumbo, the TCPA's application to text messages gets pretty convoluted. To be on the safe side, don't send unsolicited text messages to anyone.

The best practice with any of the preceding regulations is to make sure you get consumers' consent before you contact them through mobile channels.

✔ **Telephone Sales Rule (TSR)**: The FTC issued the Telephone Sales Rule and has revised it on several occasions to update its applicability to the evolving climate of the mobile channel. The TSR consists of four general requirements for telemarketers:

✔ **National Do Not Call Registry:** On October 1, 2003, the TSR gave consumers a choice about receiving most telemarketing calls by establishing the National Do Not Call Registry (see Figure 3-6). Telephone solicitors are required to ensure that they do not make telephone solicitation calls to any number listed not only on the National Do Not Call list, but also various lists containing those numbers that have changed from landline to wireless accounts and numbers that have been set aside for wireless service. Consumers can register their home and mobile phone numbers with the Do Not Call Registry at `www.donot call.gov`. Most marketers are forbidden to place telemarketing calls to any phone number listed in the registry, but some exceptions exist, such as political organizations, charities, telephone surveyors, and companies that have pre-established business relationships with a consumer. Marketers are required to check the registry at least once every 31 days to clean their internal lists. Text messaging and e-mail also fall under the umbrella of the Do Not Call Registry.

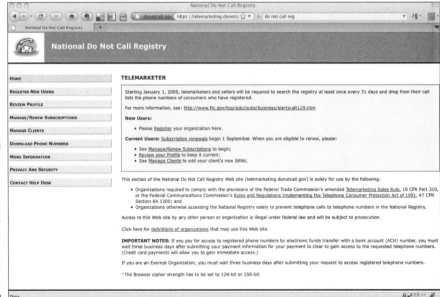

Figure 3-6:
The National Do Not Call Registry governs marketing to mobile phones.

✔ **Standards for telemarketers:** The TSR prohibits deceptive and abusive telemarketing acts and practices and sets forth standards of conduct for telemarketing calls:

- Calling times are restricted to the hours between 8 a.m. and 9 p.m., specific to the time zone you are calling, such as Eastern Standard Time (EST).

- Telemarketers must promptly tell you the identity of the seller or charitable organization and that the call is a sales call or a charitable solicitation.

- Telemarketers must disclose all material information about the goods or services they are offering and the terms of the sale. They are prohibited from lying about any terms of their offer.

✔ **Predictive dialers:** A *predictive dialer* is a computerized dialing system that automatically calls a batch of phone numbers within a given range. Telemarketers who use predictive dialers must connect the call to a live representative within two seconds of the consumer's completed greeting. If they don't, the call is considered abandoned even if it's answered by a live representative after the two seconds. Abandoned calls are generally prohibited, meaning you cannot keep someone waiting on a line longer than two seconds before they are connected to a live attendant.

✔ **Caller-ID:** To be in compliance with the Caller-ID component of the TSR, a marketer may not block Caller-ID and must list a company name and telephone number that can be called by the consumer for company Do Not Call requests. The callback number must be answered with the same company name listed on the Caller-ID.

All the rules and requirements surrounding contacting wireless devices seem like a virtual landmine. The DMA has come out with a very useful Wireless Marketing Compliance chart that helps you navigate through the rules and requirements surrounding contacting wireless devices. Check it out at www. dmaresponsibility.org/WirelessChart/.

Regulations governing automated voice campaigns

The regulations involving outbound automated voice campaigns are burdensome and important. At the federal level in the United States, the FTC and the FCC each has a series of regulations that are evolving. More than half of the states have their own voice regulations, and several of the state and federal courts have conflicting rules about pre-emption. In other words, are marketers supposed to follow federal or state laws when they conflict? You have to make your best decision among conflicting rules.

Some of the state laws are funny. For example, in Louisiana you cannot push calls on state holidays, even Creole holidays that the other 49 states have never heard of. The laws and precedents also change very frequently, so check with an attorney that specializes in telemarketing and IVR (Integrative Voice Response, or an automated call attendant) before executing your campaign. A promotional campaign is anything that attempts to sell or upsell something, even "sale notifications" and product warranty sales to consumers who have just purchased a new product. Upselling refers to the practice of inviting a client to purchase additional products and services. In the next few sections, we cover the main regulations you should be aware of before you launch a voice campaign.

Express Consent

The federal laws are broken down into general categories. If the call is promotional in nature, the FTC requires Express Consent, which is a customer's signature (digital or wet) on an opt-in form.

Call Introduction

The FTC law also requires the script to immediately state who is calling, the purpose of the call, and how to opt-out immediately.

Immediate Opt-Out

The immediate opt-out requirement is *one-button opt-out*. Generally, all the customer has to do is press a certain number to opt-out. The marketer must immediately allow the customer to opt-out, with no questions or delays.

Toll-Free CallBack

For those messages that are delivered to answering machines, every outbound IVR must include a toll-free opt-out number for consumers to call.

Caller-ID

With the right technology, you can have your caller-ID say anything and even change the number from which you are calling; however, this practice is illegal in push-based IVR programs, that is, IVR systems that initiate a phone call and then walk the answering party through a series of automated prompts).

Opt-Out

When someone opts-out, don't call them again until they opt-in on their own. Besides being obvious good sense, it is the law.

Message Length

Although the length of a message is not regulated, try to keep them short. We've observed that messages more than 45 seconds long on an answering machine are deleted, and messages more than 20 seconds long on a "live ear delivery" are hung up on.

Do Not Call

In October 2003, the U.S. implemented the Do Not Call regulations, which came with a Do Not Call Registry of consumers who do not want to receive calls from telemarketers. With the new Express Consent laws, prerecorded IVR push messages can only be delivered to people who have opted-in, but their opt-in takes precedent over their do-not-call status. In other words, a consumer who is registered on the Do Not Call Registry but later provides you their express consent to receive calls from you is eligible to receive those calls.

Cost of a Violation

At the time of this writing, the cost for violating federal laws is $16,000 *per phone call* in violation. If you placed 1,000,000 violating phone calls, you're looking at $16,000,000,000 in fines! Be cautious.

Voice campaigns where people opt-in to receive information instead of promotions are often called *informational campaigns.* These include messages such as flight delay announcements, prescription refills, and snow-day alerts. However, adding anything promotional in the content (such as, "and when you're refilling your prescription, you can save 5% on groceries") makes the call a promotional campaign. Informational campaigns have the same rules as promotion campaigns, except for the elimination of Express Consent.

Informational calls, according to federal law, can only be sent to customers who have an existing business relationship (EBR). Each state may be different, so check it out. Generally, an EBR is defined as a customer having made a purchase in the prior 18 months. The requirement of Express Consent is eliminated for informational calls, but if you can capture Express Consent, it doesn't hurt.

Safeguarding the privacy of children

Children (those 13 years old and younger) use mobile phones too, and you must be very careful when marketing to them. In the United States, rules for marketing to children are clearly spelled out in the Children's Online Privacy Protection Act of 1998 (COPPA), which you can find at www.ftc.gov/ogc/coppa1.htm. The act clearly outlines how and when you can engage children, as well as rules about gathering their personal information and gaining parental consent.

In addition to COPPA, you should pay close attention to the Cross Carrier Standards section of the Mobile Marketing Association's U. S. Consumer Best Practices Guidelines (www.mmaglobal.com/bestpractices.pdf), which details the industry-accepted methods for marketing to children via the mobile channel.

Puerto Rico Revised Sweepstakes Regulations

In November 2009, Puerto Rico became the first U. S. jurisdiction to pass a law that expressly excluded standard text messaging charges from the definition of "consideration" for games of chance. That means that in Puerto Rico, you can run a game of chance in which the only way to enter is through text messaging without having to include a free alternate method of entry.

Complying with sweepstakes rules

A chance to win a game or sweepstakes is an extremely effective incentive for collecting consumer permission, information, or participation in a marketing program. Sweepstakes and contests have strict rules that must be followed or you may face fines and even imprisonment.

One of the cardinal rules in games of chance is that you cannot require consideration in order to enter. *Consideration* is the legal term for some sort of payment or exchange of value. If consumers have to pay consideration to enter a game of chance, that constitutes a lottery — and lotteries are illegal unless they're run by a government. That's why you always see the "no purchase necessary" clause in any ad for a sweepstakes. Even when the *primary* method of entry is purchasing a product, there's always a free method of entry available for people who don't want to make a purchase.

Running a game of chance through the mobile channel presents an interesting problem when it comes to consideration. For example, say you decide to run a contest where consumers text the keyword "PLAY" to the short code 77493 (PRIZE) to find out whether they have won. Because sending a text message costs most people money — anywhere from 10 to 20 cents depending on the carrier — you need to provide a free method of entry.

 While there is debate over whether standard text messaging charges constitute consideration in games of chance, premium text messaging (PSMS) charges most definitely *do* constitute consideration. If you want to run a promotion in which consumers incur premium text messaging charges, you absolutely must include a free alternate method of entry.

 You must consult your attorney to make sure your mobile contest is legally compliant because the laws surrounding consideration in the mobile channel can be downright backwards. For example, some regulators consider a text message to be consideration, but consider a mail-in entry to be a free method for entering a contest. The government apparently thinks that a 20-cent text is not free, whereas a 44-cent stamp stuck to an envelope is free. Don't expect common sense, or common cents, to prevail when you're planning a contest or sweepstakes!

Complying with Non-U.S. Government Regulations

Mobile marketing is a global phenomenon. In fact, mobile usage penetration is deeper outside of the U.S., especially in countries that do not have high-speed broadband Internet access infrastructure in place. Although the MMA guidelines apply universally regarding standard of care (that is, the generally accepted and reasonable means of engaging a consumer), every country has its own rules, regulations, and cultural sensitivities regarding all the issues listed in this chapter. For instance, the European Union Directive 2002/58/EC explicitly prohibits spam, as do other regional directives and industry best practices and guidelines.

Each directive has different rules about what constitutes spam. The mobile channel is recognized as requiring explicit consent from mobile subscribers before you can message them, for example, but with e-mail, typical regulations allow you to e-mail anyone without their consent as long as you provide a clear and conspicuous way of opting out (telling you not to contact them).

Don't assume one set of regulations applies to all directives. Mobile, e-mail, or voice-marketing regulations may or may not vary; be sure to check for specifics before you launch your campaign!

Part II
Executing Direct Mobile Marketing Campaigns

The 5th Wave   By Rich Tennant

KENNETH BUYS HIS FIRST SMART PHONE

©RICHTENNANT

Exercise more.

In this part . . .

Direct mobile marketing campaigns involve messages sent directly to consumers, and include text messaging, multimedia messaging, and mobile e-mail. Messaging to mobile devices requires you to think about the features of the mobile devices involved and the context of the person reading the message, as well as more technical aspects such as carrier approval for your messaging.

Chapter 4 tells you how to get ready for text messaging by obtaining a common short code and getting carrier approval for your campaigns. Chapter 5 helps you execute common text messaging campaigns such as opt-ins, alerts, coupons, and other promotions.

Chapter 6 shows you how to add media such as pictures, sound, and motion to your text messages through multimedia messaging. Chapter 7 helps you adapt your e-mail marketing for mobile devices by showing you how to format your e-mails for mobile screens and how to collect e-mail addresses through mobile channels.

Chapter 4

Getting Ready for a Text Messaging Campaign

Text messaging, also referred to as Short Message Service (SMS), or just texting, is an incredibly versatile way to send a message to nearly any mobile phone on the planet. About 95% of all phones are text messaging enabled. An SMS is a 160-character alphanumeric digital message that can be sent to and from a mobile phone. *Alphanumeric* means that it consists of letters (upper- and lowercase), numbers and symbols (such as 1, 2, 3, 4, !, @, #, or $), and spaces. SMS messages can be exchanged between mobile phones and SMS-enabled devices, digital displays (like a JumboTron at a sports arena or conference), blogs, and social networking sites like Facebook or Twitter.

Text messaging is more than just a person-to-person channel; text messaging is the cornerstone of mobile marketing. You can deliver content, news, and weather; launch voting and polling programs; engage consumers in promotional offers and sweepstakes; recruit volunteers; deliver coupons and customer care alerts; and so much more.

In this chapter, we show you how to get your text messaging program organized and what you need to get started. We review how to select your text messaging partner and set up your database. We also show you how to register common short codes and tell you how to create a user flow and get your text messaging campaigns approved by carriers (U.S. carriers, at least). If you're already a pro at setting up a text messaging platform, flip ahead to Chapter 5, where we show you how to create and launch the most common types of text messaging campaigns.

Understanding SMS Basics

Launching a text messaging program takes more planning than you might expect. In order to get started launching and running text messaging programs, you need to have the following in place:

- ✔ A marketing strategy and plan that guides your decisions on what to send out. (You can read more about marketing objectives in Chapter 2.)

- ✔ A text messaging application platform that manages all the text interactions between you and individual mobile subscribers.

- ✔ A common short code, which is a shortened phone number used for addressing commercial text messages (see the section, "Understanding Common Short Codes," later in this chapter).

- ✔ Carrier approval "certification" for your campaigns (in the United States, all text messaging programs must be approved by the mobile operators; however, this requirement differs by country. You'll want to talk to local application providers in each country for help).

- ✔ A marketing program to promote your text messaging programs; you can't send text messages to people until they opt-in to receive them, and they won't know about your text messaging programs unless you advertise or promote the program to them through your mobile-enhanced traditional marketing channels.

This section guides you through the process of laying out your text messaging plans and the flow of your messaging to give you a foundation upon which to start building a platform. We show you how to add the other elements to your platform later in this chapter.

Understanding the flow of text messaging

Text messaging programs have a very specific flow to them that you must understand to get approval for your campaigns and to adapt the key capabilities of your mobile marketing application provider's platform in a logical way.

Text messaging flows involve four types of text messages:

- ✔ A *mobile originated message* (MO) is a text message that comes from your customer, the mobile user.

- ✔ An *application terminated message* (AT) is a text message that is received and processed or *terminated* by a mobile marketing application.

- ✔ An *application originated message* (AO) is a text message that is sent by a mobile marketing application to your customer, the mobile user.

- ✔ A *mobile terminated message* (MT) is a text message that is received by your customer, the mobile user.

Figure 4-1 shows you how text messaging flows between you and the mobile user. Notice how the message can flow from the consumer (a mobile originated message), through the mobile operator networks, to the application platform (as an application terminated message), and back to the consumer (as an application originated message in response to the mobile originated message).

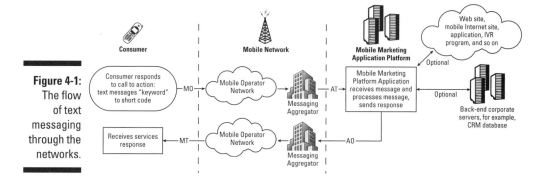

Figure 4-1: The flow of text messaging through the networks.

Trillions and trillions served

Text messaging is an extremely popular service that caught on in the United States via TV shows such as *American Idol, Survivor,* and *Deal or No Deal.* These shows gave viewers the opportunity to text in to cast votes or try to win prizes. More recently, text messaging took a big jump forward with the American response to the January 2010 earthquake in Haiti. Charities such as the Red Cross advertised a text messaging-based call for relief through all their marketing channels, including television. For example, viewers could text *Haiti* to a common short code, paying standard message and data rates, to donate $10 to Haiti relief. In just a bit longer than seven days, the Red Cross and other charities raised over $40 million via premium text messaging micro-donations (see Chapter 13); that is, donations for Haiti in $5 or $10 increments. (See Chapter 13 for more on making money with mobile.)

From these roots, text messaging has blossomed into a rich interactive medium. In the United States, billions of text messages are sent every day. In fact, text messaging has become the primary mobile communications medium. In March 2010, the Cellular Technology Industry Association (www.ctia.org) reported that U.S. mobile subscribers exchanged nearly 152.7 billion text messages a month. That's more than 5 billion a day! According to Nielsen, at the end of 2009, the average consumer sent 584 text messages versus using 180 voice minutes. Moreover, consumers are increasingly recognizing text messaging calls to action in traditional and new media marketing promotions. In 2010, consumers will exchange 5.5 trillion text messages worldwide.

Creating user-flow diagrams

One of the most important aspects of planning is creating *user flows* — documents that outline as thoroughly as possible how your users engage in your campaign. User flows are critically important for two reasons:

- ✔ **They help you design and execute your program.** You save time and money by planning ahead in the program-development process instead of fixing mistakes later. Moreover, a detailed user flow clarifies any ambiguity about interactions between mobile subscribers and your program. Finally, it helps streamline communication among members of your marketing team and any partners and vendors you may be working with to launch the program.

- ✔ **They're required for certification of your program.** As part of the certification process (see Chapter 3 or the next section in this chapter), you're required to submit your program's user flows to your mobile marketing application provider or connection aggregator. Wireless carriers test your program against these user flows. If the program works as described in the user flows, the carrier certifies the program; if not, the carrier rejects it. Also, carriers use submitted user flows for future campaign audits to make sure that your program still meets the original certification criteria.

The best way to plan your text messaging flow is to use a user-flow diagram, as shown in Figure 4-2. A *user-flow diagram* is an image that outlines the user flow introduced in the preceding section and details all the interactions that may occur between a mobile subscriber and your mobile marketing program.

User-flow diagrams typically are created with word processing software applications such as Microsoft Word, Microsoft Excel, Microsoft PowerPoint, or Microsoft Visio. Some people use standard flow-charting techniques; others use images of phones to map the user flow. Figure 4-2 shows an example of a flow-chart method. Figure 4-3 shows the phone method. Which method you choose depends on which is more useful for documenting all the possible interactions that a mobile subscriber may have with your program.

Your application provider or connection aggregator typically has the most common user flows already designed — as well as the not-so-common ones. Rather than start with a blank piece of paper, ask the provider to give you a few examples. Then you can tailor an existing user flow.

To customize a user-flow diagram for your mobile marketing campaign, start with the user flow provided by your application provider and envision all possible scenarios and interactions between mobile subscribers and your mobile marketing program. Then write down what you envision, using the following two steps as a guide.

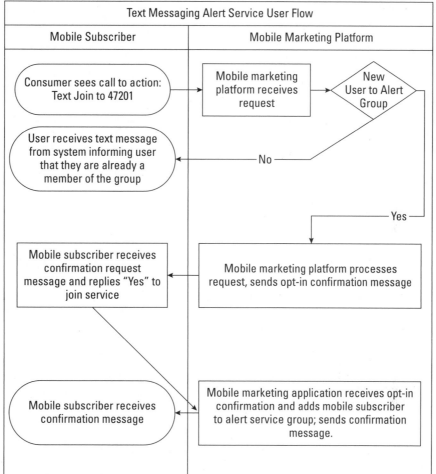

Figure 4-2:
A sample
user-flow
diagram
using the
flow chart
method.

Step 1: Paint a positive picture

Start by imagining what you want to have happen when everything works flawlessly. Picture what you want the perfect consumer experience to be. How do you want the opt-in flow to work, for example? What will the content-download experience look like?

Step 2: Map your opt-in flow

List the steps that a mobile subscriber must take to opt in to your program. Single opt-in is appropriate for programs that don't charge the consumer a premium for participation or programs.

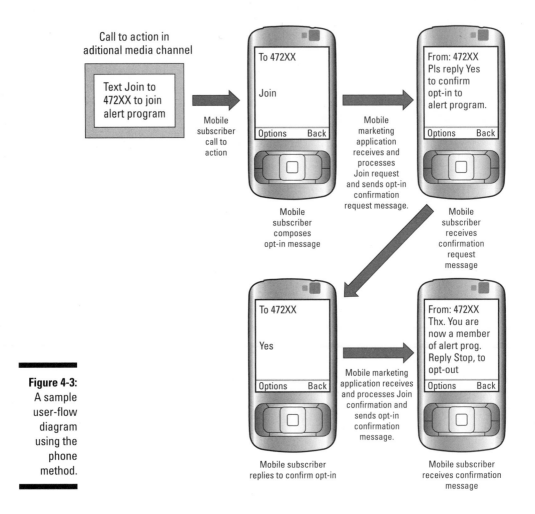

Figure 4-3:
A sample user-flow diagram using the phone method.

If you're going to have ongoing interactions with mobile subscribers, however, or plan to charge them a premium for participation, the industry's consumer best practices and regulations require you to get a double opt-in from all subscribers, meaning you have them send a second confirmation message and allow them to confirm their interest after their initial opt-in request, so you need to include that requirement in your user flow. (See Figure 4-4 for an example.) You can read more about managing opt-ins in Chapter 5. For more information about industry best practices and regulations, see Chapter 3.

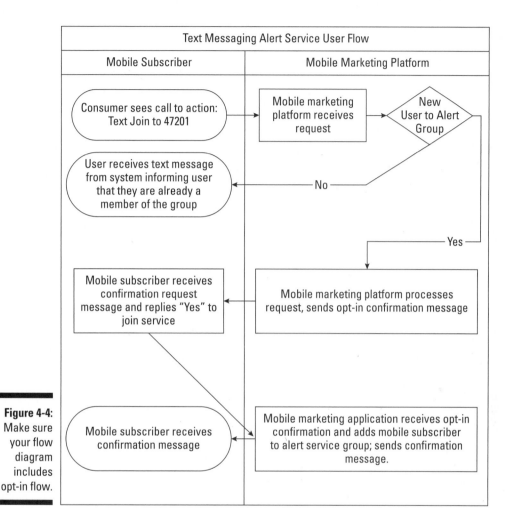

Figure 4-4:
Make sure
your flow
diagram
includes
opt-in flow.

In addition to the standard flow of messaging, you also may want to consider several common optional user flows that don't apply to all mobile communication campaigns and include them in your diagram:

✔ **Age verification:** To augment the opt-in process, you may provide the mobile subscriber an age-verification challenge — that is, require him to reply with his birth date before he can move to the next step of the program. If you're promoting content that's not suitable for children, you may want to make sure that you have the mobile subscriber's proffered birth date in your campaign's customer database. Figure 4-5 shows a typical age-verification challenge that you can send to a mobile phone.

✔ **Instant win:** You may want to award loyalty points, free content, a coupon, or some other form of incentive to participants. You could configure your mobile marketing application to award an instant prize to every third participant in the program, for example, or set it so that one in three participants wins. Ask your application provider how to configure this user flow in your system.

✔ **Grand prize:** A grand-prize winner is selected from the pool of participants at the end of the campaign. The mobile marketing application can be set up to draw the specified number of grand-prize winners automatically at the end of the campaign, or you can make the drawing manually from the list of participants, based on whatever selection criteria you choose.

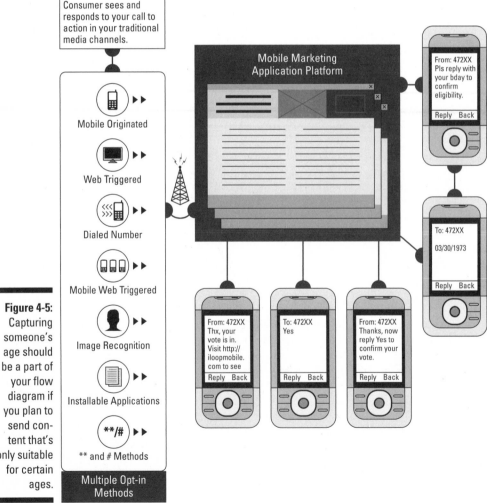

Figure 4-5: Capturing someone's age should be a part of your flow diagram if you plan to send content that's only suitable for certain ages.

Make sure that your rules are in line with both state and federal regulations.

✔ **Couponing:** Couponing is a very powerful incentive for participation in mobile programs. You may consider adding coupons within any message in your user flow to encourage continued participation in your programs as well as to encourage users to purchase your offerings.

When you send out a message, a coupon — either generated by the mobile marketing application or supplied by you to the application — can be appended to or inserted into the message.

✔ **Personalization:** If your mobile marketing program is integrated with an internal or external customer relationship management (CRM) system, you may be able to pull data from this system to personalize the messages in the program. You could insert a participant's first name in a message, such as "Hi, Mike. Pls reply *yes* to confirm."

In addition to mapping out the best-case interaction scenarios for your program, you want to map out the worst-case scenarios and edge cases for your program. Try to think through all the things that could go wrong with your program, even the most outlandish possibilities (the *edge cases*), and then map them in your user-flow diagram.

Document how both you and your mobile marketing application will react if one or more of these scenarios comes to pass. What if some of your potential customers speak French instead of English, for example? Your mobile subscriber may respond to your program's opt-in call to action by sending *oui* instead of *yes* as instructed. To prepare for that possibility, you need to configure your mobile marketing application to accept *oui, si, yup, ok, yse, yes, y,* and so on, as synonyms for *yes.*

Getting Approval for Your Text Messaging Campaigns

In the United States, all text messaging programs must be preapproved, or certified, by the mobile operator networks (this practice varies by country; check with your local application provider for assistance with certification requirements in different countries). The carriers require certification because they are ultimately liable for the traffic run over their networks and they want to ensure that their customers are receiving the highest quality service. Moreover, if one of their subscribers files a complaint or has a customer-care issue about a particular program, they want to make sure that they have on record the owner of the program and the appropriate customer support information to re-direct the customer to the campaign owner.

This section shows you what information you need to provide to the carriers in order to get approval, and how to walk through the approval and certification process.

First-time CSC and campaign certification

If you're planning to run a text messaging campaign for the first time, you need carrier approval for your campaign's message flow and for your common short code (CSC) so that your CSC is activated on all the carrier platforms. If you have already run a campaign and you have a working CSC, you only need to get approval for any new message flows.

The process for CSC activation and carrier approval is straightforward, but it does take time — about 8 to12 weeks from the submission of a completed campaign approval request form (Figure 4-6). The reality today is that most aggregators use an online tool rather than a form. You will more than likely never need to complete this form or have access to the online aggregator campaign certification tools — that is, unless you have your own applications and commercial agreements directly with an aggregator. Instead, your application provider will obtain the needed information from you and complete all the necessary forms and use the aggregator supplied tools on your behalf.

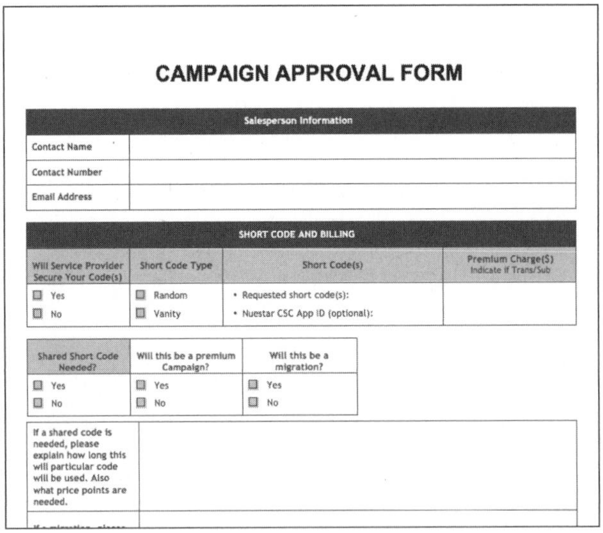

CAMPAIGN APPROVAL FORM

Salesperson Information	
Contact Name	
Contact Number	
Email Address	

SHORT CODE AND BILLING			
Will Service Provider Secure Your Code(s)	Short Code Type	Short Code(s)	Premium Charge($) Indicate if Trans/Sub
☐ Yes ☐ No	☐ Random ☐ Vanity	• Requested short code(s): • Nuestar CSC App ID (optional):	

Shared Short Code Needed?	Will this be a premium Campaign?	Will this be a migration?
☐ Yes ☐ No	☐ Yes ☐ No	☐ Yes ☐ No

If a shared code is needed, please explain how long this will particular code will be used. Also what price points are needed.	

Figure 4-6: A sample campaign approval request form.

You can't submit an approval request form directly to the carriers; instead, you need to submit the necessary information to your application provider, who in turn completes the forms and submits the information to the aggregator, who then works with each individual carrier to get your program approved. Because so many people and steps are involved, you'll want to make sure that the information you provide is complete and accurate at the time of submission. If it's not, you'll have to fix any errors and you may need to start the approval process over.

You need to submit the following information to your application provider, who then uses it to complete the approval form that is submitted to the aggregator:

- **Sales contact:** This is your primary contact at the application provider.

- **Common short code (CSC) owner:** Specify who will own/owns the CSC — you or the application provider. (You can read more about CSCs in the next section.)

- **Type:** Specify whether you're using a random or vanity code. (Discover more about random and vanity codes in the section "Deciding what type of CSC to use" later in this chapter.)

- **Billing:** Specify whether the code will be used for standard rate or premium rate messaging.

- **Migration:** Specify whether you're moving the CSC from another application provider, or whether this is a new code.

- **Campaign duration:** How long will your campaign be running (for a few months, or forever)?

- **Type of campaign:** What type of campaign will you be running on the CSC; for example, alerts, couponing, polling/voting, sweepstakes, or other?

- **Which carriers the code will be run on:** Here's a word to the wise: Say all. It doesn't cost you any more money than picking just a couple, and you want to go through this process as few times as possible.

- **All the details of your campaign:** What is it intended for? What are its objectives and dates? How will you promote it? How much traffic do you intend for it to generate? What will the program user flows look like? and so on.

- **Up and running:** Prior to submitting your program for approval, all aspects of the program will need to be live and running (all user flows, all support, all marketing material, and so on) so that the carrier can run end-to-end testing of the program before approving it.

Re-certifying and getting updates

Every single user flow and campaign on your CSC must go through the approval process. Whenever the current campaign user flows change or when you want to add additional consumer interactions (that is, new user flows) on the CSC, you have to go through the previously discussed certification process again. Although all the same information is still needed for new programs on an active short code, the approval process tends to be faster, above six to twelve weeks, compared to the eight to fifteen weeks. (These are U.S. estimates; every region varies.)

Auditing programs and maintaining compliance

All text messaging traffic going through U.S. carrier networks is regularly audited by the carriers, meaning that it is compared to the information you supplied during your initial campaign certification. If the carriers find any discrepancies between your approved program and the actual live program you're running, they may choose to flag your program as being out of compliance. If they do, they will notify you of any infractions they find and give you a grace period to fix them. If you don't, the carriers may shut off your CSC temporarily or permanently, depending on the nature of the infraction.

Many campaign infractions are easy to fix and the carriers may show some leniency. For example, if your opt-in language needs adjustments, you just need to change a few words. Of course, fraud, improper disclosures, or any programs inappropriately delivering adult-, tobacco-, or alcohol-related content will get your CSC terminated. Read Chapter 3 for more information about regulations and rules governing text messaging campaigns to make sure you're in compliance.

Understanding Common Short Codes

When it comes to commercially addressing text messages, your common short code means everything. In the United States, all commercial text messages (text messages for the purpose of mobile marketing) must be addressed and sent via common short codes.

A *common short code (CSC)* is simply a short (five or six digits) phone number used to address and route commercial text or multimedia messages through wireless operator networks (see Figure 4-7). CSCs are critical because nearly all effective mobile marketing programs leverage text messaging in one way or another.

Common short codes are effective for mobile marketing because they're all of the following things:

- **Bidirectional messaging:** Messaging traffic can be addressed both ways with CSCs, both to and from the mobile subscriber and you.

- **Cross-carrier enabled:** After they're activated on a carrier network, CSCs work across most of the leading U.S. carriers, extending a marketer's reach to more than 235 million mobile subscribers in the United States.

    CSCs are country-specific, unlike Internet domains, which work worldwide. You need to lease a CSC in each country where you want to run your mobile marketing (see "Acquiring a common short code," later in this chapter).

- **Billing engines:** You can use premium Short Message Service (SMS) messages and charge people for participation in your programs. (For more information about premium SMS, also called PSMS, see Chapter 13.)

- **Effective mechanisms for permissions marketing:** CSCs are the primary means of obtaining opt-ins in mobile marketing.

- **Useful:** CSCs are useful for a wide range of marketing campaigns and services.

From: 20222 ———— Common short code
Help

Send   Menu

Figure 4-7:
A common
short code
(CSC) is a
shortened
phone
number.

The following sections show you how to acquire and use CSCs for your text messaging campaigns. We show you how to launch and run those campaigns in Chapter 5.

Although you may have heard of them, we highly encourage you not to consider using either long codes or SMTP messaging methods for your text messaging. *Long code* is the term used for a full 10+ digit phone number. It is technically possible to connect a mobile phone modem with its own mobile phone number to a device like a PC to send text messages to another phone number. Although this is technically possible, it is not commercially prudent. This solution can only support very low volumes (some hundreds of text messages), and moreover it circumvents all the commercial regulations, like the mobile Marketing Association's Consumer Best Practices Guidelines. *SMTP messaging* refers to addressing text messages with an e-mail format such as usersphonenumber@carriermeailcomain.com and sending those messages from a PC or similar platform. Like long codes, SMTP messaging is technically possible, but does not provide a sustainable quality service in terms of volume support or delivery reliability, nor does the practice adhere to industry best practices guidelines and regulations.

Acquiring a common short code

You have two ways to gain access to a CSC for your mobile marketing program:

- ✔ **You can lease a CSC directly.** Choose this option when you want to run lots of different campaigns with no limit to the complexity of the campaigns.

- ✔ **You can rent access to an existing CSC.** Choose this option when you're on a budget or you need to run a minimum number of simple campaigns.

If you'd like to lease your own CSC directly, you can obtain it from one of the few short code administration bodies:

- ✔ **United States:** Common Short Code Administration (www.usshort codes.com; see Figure 4-8).

- ✔ **Canada:** Canadian Wireless Telecommunications Association Common Codes Administration (www.txt.ca/)

- ✔ **Latin America:** Administracion de Codigos (www.latinshortcodes.com)

- ✔ **United Kingdom:** U.K. Mobile Network Operators (www.short-codes.com)

- ✔ **France:** SMS+ (www.smsplus.org/index.php)

- ✔ **China:** Ministry of Information Industry Short Code Administration Group (www.miit.gov.cn)

To lease a short code or obtain access to one in other countries, you need to go through your application provider or a local aggregator. Ask your mobile marketing provider or local aggregator for assistance.

Figure 4-8:
The U.S. Common Short Code Administration provides CSC leasing in the U.S.

If you do decide to lease a short code, it's a pretty easy process. The following are the steps for doing so in the U.S. Remember that every registry may have a slightly different process:

1. **Go to the Common Short Code Administration Web site at www. usshortcodes.com.**

2. **Click on the Get an Account Now button, complete the form that appears (create a user ID, password, enter your address, and so on), and register your account.**

   If you're the marketer (as opposed to the application provider), select the role of content provider from the drop-down list and click Create Account.

3. **After you've created the account, you are asked to log in. After you log in with your user ID and password, click on the Apply for a New CSC link (on the left) and fill out the form that appears. Click Submit.**

   If you're having your application provider do this for you, be sure it puts your contact info in as the content provider. That way, if you leave your application provider, you will own the common short code, as opposed to the provider. In addition, you need to specify whether you want to lease the code for 3, 6, or 12 months, as well as the type of code (random or vanity) that you'd like. (See the following section for an explanation of random and vanity codes.)

4. **Read the terms and conditions and click the I Agree check box.**

5. **After you've accepted the terms and conditions, you are invited to confirm your purchase.**

   If you do not complete the payment for the common short code immediately, they hold it for 60 days. If you do not pay within 60 days, the code goes back into the pool of available codes.

Leasing your CSC is just the first step. After you've leased your CSC, you then need to have it activated on the mobile operator networks and bound to an aggregator who in turn binds it to a mobile marketing application. After this binding is complete and your CSC is registered in the carrier networks, all messaging traffic addressed to the CSC must be routed through a carrier network, who hands it to the registered aggregator, who in turn will route it to your specified application provider's text messaging platform. (The process for doing this is called the carrier approval process, which we detail in the section, "Getting Approval for Your Text Messaging Campaigns," earlier in this chapter.)

Leasing your own CSC can cost anywhere from $500-$1,000 per month, and it takes many months to get a new CSC approved. If you're not prepared to get your own short code — due to the expense or due to the time it takes to activate one — you can ask an application provider or connection aggregator to rent you access to one of their CSCs.

Many countries don't have a centralized short-code administration body, in which case you must rent access to a short code. Although this approach may get you up and running faster, at less expense, you want to take care with using this model. Depending on the relationship you forge with the application provider, the application provider may end up owning all your customers (all the opt-ins) on the code. Also, if the application provider does not pay the short-code lease or if a program on the code in a shared model runs afoul of the carrier requirement, the carriers may turn off the code and your programs along with all the other programs running on the code. If you're going to be doing any mobile marketing beyond one-off campaigns here and there, take it from us: Make the investment and get your own CSC.

Deciding what type of CSC to use

When you lease or rent access for your CSC, you have some other choices to make — namely, choosing the type of CSC to use. Here are the options you have and some tips for making the right choice:

✔ **Choosing random or vanity codes:** You'll need to choose between two short-code schemas:

- **Random short code:** A short code is considered to be *random* when the code-administration body assigns a random number sequence to the company leasing the code.

- **Vanity short code:** A short code is considered to be vanity when the code-administration body allows the company leasing the code to pick the numbers. An example of a vanity short code would be 46445, purchased specifically to spell *googl*. A company may choose to lease a vanity code to facilitate easy recall (77777) or to build its brand (57238 = kraft).

✔ **Deciding on five or six digits:** In addition to choosing a random or vanity short-code schema, you need to pick how many digits you want to use in your code: five or six. In the United States, you can lease five-digit codes as either random or vanity short codes, but six-digit codes can be leased only as vanity codes.

You may see four-digit short codes, but these codes tend to be reserved for the sole use of wireless carriers. Codes greater than six digits are called *long codes* and they're primarily used for running cross-border international programs.

Going dedicated or shared

You can choose to run multiple mobile initiatives on a single short code simultaneously or to run only one at any given time. When multiple mobile marketing campaigns are run on a single short code, the code is referred to as *shared*. When only one service is running on the code at any given time, the code is referred to as *dedicated*.

In short-code terms, *dedicated* and *shared* have nothing to do with who owns or leases the short code; they apply solely to how the short code is being used. Therefore, you can use your own dedicated code, rent a dedicated code, use your own short code in a shared model, or rent access to a shared code.

Both dedicated and shared short-code models have pros and cons, as you see in Table 4-1.

Table 4-1	Short-Code Models	
Model	*Pros*	*Cons*
Shared	Multiple initiatives can be run under one short code for a lower cost per initiative.	You need to include keywords in SMS messages to identify the initiative. User flow and instructions for initiatives are more complex. One noncertified "outlaw" initiative could shut down all other initiatives on a shared short code.
Dedicated	End-user task flow is easy. End users can text without having to include keywords to identify the initiative. You have more flexibility in initiative tactics. Reporting is easier.	The company is not amortizing short-code costs over multiple initiatives. All metric data can belong only to the initiative on the dedicated short code.

The shared and dedicated models are not cast in stone. As part of a company's CSC strategy, a short code can be used as dedicated for a certain period and then used as shared with multiple initiatives running on it. Consult your application or connection-aggregator partner for details.

Choosing an SMS Application Platform

The heart of your text messaging endeavors is your text messaging application (also often referred to as a text messaging platform). There are three approaches to gaining access to a text messaging platform:

✔ **Agency:** You work with a marketing agency and they handle everything for you.

✔ **Do-it-yourself:** You pay for, develop, and maintain your own solution yourself (this is a fairly expensive and risky endeavor given the fact that the technology and industry standards are often changing).

✔ **Platform:** You license access to a mobile marketing platform and either use this platform yourself or contract with the platform provider to manage it on your behalf.

Regardless of the approach you take, you should understand how text messaging platforms work and what they can and cannot do for you. That way, whether you license a platform, build it yourself, or contract with an agency, you know what to ask for, what features to consider, and what to evaluate your partnerships on. This section explains what to look for in a text messaging application platform, no matter which approach you take.

Building your own text messaging platform is beyond the scope of this book. If you're up for that challenge, get to know a venture capitalist and start your own mobile marketing business.

Understanding SMS application platform capabilities

The text messaging application platform manages all the interactions between you and your customers. Regardless of what your specific text messaging campaign is about, your text messaging platform performs three primary functions:

✔ Manages the connection between the application and the mobile operator's networks. This is typically done through a message aggregator, but sometimes the application provider may have one or more direct connections to a mobile carrier.

✔ Provides an Internet-accessible administration interface so that you can manage all your text messaging campaigns, common short codes, keywords, or reporting. See Figure 4-9 as an example.

✔ Has a database that stores all the transactions you've had with your customers through text messaging (the data will include time of day, type of program, and customer response). It will also have application interfaces that can be used to export and or achieve (manually, periodically, or in real time) the customer transaction data to third-party databases, like your company customer relationship management systems.

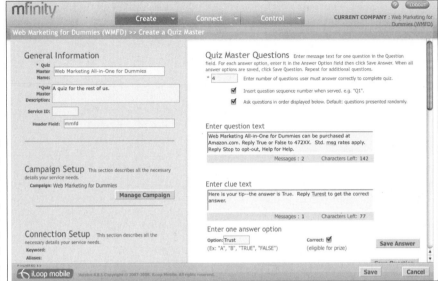

Figure 4-9:
Applications
provide
access to
manage-
ment tools
such as
templates.

In addition, providers of text messaging applications tend to provide the following consulting services as well:

✔ **Platform training:** To the extent that you want to learn, they can teach you how to use their platform.

✔ **Common short code registration services:** They'll help you rent or lease your codes, and get them activated and approved on carrier networks.

✔ **Campaign approval processes:** They'll help you get your campaigns approved by the carriers and assist you with navigating the myriad industry best practices and regulations, and help you respond to carrier audits.

✔ **Campaign consulting:** Although most leading technology providers do not make the best campaign consultants — use your agency for that instead — they can provide you with insights around what type of programs will be most effective to help you deliver value to your customer and to achieve your company objectives.

Selecting your SMS provider

A tremendous amount of expertise goes into developing and maintaining a text messaging platform. When you're looking for a provider, be sure to ask about or consider the following:

✔ **Experience:** Does the provider have extensive mobile experience and relationships within the mobile marketing industry? Ask for references; review campaigns that they've run before. Don't take their word for it. Also, it seems like everyone has done something with one of the largest brands at some time in their past, like Coca-Cola or Procter & Gamble. Make sure their references are current.

✔ **Industry leadership:** Make sure the provider is a member of the Mobile Marketing Association, or at least is following the MMA best practices and standards of care. You should also check whether it is a member of the related trade associations that are pertinent to your business, like the Direct Marketing Association for direct marketers, the Internet Advertising Bureau for Internet adversities, Shop.org for retailer, Online Publishers Association for publishers, and so on. Being members of one or more of these organizations demonstrates that the provider is continually learning and adapts to the changes in the industry.

✔ **Area of expertise:** Confirm which areas of mobile marketing the provider is an expert in. Some only provide SMS services and others offer a range of mobile marketing services including platform, analytics, strategy, creative, or execution. If the provider representative says that they are experts in all of these areas, make sure you drill down and find out who they work with or who they've recently bought. Be skeptical when one firm says they are an expert in everything.

✔ **Capabilities:** Does the provider have the capabilities you need to deliver or will they have to custom develop something special for you? If they have it on-hand, they can show you immediately.

✔ **The throughput/messaging capacity of the platform:** Ask how many text messages per second/per hour the platform can handle before it crashes and floats up to the top of the fish bowl. For example, if you're a successful national brand running a national television ad, you better make sure that your platform can handle millions of messages an hour. Even if you're a small company running a program, you still may run into capacity problems if the platform has a thousand other small companies each running a message. Don't be shy: Ask about throughput/capacity, ask to see reports, and have your provider prove that they can support your messaging traffic. Also, don't just ask about total volume, but peak spikes too. You want them to test for the maximum number of messages that may come in or go out at a specific period of time, not just the average.

✔ **Failover and disaster recovery plans:** Ask your provider representative if they're prepared for a catastrophe; for example, ask them what they'll do if their data center (where their servers are hosted) loses power or if a server or database fails? Ask them how quickly they can get back in service. If they are industry leaders, they'll have a redundant data center and can be back up in minutes with no loss of data. If they're not, your programs may be running on a computer under someone's desk, and you could risk losing everything and being down for a very long time.

🖊 **Pricing:** Pricing should be one of the last criteria you consider. Keep in mind that you get what you pay for. If you pay a little for your platform, don't expect a lot of service or support.

With the popularity of text messaging the mobile marketing increasing, both niche-market point solution providers and multi-capable platform providers are popping up all over the place. At the time of this writing, the leading text messaging providers include iLoop Mobile (www.iloopmobile.com), Hipcricket (www.hipcricket.com), Waterfall Mobile (www.waterfall mobile.com), Vibes Media (www.vibesmedia.com), Velti (www.velti.com) 2Ergo (www.2ergo.com), Telescope (www.telescope.tv), BookIt (www.bookit.net), and SMaSh (www.smashcode.com). There are also some very good smaller players, like mobileStorm (www.mobilestorm.com), Cellit (www.cellit.com), and Mobile Card Cast (www.mobilecardcast.com).

If you want to do some additional research on SMS providers, we recommend that you start by contacting the Mobile Marketing Association (www.mmaglobal.com) and getting a list of their members specializing in SMS. You should also check out the partners page at U.S. Short Codes.com (www.usshortcodes.com/csc_applicators.html) or simply conduct some Google searches.

Setting Up Your SMS Database

SMS campaigns have the ability to collect all kinds of valuable data on the people who interact with your campaigns. For example, a simple SMS campaign can tell you

🖊 Your customer's mobile phone number

🖊 Your customer's carrier

🖊 Your customer's phone model (if a Web URL is in the message and is clicked on by the consumer)

🖊 Your customer's interests

🖊 Any data you collect by asking your customers during a campaign

Be sure you confirm that your own database or your application provider's database can capture and store all that data so you can use it to target your marketing campaigns and follow up with customers. In addition to capturing and storing it, you also need to be able to manage your data.

This section shows you how to capture, store, and manage the data you collect from your SMS campaigns.

Read this section with care. Concern over personal information and privacy is at the forefront of many consumers' minds. Be careful with how you use information collected and be sure to stay current with local and federal laws regarding consumer privacy. Also, stay true to your mobile marketing code of conduct we discussed in Chapter 3.

Creating consumer profiles

An important aspect of marketing is developing profiles of the members of your audience so that you can target different audiences. When setting up your database, make sure it is set up to collect enough information to build a profile of each type of person or group you want to target. You can develop these profiles by amassing several types of data from a wide range of sources, including

- **Demographic data:** Age, gender, race/ethnicity, religion, marital status, number of children, level of education, occupation, income, nationality, and location/place of residence.

- **Psychographic data:** Lifestyle/activity, attitudes, interests, purchasing motives, and products and services used frequently.

- **Preference data:** Consumer preferences for when and how many times they want to be communicated with, preferred modes of communication (SMS, print, e-mail, and so on).

- **Behavioral data:** Purchasing history, criteria for choosing products, effect of the environment (location, culture, family, media exposure, and so on) on their choices, Internet sites visited, ads and links clicked, customer-support interactions, and so on.

- **Situational data:** Situational data about the consumer; for example, where the consumer is, what the weather is, what the stocks are doing, and so on.

- **Syndicated data:** Consumer purchasing data compiled from individually scanned consumer transactions at thousands of locations.

In tech speak, all this data is commonly called *metadata* — data about something. If a database engineer asks, "What kind of metadata do you want to capture?", you can answer, "I need demographic metadata: age, geography, psychographic data, and so on." You can use that to impress people at cocktail parties, too!

Amassing all these data types helps you develop a clear picture of the needs, wants, and desires of your target audience; thus, you have a better chance of giving your customers excellent service and providing them value.

Collecting data automatically through SMS

When a consumer opts in to your campaign via SMS, the mobile marketing application captures her mobile phone number. From this mobile phone number, your application provider captures the following data points, all of which you need to support the interaction with the subscriber and analyze your programs:

- ✔ **Previous participation in other programs you've run:** You can match the number to see whether it has been used in other campaigns.

- ✔ **Wireless carrier:** The number can identify the wireless carrier that the subscriber is using.

- ✔ **Crude location:** From the number's country and area codes, you can make a crude estimate of the subscriber's location: country, state, city, time zone, and so on.

  You can't use this method for real-time location detection, however, because it doesn't tell you where the person is at any given time — just where his phone is registered.

- ✔ **Porting status:** You can find out whether the number has ever been moved from one wireless carrier to another.

- ✔ **Technical information:** You can find out whether the subscriber's phone supports binary data (such as pictures and video).

Collecting data manually through SMS

You can ask campaign participants to submit any number of data points via SMS, including demographic, physiographic, and preference data. For example, you may ask a user to submit her birth date as an opt-in challenge. You simply need to make sure that your text messaging application allows you to collect the data appropriately. To collect data this way, your message flow has to allow for participants to text the information you want to collect to your short code in reply to a message. For example, your text message might say, "What's your first name? Reply with your first name."

Accessing your mobile marketing data

For basic reporting purposes (such as number of votes, opt-ins, opt-outs, purchases, content downloads, or mobile Internet page views), you can access this information in the mobile marketing application's database via standard reporting tools in the application provider's software, as shown in Figure 4-10.

Figure 4-10: Application providers or other partners can give you access to your data.

For advanced reporting and data analysis, and to build your marketing database, most mobile application service providers allow you to export the information from your account in their systems.

After you've exported all the information from the mobile marketing application, you can combine it with other data you've collected on individual members of your audience or on your audience in general (see the following section). In other words, you can use your mobile marketing data to enhance the profile of your audience as a whole as well as profiles of individual members of your audience.

Integrating SMS data with your CRM

Someday — maybe even today — you'll want to merge your mobile campaign data with the data stored in your company's customer relationship management (CRM) system. That way, you can follow up on the data you collect within the context of your normal sales or marketing operations. This process is easy enough and typically can be handled in any of three ways:

- ✔ **Manually:** You can ask your mobile marketing application provider to give you a report (in an Excel worksheet or an XML data structure, for example) so that you can combine your data with that of the CRM database manually.

- ✔ **Via data feed:** Your mobile marketing application provider should be able to give you access to an XML data feed. Then you can pull data from this feed on a regular basis (such as once a day or every five minutes) so that you can combine your data with that of the CRM database automatically on a set schedule.

- ✔ **In real time:** You can ask your mobile marking application provider to send you real-time data as your participants interact with the system. (For example, maybe you need to know immediately if someone opts out of your campaign so that you can update permission marketing management systems in other parts of your company.)

Chapter 5

Executing Common Text Messaging Campaigns

At first glance, text messaging seems to be a very simple service. I mean, really, what can be accomplished with 160 characters? If that's what you think, you will be surprised to discover just what text messaging can accomplish. You can

- Build awareness for your brand and products
- Stimulate engagement in your loyalty programs
- Sell goods and services and raise money
- Inform and entertain
- Recruit volunteers and build community
- Direct people to your store or events
- Provide real-time and asynchronous customer care and support
- Stimulate social media engagement
- Send last minute alerts and special VIP offers

These benefits are just the tip of the iceberg. You can do even more.

In this chapter, we focus on showing you how to set up text message-based mobile marketing programs, including promotion services, quizzes, polls, surveys, alert services, couponing, and more.

In the following pages, you discover how to manage consumer opt-ins for your text programs as well as how to gracefully handle the opt-outs when your customers tell you they don't want to hear from you via text anymore. You also find out about the common mobile marketing text programs, such as direct response, trivia, polls, surveys, mobile giving, alerts services, and more.

After reading this chapter, you'll have a clear, concise picture of exactly what it takes to run a text messaging program.

Getting Permission: The Opt-In

So what's an opt-in or an opt-out? An *opt-in* is the step someone takes to give you permission to proactively send him text messages. An *opt-out* is the steps someone takes to let you know that he no longer wants to hear from you; that is, the steps he takes to revoke his opt-in permission.

Sometimes, mobile marketing interaction occurs only once, such as when a customer requests some information through a mobile interaction and you send the information in return. In the case of single interactions, you don't need to make your customers formally opt-in because there is no ongoing interaction between you and the customer. In this case, the consumer initiates the interaction, so he is, in effect, opting in to one communication by requesting the information in the first place. If you want to initiate a future interaction (that is, send the consumer messages on an ongoing basis), you must get the consumer's permission with a formal opt-in.

The process of obtaining opt-ins is crucial to your long-term success in mobile marketing, especially with text messaging. Industry self-regulation and government laws alike require that you receive opt-ins from everyone before sending them text messages that you initiate.

The following sections show you how to gain formal opt-in permission and how to provide opt-out for subscribers who no longer want to receive your information.

Placing an opt-in call to action in media

A request for an opt-in is called an *opt-in call to action*. You can place an opt-in call to action in any traditional, new, and mobile media channel, including the following:

✓ Television

✓ Print (including magazines, coupons, package labels, and so on)

✓ Radio

✓ Point-of-sale displays (see Figure 5-1)

✓ Face-to-face encounters

✓ Outdoor advertising

✓ A Web page or advertisement

✓ An advertisement in a voice, text, or multimedia message, application, or mobile Internet site

✓ An e-mail

✓ A customer-care call

When you place a call to action in media, you're asking the members of your audience to pull out their phones, respond to your offer (opt-in to the campaign), and receive the benefits of your offer.

Figure 5-1:
You can prompt customers to place an opt-in call using traditional media.

Collecting mobile-originated opt-ins

A *mobile-originated opt-in* happens when someone uses her phone to send a text message in order to opt-in to receive future messages in return. The messages are called mobile-originated because they originate from the phone belonging to the person opting in.

When someone sends a mobile-originated (MO) message, your text-messaging application can respond with a mobile-terminated (MT) message that confirms the opt-in and gives additional information. Here's a summary of these two important message flows so you can better understand the information that follows in this section (read even more about message flow in Chapter 4):

- ✔ **Mobile-originated (MO):** A mobile subscriber composes *(originates)* a message on her phone and sends it to you.

- ✔ **Mobile-terminated (MT):** A message goes from an application provider's service to a mobile phone, so the message ends *(terminates)* on the phone.

When someone opts in to your mobile campaign with an MO message, you return an MT. Here are the three basic methods for collecting opt-ins using MO opt-in:

- ✔ **Single opt-in:** In a *single opt-in,* someone sends an MO in, and you simply send an MT back confirming the opt-in. Mostly, this process is used for one-time interactions; when the initial interaction is done, no future interactions will occur. However, if you want to continue to send messages in the future, you can use the single opt-in method only for standard rate messages where the opt-in is originated from the phone. (A *standard rate message* is a message billed to the consumer under the consumer's carrier messaging rate plan.) If the opt-in is originated from the Web or an app, or the like, you must get a double opt-in before you can send messages on an ongoing basis.

- ✔ **Double opt-in:** In the *double opt-in* scenario, someone sends an MO in, and you send an MT back requesting confirmation for the opt-in. For example, the system might respond with a text message that says, "Thanks, pls reply *Yes* to 12345. Std Msg&Data rates apply. To opt out, reply *stop,* or for help reply *help.*"). If the user sends the confirmation, he is opted in to the program and the mobile marketing application processes the request and sends back a welcome message, such as "Thank you. You're now in the group. To opt out reply *stop,* or for help reply *help.*" Double opt-in is best for standard rate and premium rate text messaging programs, and when the opt-in is initiated from a source other than a text message (such as a Web site or another application).

- ✔ **Multistep opt-in:** Use *multistep opt-in* when you want to challenge consumers with additional questions before they can participate in your program. For example, you may ask users for their ages if you're running a program suitable only for users 17 and older, or you may ask a series of questions to collect additional *metadata* (data about themselves). After a user responds to the additional challenges, the interaction may end, or you may follow up by triggering a double opt-in as well to get express consent for future marketing.

Collecting opt-in through the Internet and applications

Another great way to invite someone into your text messaging-based mobile marketing program is to present her a form on an Internet page, mobile Internet page, or in an installed application, as shown in Figure 5-2. For example, a customer can opt-in to receive text alerts.

In addition to capturing a mobile phone number on your opt-in form, collect additional consumer information and preferences, such as areas of interest, address, birthday, and so on.

Figure 5-2: Have customers opt-in on the Web using a form to collect information.

Collecting opt-ins through snapping and scanning

Cameras on mobile phones are wonderful tools for gathering opt-ins. You can instruct audience members to take a picture of an object, a soft-drink can, a magazine ad, a movie poster, or branded icon or almost anything else that has clearly defined edges and then instruct them to e-mail or text (via MMS) the picture to your mobile marketing program; some applications can also recognize the image locally on the phone, thus skipping the step of sending the picture in. When your program receives the picture, or the application decodes it, it processes the picture and then opts the mobile subscriber in to the program (see Figure 5-3). This process is sometimes called *image recognition, visual search,* or *digital watermarking.*

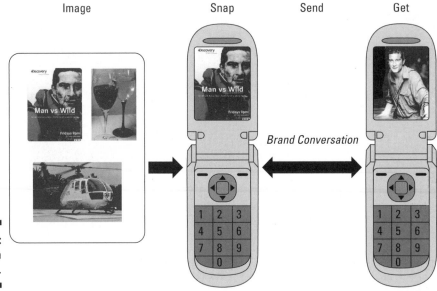

Figure 5-3: Opting in via the camera.

Courtesy of Snaptell

 The camera can be used for so much more, including the emerging practice of augmented reality (AR). *Augmented reality* refers to the effort to enhance a physical real-world image with computer generated imagery. For example, after downloading an application designed for augmented reality to their phones, your customers' camera viewfinders might depict the real world, as it always had — but with directions to your business or with three-dimensional images of your products superimposed over it. Stella Artois, the brewer, has an AR application that points the way to the closest bar to get a Stella Artois beer. Pizza Hut has one you can use to find the nearest Pizza Hut. I-PoP (www.i-pop.net) recently launched an AR dressing room in which an Adidas shirt is superimposed on any person standing in front of an augmented-reality-enhanced display or mirror — and with the click of a button, the shirt can be changed.

There are a number of companies you can look at to help you with these services, including: Amazon's SnapTell (www.snaptell.com), based in Palo Alto, California, Los Angeles-based SnapNow (www.snapnow.com), The Hyperfactory (www.hyperfactory.com), and Digimarc (www.digimarc.com). Google has also launched Google Goggles (http://www.google.com/mobile/goggles/) for visual search. You should also check out Layar (www.layar.com) and i-Pop (www.i-pop.net). Do some online research and you'll find even more options in this expanding field.

Collecting opt-ins through dialing and pressing

Dialing and pressing is all about consumers using their phones' keypads and the voice channel. You can encourage people to call a phone number by asking them to "dial 1-800-XXX-XXXX to experience the sounds of the movie" or "call 408-XXX-XXXX to listen in on the game," for example.

You don't have to answer the calls yourself; you can use an IVR (Interactive Voice Response) system to ask the caller to make selections. Selection options in an IVR session could include "Press 1 to receive a ringtone," "Press 2 to get your last five transactions," or "Press 3 to get the movie listings sent to your phone," or something similar. You can read more about IVR in Chapter 11.

Mobile marketing programs and any other programs that use text messaging (such as IVR, Internet, or mobile Internet) must use common short codes (CSCs) to address and route the message traffic. For details on CSCs, refer Chapter 4.

You can also collect opt-ins with key touches. Two companies — Zoove (www.zoove.com) and Singletouch (www.singletouch.com) — have developed two alternative opt-in channels.

Zoove's method uses the star (*) key on the mobile phone. A mobile subscriber on the Sprint network, for example, can press **267 — that is, **AOL — and the Send/Talk button on his phone (typically, the green button). In return, an AOL promotional mobile Internet site is sent to the phone. Singletouch's solution works the same way but uses the pound (#) key instead.

Both services are still limited in their deployment across wireless carriers, but you can see the possibilities of these methods of opt-in.

Gracefully Saying Goodbye: The Opt-Out

Breaking up is hard to do, but sometimes people just want to leave. They want to opt out and stop interacting with you. Maybe they'll come back, and maybe they won't, but you need to handle their requests with grace. Accept each request, reply politely, and *never contact the person again.* Otherwise, you'll become a spammer, and you don't want that.

Every best-practices guideline on calls to action covers opt-outs. You must include opt-out instructions that explain your program in your media and in the legal terms and conditions.

Industry best practices and regulations require all text messages to contain opt-out instructions, such as a *stop* keyword. You can read more about the industry best practices and legalities of obtaining permissions in Chapter 3.

You can use any of the opt-in methods discussed earlier in this chapter to capture opt-outs, but the most convenient way to gather an opt-out is simply to have the mobile subscriber send the mobile marketing application a text message that includes the keyword *stop* (or any other reserved opt-out keyword, such as *end, quit,* or *cancel*). When you receive the opt-out request, send a final reply, such as, "Thank you. Your opt-out request has been processed. We'll miss you. If you'd like to join again, reply *join* to 12345." Figure 5-4 shows an example.

Figure 5-4:
Replying
stop to
an MT
message is
the easiest
way to
opt out.

Courtesy of iLoop Mobile

Sending Information and Alerts via SMS

One of the simplest and most effective forms of text messaging is sending text messages on a periodic or regularly scheduled basis. You can send messages once a day, a couple times a week, or just once in a while, depending on the type of information and the frequency your subscriber expects.

You can also send alerts that are triggered as a response to an event, such as a birthday, recent purchase, or the availability of an overstocked item at a discount. The following sections help you understand when and how to send information and alerts via SMS.

Scheduling and sending SMS information

You can send your text messaging content to your mobile marketing agency or application provider and ask it to send it out, or if you have licensed access to a mobile marketing application platform, you can do it yourself, as shown in Figure 5-5.

Figure 5-5:
Sending
SMS
messages
is easy
using an
application
platform.

If you're going to do it yourself, you can follow these steps. These are generic steps, and are not specific to one application. Most application providers have a similar process:

1. **Launch your Internet browser and log in to the application.**

2. **Select the alert service feature.**

3. **Select the Schedule a Message button.**

4. **Fill out the message scheduling form, including your 160 character message, the keyword, and common short code associated with the program.**

5. **Select the database lists you want to send the message to and apply any filters (see the section titled "Sending filtered and automated SMS alerts" later in this chapter for more information).**

6. **Select the Send Now button to send the message immediately, or the Schedule/Calendar button to schedule the date and time you want the message to be automatically delivered.**

7. **Select the Send/Save button.**

The above is a generic user flow that is supported by most text messaging application provider solutions. If your messages change frequently, you may want to look for an application provider that lets you manage the content. This gives you more control over the timing of changes made, which is useful, but on the other hand it requires more work from you. Again, most applications offer similar user interfaces, and many providers can write one that is customized for your needs.

After you've sent your message, be sure to keep an eye on your reports (see Chapter 14 for more on reporting and analytics). Pay special attention to response rates. Did people reply to your call to action, like clicking on a link? Or did many people opt-out immediately upon receiving your message? If so, maybe your message was not targeted well enough and you need to work on the relevance of your content. Paying attention to these reports and adjusting to the results you see is the key to ongoing success with your text alert programs.

Sending filtered and automated SMS alerts

Most mobile marketing application providers give you the ability to filter your list of opted-in customers before you send a message. *Filtering* means you can select only those people in your list that meet a specific set of criteria. For example, say you're a concert promoter and you have a database of 100,000 subscribers, but you only want to send a message to the 15,000 people in the database who like hard rock, are between the ages of 25–30, and live in the San Francisco Bay area. All you need to do is log in to your provider's application, select the criteria you are interested in filtering the list for, and then press the filter button (see Figure 5-6).

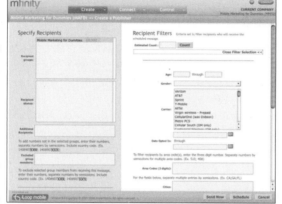

Figure 5-6:
Filtering allows you to send SMS messages to specific groups of subscribers.

Courtesy of iLoop Mobile

In order for filtering to work, your database must contain identifying information about your list. You can read more about building database profiles in Chapter 4.

If your database also contains information that pertains to event dates, you can use your application's filter to automatically send an SMS to a single subscriber or a group of subscribers when a certain date in any database field coincides with the date you specify in your filter. For example, you might want to send a birthday announcement to anyone whose birthday field contains the date July 4.

Filtering by date starts to get really interesting and powerful when you have a content management system or data service that sends information to your SMS application, which is in turn programmed to send an SMS to the customers in your database who are affected by that information. For example, if you subscribe to a weather service, stock quotes, or holidays, your SMS application could be programmed to send alerts to the customers who request alerts related to that information.

You can also use filtering to set parameters for your messages. For example, if you have some customers who only want to hear from you on the weekdays, or between 9 and 5, on their birthday, or only about specific topics in their immediate vicinity (a particular band, promotion, news or event category, for example), you can set your filters to send or withhold a particular message based on those customized options.

If your text messaging application provider does not let you filter your database, or if it can't help you do it, find another provider. This is an incredibly important capability because it's the primary tool at your disposal to help you in sending relevant messages to your subscribers.

Following best practices for SMS timing and content

When employing alerts services in your marketing programs, keep these things in mind:

- ✔ Always get permission first by obtaining an opt-in (see "Getting Permission: The Opt-In" section earlier in the chapter).

- ✔ Think about how often you send someone a message. Send too few and your relationship gets stale; send too many and you run the risk of annoying your customer. Make sure your content is relevant to the frequency you choose. For example, weather is a daily event, so a daily weather alert is appropriate.

- ✔ Keep the content fresh. No one wants to get the same discount or coupon code every single time he hears from you. Keep your content informative and entertaining with current events and news about your business, the industry, trivia, sweepstakes, and related promotional incentives and programs.

- ✔ Keep your content relevant to your audience by targeting and filtering your list as described in the previous section.

- ✔ Remember the character limits and formats. Text messages only support alphanumeric characters (such as A, B C...; 1, 2, 3...; !, @, #, and so on).

- ✔ Make sure you include the required industry language, like Std Msg&Data rates apply. (See the Mobile Marketing Association Consumer Best Practices guidelines at www.mmaglobal.com/bestpractices.pdf for more details.)

Engaging with Mobile Coupons

Text messaging is a great way to get offers, coupons, rebates, samples, vouchers, and gift cards into the hands of your customers. The concept is simple. The user sends a text message to request an offer or opts in to an alert service group to receive offers and similar content from you on a periodic basis.

There are two types of mobile coupon types you need to know about:

- **Closed systems:** *Closed system offers* refer to offers that are issued and redeemed by the same organization, for example, when your local pizza chain issues a coupon and redeems the coupon at one of its stores.

- **Open systems:** *Open system offers* refer to the situation when the issuer of the offer (such as your favorite soft drink brand) and the redeemer of the offer (such as a grocery store selling that soft drink) are different. For example, the soft drink brand issues a 2 for 1 coupon or offer and your grocer honors the coupon. You grocer takes your money, less the discount. The grocer must then work with an open system intermediary, like Inmar (www.inmar.com) or Valassis (www.valassis.com) to coordinate with the soft drink brand to receive reimbursement for having honored the coupon.

In the following sections, we explain how to set up the two types of mobile coupon systems and provide tips for getting the best results from your mobile coupon program.

Setting up your couponing program

To set up a closed system coupon program, you have two choices:

- **You can manage the program yourself.** This is done by using a general text application provider's direct response or alert service applications. In order to send coupons, you need only send text messages that contain the offer you want your audience to redeem. The offer can be all text with instructions on how to redeem the coupons, and you can also include offer codes and other information that give the coupons specialized features.

- **You can work with a specialized mobile couponing firm.** Companies that enable mobile coupons include lots of specialized features such as offer codes, personalization, and database integrations. Some of the best mobile coupons companies are iLoop Mobile (www.iloopmobile.com), Hipcricket (www.hipcricket.com), Money Mailer (www.moneymailer.com), Where (www.where.com), eKwipper (www.eKwipper.com), and 8coupons (www.8coupons.com).

Setting up an open system coupon program is a bit more complicated because you need to work with solution providers that can tie all the pieces together. You'll need to work with your solution provider to make sure all of the following participants in your program can work together:

✔ **The issuer of the coupon:** If that's you, your coupon needs to have all the features that the rest of your participants need to use. For example, if your coupon is redeemable at a point of sale, the point-of-sale computer has to be able to use the information you put in the coupon.

✔ **The redeemer of the coupon:** Your customer has to be able to receive, view, and interact with the coupon. This requires making sure the coupon works on the customer's phone and incorporates the capabilities of the phone such as touchscreen or Internet browser.

✔ **The point-of-sales solution:** The coupon has to be redeemed by someone and usually entered into a database to track the coupon and record the sale at the same time. Some coupons are redeemable online and others at a register in a store, so your coupon needs to be able to accommodate whatever form of entry is required. (We discuss redemption methods in the next section.)

Setting up coupon redemption at a point of sale

When someone receives a text coupon from you, you're going to have to tell him how to redeem the coupon. Several methods are available for point-of-sale redemption, including

✔ **Asking the customer to show her coupon to a clerk in the store.** With this method, the store clerk simply reduces the price of the purchase and maybe records the coupon in the system or on a less formal record-keeping tool, like a clipboard with a place to write down the details of the transaction.

✔ **Giving the customer an offer ID to share with the person in the store (see Figure 5-7).** Use your coupon system to generate a randomly assigned code that is unique to each customer, and then record each redemption code to prevent people from redeeming a coupon more than once.

✔ **Sending a special mobile bar code that can be scanned at the counter.** This is the most automated method, but it's also the method with the most technical challenges (we discuss these challenges in the remainder of this section).

Figure 5-7:
Offer IDs in
a coupon
can be
assigned to
each
customer.

From: 472XX
Boots Sale! Take 20%
all boots @ boots for
less now through
Sunday, 09/1/2010.
show your phone in-
store to save on fall's
most fabulous
footwear! Your ID:
1234.
Options   Back

Any of the aforementioned methods of point-of-sale redemption require some type of system for recording the details of the coupon. Methods for recording the coupon can get pretty sophisticated, and you *should* get sophisticated if you want to track interactions with your customers. Any information about coupon redemption can tell you a lot about what your customers are buying and how they are buying.

The most sophisticated way to redeem and record mobile coupons is by delivering a bar code to a user's phone (Figure 5-8). Mobile bar codes are a bit different from the bar codes you typically see on packaging or paper coupons, and scanning them requires a special POS scanner. (Traditional in-store scanners can't read a mobile phone's screen reliably, and phone screens are very small, so bar code data footprints are limited.) Mobile bar codes are often referred to as 2D or 3D codes. As of this writing, Target and Starbucks are the only two companies that formally accept these codes.

One challenge with this method is that the 2D and 3D scanners can be quite expensive. Although they're common in some countries, such as Japan, they're not yet widely deployed in the United States. Another challenge is that mobile phones and networks must be configured to support 2D and 3D bar codes.

Figure 5-8:
2D and 3D
mobile bar
codes can
be scanned
at a point of
purchase.

One mobile couponing company, bCODE (www.bcode.com), combines text and scanning. You should also check out Scanbuy (www.scanbuy.com), NeoMedia (www.neom.com), and Neustar (www.neustar.com) for more on the latest in 2D barcodes. These companies send the coupon via text, MMS, Web sites, and applications, and they can provide you with a scanner that you can put in your store to scan phones and redeem coupons.

Keep in mind, however, that just having the scanner isn't enough to enable your mobile coupon codes to work effectively. Your coupons and scanners also need to be incorporated into other POS systems features such as computing taxes, generating a receipt, and communicating with various other software modules or applications for things like inventory management, loyalty applications, and forecasting. Your mobile coupon scanning system also needs to integrate with your POS system's traditional bar code readers, credit card readers, and other external devices for recording items purchased, identifying customers, and collecting electronic payments.

The mobile marketing industry has made great strides in delivering mobile POS technology and gaining consumer acceptance of mobile coupons. The companies that are leading the way include mDot Network (www.mdot network.com), Hipcricket (www.hipcricket.com), iLoop Mobile (www.iloopmobile.com), and Infinian (www.infinian.com).

Bar codes: More than just for coupons

Coupons are just one of the many uses of bar codes on and with the mobile phone. In addition for point-of-sale redemption of coupons, vouchers, gift cards, and so on, they can be used in mobile-enhanced traditional media to stimulate consumer opt-in and participate in mobile programs. The reason why they're so useful is you can cram a lot of data into one small bar code. Some of the more popular uses include airline check-in, business cards to share contact information, calendar/event promotion, URL/e-mail address promotion, Geo-location map links, text or pictures, and more. One major challenge with bar codes is that the industry has not yet adopted a common standard. There are 1D, 2D, and 3D bar codes and countless implementations of each. Just a few of the standards include QR-Codes, DataMatrix Codes, Cool-Data-Matrix, Semacodes, UPCODE, Trillcode, Quickmark, Shotcode, Connexto, Beetagg, Qode, JagTag, and others. Some of the leading companies enabling bar codes for mobile include ScanBuy (www.scanbuy.com), NeoMedia (www.neom.com), JagTag (www.jagtag.com), Microsoft (http://tag.microsoft.com) and others. In the United States, Neustar (www.neustar.com) is actively helping to drive a common standard for bar codes. You can also find out more about 1D and 2D codes and Google's project zxing at http://code.google.com/p/zxing. On the flip side, a number of companies enable consumers to scan the bar codes on products for price comparison shopping and for gathering information, including Redlaser (www.redlaser.com) and Big In Japan's ShopSavvy services (www.biggu.com).

These companies are working with numerous POS vendors to create an Internet-enabled network that allows mobile marketers to execute seamlessly and securely at the POS without requiring the retailers to replace POS hardware and software. Companies like Microsoft are working on the next generation of POS systems which will run on the Internet as opposed to being installed on proprietary hardware in the store. These companies will provide connectors (called APIs or Application Programming Interfaces) so that mobile marketers can integrate directly with the POS software.

In the next few years, you will see mobile marketing at POS take off as the technologies for connecting mobile devices to the POS systems in real time become mature and widely accepted. Just like with ATM machines in the 1970s and 1980s, adoption and maturity of these technologies will take time, but eventually will become second nature to us.

Getting technical with text coupons

Mobile coupons can get pretty technical behind the scenes. Suppose you want your coupon to only be redeemed once, or you want to give everyone on your customer list a unique offer code so only that person can redeem the coupon. Complex databases are sometimes required to generate all kinds of parameters and functions that generate the messages, the associated offer codes, and the relationship between the offer and the interaction with a real person. Mobile coupon application providers take your coupon requirements — and those of your program participants — and put them into a database so that the system that generates the coupons knows how to formulate the features of the coupon when it is sent out. Talk to your mobile application provider about its solution and how configurable it is.

Setting up Internet and application coupon redemption

In addition to point-of-sale redemption, mobile coupons can also be redeemed on a mobile Internet site or through a mobile application. Companies such as Cellfire (www.cellfire.com) can enable coupons through the download of their applications. The application maintains all the coupons locally on the phone and continuously reaches out to the coupon server via an Internet connection on the phone to update itself automatically. Companies like mDot Network enable coupon redemption at the point of sale. (See Figure 5-9.)

Redeeming coupons through a mobile Internet site requires the customer to enter a code contained in the coupon or click a link with the code embedded. This method of coupon delivery can be very effective, but it isn't as universally applicable as text messaging for delivering coupons, for several reasons:

✔ The mobile subscriber has to have a phone that supports applications.

✔ The subscriber has to want to install the application.

✔ The subscriber has to know how to use the application.

✔ The subscriber has to be on a data services (Internet) plan with the mobile operator.

These limitations are disappearing fast, however, as mobile subscribers continue to adopt more advanced phones and services.

Figure 5-9:
MDot, a
leading
mobile
couponing
provider for
retail.

Courtesy of mDot Network

Offering incentives: Gifts, freebies, and samples

It should come as no surprise to you that people respond to incentives. Offer them something of value, and they'll be more inclined to participate in your program and initiate communication with you. Continue offering them value, and they may become customers. Keep offering them value, and they'll become loyal customers. Keep offering them value after that, and you'll turn them into evangelists who'll start doing your marketing for you. This process starts with the first engagement, and an incentive is a great way to kick-start the interaction.

The most common forms of incentives are

- **Money:** Coupons, discounts on services, or even hard cash
- **Content:** Free ringtones, wallpapers, images, and so on
- **Free stuff and experiences:** Tickets for trial and sample products, free movie admission, a chance to go backstage and meet the star, and so on

In the United States, wireless carriers tend to frown on your offering free content such as ringtones and wallpapers, especially if they're selling the same content via their branded content storefronts on the phone. Free content programs must be preapproved and certified with the wireless carriers, and your best shot at getting approval is offering content that isn't available anywhere else.

Not surprisingly, offering free content (like a ringtone, wallpaper, game, application and so on) is also often your best shot at getting mobile subscriber participation; many subscribers value unique or personalized content.

Managing prize promos, contests, and giveaways

It's common practice in marketing to offer prize promotions, run contests, and give stuff away as incentives to encourage people to participate in marketing programs. You could run a program that gives out small prizes instantly throughout the campaign period and ends by awarding one lucky participant a grand prize, such as a new car or a vacation. This format works well in traditional marketing programs, and it works well in mobile marketing programs too.

You can enhance any of your mobile marketing promotions — text-based communication programs, voice programs, mobile Internet programs, and so on — with incentives. The process is simple:

1. **Promote the incentive along with the call to action to participate.**

2. **Set the odds of winning (often a configurable element) in the mobile marketing application.**

   If you're going to have an instant-win component or a grand prize, configure the odds for that too.

3. **Coordinate with your prize fulfillment house if you're going to be giving away physical goods or services, or configure your mobile marketing application to award content to be consumed on a mobile phone (such as a ringtone).**

When you run any type of contest, sweepstakes, or giveaway program, you absolutely must work with your legal team to document the rules and the related terms and conditions of your program. The law requires you to provide this documentation, such as start and end date of the program, alternative forms of entry, value of price, who is eligible, and so on. Every state has its own laws about these types of programs, so if you're running a campaign, make sure that you're compliant with all the individual state laws. You can read more about legalities of mobile campaigns in Chapter 3. Also, you can contact ePrize (www.eprize.com), one of the leading sweepstakes providers in the United States.

Giving people a taste: Product-sampling programs

Sampling is another fantastic tool you should consider using in your marketing communications programs. For many products, all it takes to get a consumer hooked is that first use. Mobile marketing is a good vehicle for sampling. For digital content, you can deliver a clipped version of the song, a photo with *Preview* stamped on it, and so on. You can't get physical goods (such as a new sports drink) into a phone, however, so your best bet is to mail product samples to program participants or mail them a card that they can use to get the samples free at a local store.

To run a sampling program, promote it in traditional media. When a mobile subscriber responds, you can query him for his address via interactive voice response (IVR, see Chapter 11 for more) or text messaging. When you have all the information, you can thank the user and send him a text message saying that he'll get his sample in a few days, barring any delays in shipping.

The mobile marketing company ShopText (www.shoptext.com) has refined this process to an art. With ShopText, you can set up not only sampling programs, but also commerce programs.

Offering Quizzes and Trivia

Mobile subscribers interact with quizzes and trivia programs by responding to questions sent to their phones. You can use text messaging in quiz programs to gather feedback, consumer opinions, or votes, as well as to inform and entertain. Your customers can have a great time with trivia programs, for example.

A *closed-ended* quiz is a program that gives mobile subscribers a fixed set of response options, such as *a, b, c,* and *d* or *true* and *false.* (See Figure 5-10 for a sample quiz.) If a user gets the answer right, you can send a response message saying "You're correct" or "You win." But if the user sends an answer that doesn't match any of the predefined answers, you should send back an error-response message with instructions for answering the question correctly. If the user tries to answer a question twice, you could send a reply like "I'm sorry, you've already answered that question," or "We did not understand your answer."

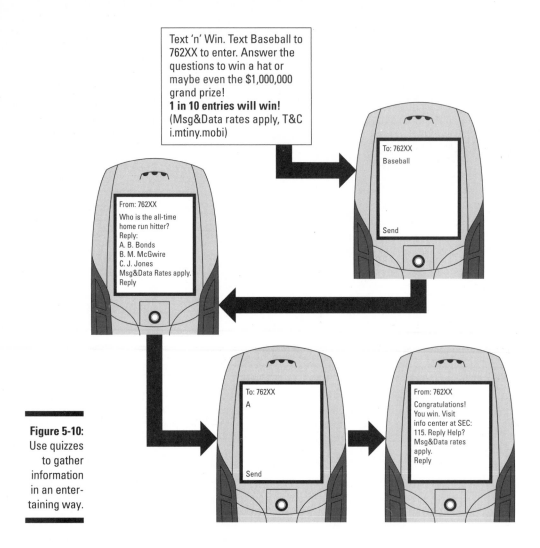

Figure 5-10:
Use quizzes
to gather
information
in an enter-
taining way.

Setting up quiz options

In addition to the typical user flow (see Chapter 4 for more on user flows), your mobile marketing application provider should be able to provide the following configurable options for a quiz program:

✔ **Question-response format:** Decide which format you want to use for user responses, such as alphanumeric selection (*a, b, c,* and *d* or *1, 2, 3,* and *4*), binary choice (*true* and *false* or *yes* and *no*), or individual items (*red, green, blue,* and so on).

✔ **Question order:** Decide whether questions should be delivered in fixed linear order or pulled randomly from a pool of questions. You may want your audience to answer the same five questions in a specific order, or you may have the service pull five questions randomly from a pool of 500, generating a random set of questions for each participant.

✔ **Question count:** Decide how many questions a user must answer to complete the program. If the quiz is configured so that the user has to answer five questions, for example, the mobile marketing application will send the next question in the sequence or pull one randomly (see the preceding item) until all the questions in the campaign sequence are sent or the user opts out of the service.

✔ **Auto-response format:** Decide whether each question has a correct answer or is simply being used to collect user input (see the next section, "Setting quiz response options"). In either case, you also need to decide when to send an individual text message to the mobile subscriber: after each answer (correct or incorrect) or upon completion of the quiz, for example.

Along the way, include opt-in and opt-out options and a reminder about how standard messages and data rates may apply if you plan to ask a lot of questions. Refresh your memory of this in Chapters 3 and 4.

Setting up quiz response options

You may run a quiz that doesn't have correct or incorrect answers; you just want a response. In this case, you don't have to specify the response options as being correct or incorrect. All responses are simply accepted and recorded. Following are a few examples of response options you can set (see Figure 5-11):

✔ **Clue:** If your program supports a clue element, users can request a clue to answer a question. Suppose that a user is stuck on the third question. If he texts *clue* or *hint* to the mobile marketing application, the application sends back a clue for the question.

✔ **Action on incorrect response:** Decide what happens when users give incorrect responses. If a user gets the third question wrong, for example, does she simply start over or move on to the next question until the campaign question count is reached? (For more information about question count, refer to "Setting up quiz options," earlier in this chapter.)

✔ **Response timing:** You can choose to run a speed quiz that measures the speed of user responses. The fastest responder may win, for example.

✔ **Participation cap:** You may want to set a participation cap to limit how many times users can participate in the program during a given period — one to ten times a day, once a week, once a month, one time only, or unlimited times through the entire program, for example.

✔ **Repeat questions:** Decide whether to configure the service so that users receive some questions more than once or whether they always get different questions.

✔ **Premium billing:** Decide whether to bill mobile subscribers for participation in the program. (For details on making money with your mobile marketing programs, see Chapter 13.)

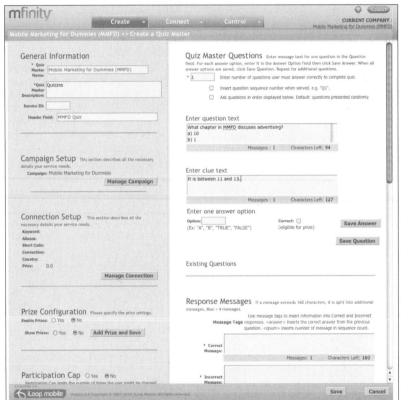

Figure 5-11:
Some example quiz-response settings.

You can also use the application for quizzes to direct mobile subscribers to a particular next step in an application user flow, such as a product offering (a content storefront, for example) or another text messaging campaign or service. You can use the response to a question to initiate a mobile subscriber into a horoscope program, for example. When the subscriber answers the question, his response is used to configure the next question to be sent to his phone.

Ratings by the pint: An interactive Guinness program

The Great Guinness Pint contest is an example of an interactive program. The program, which ran in 2008, allowed consumers to rate their pints of Guinness directly via mobile phone. Each time a consumer rated a pint, she was entered for a chance to win a trip to the Guinness brewery in Dublin, Ireland, for the company's 250th anniversary celebration. Participating accounts received recognition for the quality of pints they served. Each account owner, along with the Guinness team, tracked ratings in real time directly on a mobile phone as well as online. In addition to tracking progress, the Guinness team added or edited an account on the fly. When a new account was added, a keyword was generated automatically, allowing consumers to participate immediately.

Here's how the program worked: Throughout a participating account's bar, various point-of-sale (POS) materials, such as coasters, table tents, posters, and custom pint-rating cards, were displayed. These POS materials encouraged customers to help Guinness find the greatest pint in America. Consumers were directed to text the word *great* (or a unique keyword assigned to each account) to 88500; when they did, they were prompted to rate the pint of Guinness that they were just served. Each POS material educated consumers on what makes a pint great, above and beyond taste.

In developing this program, John Lim, chief executive officer of Mobile Card Cast, knew that its success would be driven by the competitive nature of Guinness accounts and by high participation levels among consumers. Therefore, he used simple Short Message Service (SMS) technology to create ease of use for consumers and to allow account owners to access rankings through a simple mobile landing page. The following figure shows an example of the marketing materials used to promote the program within an establishment.

Courtesy of Mobile Card Cast

Capturing Sentiment with Polling and Surveys

In *polls* (also referred to as *votes*), as opposed to quizzes and surveys, the questions you want your audience members to answer are placed in traditional or new media: billboards, in-store end caps, newspapers, television, e-mail and radio programs, and so on. Like quizzes and surveys, however, polling allows you to gather audience members' opinions and feedback as well as to inform and entertain.

In mobile marketing, a poll poses questions not in a text message but in traditional media. Mobile subscribers see or hear the call to action (such as "Text *a* or *b* to cast your vote"), and when they respond, the mobile marketing application sends a reply (such as "Thanks. You voted *a*. Total tally: *a* 35%, *b* 6%, *c* 59%"). See Figure 5-12 for a sample poll user flow.

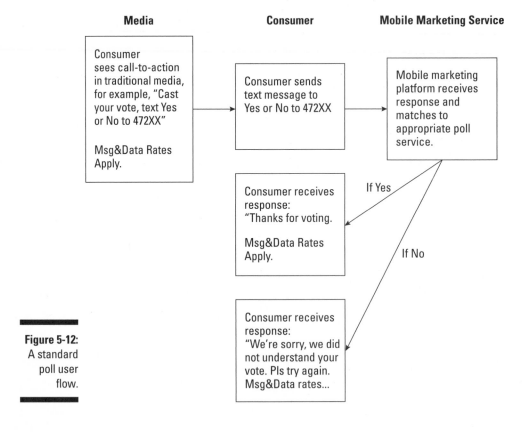

Figure 5-12: A standard poll user flow.

Planning the survey

In planning a survey program, you need to consider the following points:

- ✔ **How many questions to ask:** Don't go overboard. If you ask too many questions, people will simply drop out without completing their participation in your program.

- ✔ **The order in which questions will be asked:** Think about the order in which you ask the questions. Does some flow make particular sense?

- ✔ **The required length of answers:** Remember that most people don't have mobile phones with full keyboards, and pecking out long messages can be tedious for them. Try to limit the information you need to short responses.

Using open-ended questions

You can use open-ended text messaging survey programs to gather information such as consumer, candidate, or employee feedback. After a job interview, for example, you could send the candidate a text message like this: "Please give us your feedback on the interview process. Reply to this message with your feedback."

Unlike questions in quizzes (refer to the section, "Offering Quizzes and Trivia," earlier in this chapter), survey questions sent to mobile subscribers' phones don't have preconfigured response options, such as multiple choice or true and false. Rather, subscriber are asked a question and invited to send free-form responses. You may ask a mobile subscriber "What's your e-mail address?", for example. When he answers this question, the mobile marketing application automatically sends out the next question, and the process repeats until all the required questions have been sent and answered.

Ask your mobile marketing application provider whether you can chain your survey program, or even your quiz programs, with any other mobile marketing programs you're running. When you chain one program to another, you can do really cool things. Suppose that a user is opting in to your couponing program. If you chain a survey template to the coupon service, you can collect the user's preferences and other personal information before you allow her to opt-in and get the coupon.

Setting survey options

Your mobile marketing application provider should be able to provide the following configurable options for your survey program:

- ✔ **Number of questions:** Decide how many questions a user must answer to complete the program.

- ✔ **Question order:** Decide whether questions are always delivered in fixed linear order or pulled randomly from a pool of questions.

- ✔ **Question labels:** Make sure that your mobile marketing application allows you to use a configuration tool to label your survey questions. Later, when you data-mine and report on the survey responses, the labels will help you sort and organize the data. (For details on reporting on your programs, see Chapter 14.)

Choosing a poll type

Following are some of the most common uses of mobile polling and voting:

- ✔ **Television voting/polling:** During the 2008 season of *American Idol* season, the show's exclusive mobile-carrier sponsor, AT&T, reported that more than 78 million votes were submitted over its network. Another popular show, *Deal or No Deal,* uses voting for mobile sweepstakes campaigns. Sports and news shows use polls to discern the opinions of audience members.

- ✔ **Live-event polling and voting:** Increasingly, polling and voting are being used in live events such as sporting events, keynote speeches, and radio broadcasts. The call to action for the poll is placed in traditional media, and people respond. Then the results of the poll are displayed on the stadium's in-venue display screens, on a screen behind the speaker, or on the radio station's Web site.

If you expect high-volume interactions — hundreds of thousands or even millions of messages in just a few hours — be sure to consult your mobile marketing application provider and connection aggregator. They can fine-tune their systems to ensure that high-volume traffic is processed efficiently. Often, in the case of high-volume programs, the marketer opts to turn off the poll's immediate message-response feature so that the mobile marketing application can spend all its time processing poll responses. Responses can be sent after all the poll responses are processed.

Be sure to take time zones into account when you decide when the delayed responses should be sent. You don't want to wake people up in the middle of the night.

Setting poll options

Your mobile marketing application provider should be able to provide the following configurable options for your poll program:

✔ **Question-response format:** Decide which format you'll use for user responses, such as alphanumeric selection (*a, b, c,* and *d* or *1, 2, 3,* and *4*), binary choice (*true* and *false* or *yes* and *no*), or individual items (*red, green, blue,* and so on).

✔ **Response message:** Decide whether you want to include poll statistics in your response message (such as "Thank you. You voted *a,* and so did 60% of the other participants"). Ask your mobile marketing application provider whether it can support real-time results in your response messages.

Discovering Text-to-Screen and Experiential SMS Campaigns

Another popular form of consumer interaction via text is text-to-screen, a simple idea that can create a lot of interaction with live audiences at sporting events, concerts, television broadcasts, and the like. In a text-to-screen program, you place a call to action in traditional media (the giant video screens at a sporting event, a public-address announcement at a concert, or a ticker at the bottom of the TV screen, for example), inviting mobile subscribers to send a text message (such as encouragement for the team or a shout-out to a friend), a photo (such as a picture of a group of friends watching the event), or some other content. When it receives a message of this type, the mobile marketing application places the message in a moderation queue. Then, after the message has been moderated by an automated system or a live person, it's displayed onscreen at the event for a few seconds.

Examples of text-to-screen services go as far back as 2005 in the U.S. When U2 toured the United States in 2005, for example, the band used text-to-screen during shows to support the Live 8 antipoverty initiative. U2 asked audience members to text their names to a short code. The mobile subscribers' names, along with thousands of other participants' names, were displayed onscreen at the concerts. Later, U2 added up all the names and total participants recorded at all its events and used these figures to show the world that people care about poverty issues.

Another useful application of text-to-screen is to poll audience members during live presentations. For example, an organization out of Chicago, Jarbyco (www.jarbyco.com), enables parishioners to text their pastor during sermons. Unlike mobile polls, in which mobile subscribers answer questions, in text-to-screen programs, mobile subscribers ask the questions. You present the call to action during the event, and subscribers text in their questions, which you moderate and display onscreen. Then the presenter can look at the screen and provide answers to the audience. This same capability has been used in live events to provide real-time feedback to speakers, but as you might expect, feedback sometimes distracts the speaker, especially if the feedback is negative. Leading text-to-screen applications providers include Aerva (www.aerva.com), iLoop Mobile (www.iloopmobile.com), Vibes (www.vibes.com), and so on.

Text-to-screen programs can support interactions with almost anyone. During its annual conference in 2008, for example, the Direct Marketing Association offered a mobile concierge service. Attendees could text in their questions (such as "When will the exhibits close?"), and a person in the information booth would text back the answers via a Web browser.

This chapter just scratches the surface of what is possible with SMS. There are so many topics we haven't covered, including customer relationship management loyalty programs, customer support and care programs, or more advanced secure SMS programs, or "intelligent" programs like those offered by iLoop Mobile and its Smart SMS solution (www.iloopmobile.com).

Chapter 6

Sending Multimedia Messages

● ●

● ●

Multimedia Messaging Service (MMS) gives marketers the ability to deliver messages to mobile phones that tell a story with captivating images, sound, and full motion video. You can even use MMS to write long descriptions in alphanumeric text and to include links to mobile Web sites and other stuff without the 160 character limits that SMS messages impose.

In this chapter, we tell you all about using MMS for marketing. We show you how it is different from SMS. We also explain the types of content you can include within MMS messages and how to use this content to script compelling and engaging messages within your mobile marketing programs.

In addition, we show you the types of applications you can use to create your MMS content and explain how it is important for you to use a mobile marketing application provider that specializes in MMS to power your MMS programs. We also show you a number of MMS marketing examples to help stimulate your creative juices on how to use MMS for your business.

Comparing MMS to SMS

Multimedia Messaging Service (MMS) can be used to send messages in the same manner as *Short Messaging Service* (SMS), but MMS messages can contain a lot more content because MMS messages aren't limited to 160 characters of text and links as SMS messages are. The MMS messaging standard was created in 2001 after the huge commercial success of text messaging, and today's MMS features continue to grow in popularity every day all over the world.

The next sections explain the differences between MMS and SMS messages. (You can read about SMS in Chapters 4 and 5.)

Discovering the content capabilities of MMS

Compared to SMS, MMS has the ability to send a lot more interesting, engaging, and feature-rich messages that people can interact with. Here are the main content capabilities of MMS:

- **Text:** You don't have to worry about running out of characters with MMS (and your customers won't have to learn some new teenager language that allows meaningful expression within 160 text characters). You can include a practically unlimited amount of text (up to several thousands of characters) in an MMS message. Additionally, you can format your text in many ways, from adding color to changing fonts and styles.

- **Images:** This is the most familiar type of MMS message for personal communications. People love to take pictures with camera phones and send them immediately to friends and family. For mobile marketers, you can send images and have them integrated into an MMS delivered directly to your customers' mobile phone inboxes. As you know, a picture is worth a thousand words, so inserting a compelling picture truly helps to get your message across!

Think about all of the ways that adding images can help you communicate with your customers. You can send out a message with your logo in it, which helps to distinguish and showcase your brand. Or, you can send a picture of the new product — the hot new shot — that you want people coming to your retail store to shop for!

- **Audio:** MMS messages can include audio clips that play like a soundtrack during a slideshow, or the sound can be inserted as a standalone feature of the message.

- **Animations:** MMS technically functions like a slideshow, so animations look great in an MMS (imagine flipping through a flip book). These animations can range from animated icons, cartoon figures, or rotating images and are easily assembled into an MMS. An animation can be created in either an animated GIF file or video format and delivered to a phone as an MMS! (An *animated GIF* is a series of images displayed one after the other, like an animation. They look just like you are watching a slideshow or movie.)

- **Video:** Nearly all MMS-enabled phones can receive video files. You should use an application like Final Cut Pro, iMovie, or QuickTime Pro to encode your video clips in H.263 and MPEG-4 formats, which ensures that your MMS video message will have compatibility with most devices. MMS messages can contain a lot of content, but file sizes are not unlimited. Make sure videos are no more than 15 frames per second and roughly 30 seconds in length. This ensures that the video can be delivered to nearly all MMS-enabled phones and that it's still high quality enough for the person who receives it to enjoy it on her phone! Check out the manual of your software application to understand how to save your content in these recommended formats (Hint: With most programs, you typically use the Save As for Web or Export feature.)

Examining MMS compatibility and reach

Although SMS text messaging has the greatest reach of any form of mobile messaging in the U.S., MMS is not far behind. Of the 230 million folks in the U.S. who send text messages today, roughly 85% of them (or 200 million) can send and receive MMS messages. For us marketers, 200 million is a big number — it's twice the size of the audience who watched the 2010 Super Bowl!

Most consumers do not need a data or Internet plan (that is, a contract with their carrier to connect to the Internet or download applications from their phone) to send and receive MMS on their phones — MMS messages are considered part of the text messaging plan provided by wireless carriers.

In 2009, consumers were sending about 5 billion MMS messages per month in the United States, compared to around 1 billion SMS text messages per day. (By March 2010, more than 5 billion text messages were sent daily in the U.S.) The important thing to note is that enough people are using MMS to make it worth a marketer's while to invest in MMS messaging.

There are two types of MMS-capable phones: those that just receive pictures and those that receive all forms of MMS, including pictures, video, and audio files. When MMS was brand-new (way back in 2003), most phones could only receive pictures via MMS. In 2010, 95% of MMS-capable phones can now receive all forms of MMS messages, enabling everyone, including consumers and marketers, the full suite of multimedia options when creating MMS mobile marketing campaigns.

If you want to know whether your customers are capable of receiving your MMS marketing messages, ask them if their mobile devices take pictures. If the answer is yes, your customers probably have MMS-capable phones (some devices without a camera may accept MMS, but they're few and far between). The mobile phone manufacturers started years ago to integrate MMS capability into nearly all their phones (not just the high-end ones) that they ship. Only a handful of phones still around today in the U.S. can't receive MMS.

Paying attention to MMS pricing

Starting in 2008, nearly all the wireless carriers in the United States made one significant change that jumpstarted the MMS mobile marketing industry. (MMS has been in Europe since the early 2000s.) The wireless carriers decided to charge consumers the same rate for MMS as they did for SMS messages if they had a text messaging plan (which most mobile users do today).

Prior to this change, you were charged an extra fee to receive a picture or video message on your phone. Fortunately, this change enabled all messages to be treated equally (regardless of size, content, or type, a message is a message), which means that mobile marketers can deliver video to consumers via MMS for the same price as a text message! Because people love telling stories with visuals and sounds, marketers can now get much more creative with personal and business communication using MMS.

Even though the pricing for consumers has been lowered so that the cost to a *consumer* to receive an MMS is the same as that for receiving a text, mobile *marketers* do pay a tiny bit more to send MMS messages to their customers. (It's like why those rental car places charge us a little more to drive the luxury car with a GPS unit versus an economy car with manual windows!) Fortunately, the price difference isn't too great. Many marketers find it a small price to pay to send a message with color, action, sound, and even animation!

On average, MMS message campaigns cost from 25–50% more than a standard SMS campaign. Using do-it-yourself tools (see the section titled, "Delivering your MMS content" elsewhere in this chapter), you can expect to pay roughly $.10–$.20 to send an MMS to one of your customers versus about $.05–$.10 for an SMS message.

Preparing Your MMS Campaign

Setting up an MMS mobile marketing program can be simple, although it is more complicated than just setting up a similar text messaging–only campaign (as we discuss in Chapters 4 and 5). To properly execute an MMS mobile marketing campaign, you need the following:

- ✔ Properly formatted and scripted content files.
- ✔ An MMS application (a software solution) to create your MMS message.
- ✔ An MMS mobile marketing partner to manage your campaign and help you deliver it to your customers. (Believe us; you don't want to try this on your own.)

Putting together an MMS message is a lot like putting together a slide presentation or a commercial. Your MMS messages can be as simple as one static image, or as intricate as a series of fully interactive images, movie clips, and sounds, as shown in Figure 6-1.

Figure 6-1:
MMS messages can include multiple media in one message.

Powered by Mogreet. Courtesy of the Mobile Marketing Association

Don't think of MMS messages as simply a way to deliver a message. Instead, MMS gives you the opportunity to tell a complete story. In the following sections, we explain how you can quickly and easily set up an MMS-based mobile marketing campaign.

Putting your MMS storyboard together

A storyboard is like a map of your entire MMS message that includes a beginning, a middle, and an ending — just like a story. You need to use a storyboard to explain to the person or company who is building your MMS message what you want your message to say and how you want it to look.

Creating a storyboard is easy. All the best stories start with one — even Steven Spielberg and Alfred Hitchcock created them before finalizing their masterpieces! Yours doesn't have to be this intricate, though. All you need is a pencil, a pad of paper, and a little imagination to get started. If you want to use a computer application to do your storyboard, several are available, such as StoryBoard Pro Software by Atomic Learning. You can download it for free from www.atomiclearning.com.

To create a storyboard, write or draw the story in frames or scenes, just like a comic book. Be creative and try to visualize how you want your message to grab your customer and how the story should flow from one scene to another. For example, imagine if you were starting a band and wanted to create an MMS message to send to your fans to tell them to buy tickets to tonight's show. The first scene of the storyboard might open with an image of you backstage and a hint of music playing in the background. The next scene includes an image of the band tuning up their instruments and slightly louder background music. The final scene has music at full volume, an image of a crowded nightclub, and the band on stage with a call to action to come see the band tonight! You get the idea.

Here are a few other things you should include in your storyboard to make sure that your MMS message is as effective as it is attractive:

- ✔ **Determine the purpose of your story.** Are you trying to entertain, inform, or drive a specific action (like encouraging someone to buy something)?

- ✔ **Think about how to tell your story in 30 seconds or less.** Because the size of the message has some limits, you've got about thirty seconds total to tell your story.

- ✔ **Include a call to action in your storyboard.** Make sure your MMS message tells your customers the action that you want them to take. (For example, come see my band, or come check out the sale at my store!) This call to action should be simple, strong, and easy to remember so that you leave a lasting impression on your customer!

Collecting and formatting your media

Before creating your MMS, you need to collect or create the images, text, music animations, and video that will make your story engaging. When creating a series of media animations for an MMS, select the pictures that you want to weave together into a mini story and use an application like Corel's Paint Shop Pro (www.corel.com) or Adobe Photoshop or Adobe Illustrator (www.adobe.com) to convert it into an animated GIF.

If you want your animations to look like a video, you can use a video editing program like Apple's iMovie or Final Cut Pro (www.apple.com) to convert the animated GIF into a mobile video. Eventually, when you create your MMS, it will look like you're reading a flipbook as the slideshow appears before your eyes. Keep in mind, however, that your MMS application provider will probably have to adjust or modify some of your files to ensure they are compatible with market requirements. Ask your application provider whether creating your own media will save you any time or money before you do it yourself.

When creating an MMS, the video part of an MMS should be around 200KB in size for optimal performance across the majority of mobile devices and networks. Here's why: In the process of creating an MMS, a few components are added to create the MMS, which doubles the size of the total file. Think of the process as like shipping a valuable item across the country. Before you ship it, you need to surround it with packing peanuts and put it in a secure box before dropping it off at the post office. The packing peanuts make your package a little heavier. MMS works the same way: Your video gets bigger as an MMS wrapper is assembled to protect the MMS and deliver it to a mobile phone. Most carriers require that videos are smaller than 400KB for MMS, so make sure your video is less than 400KB (shoot for 200KB for the fastest delivery); otherwise, it might not get delivered!

If you're using an application provider to create and send your MMS messages, they may also offer creative services. In that case, you won't have to build the message yourself, but you should still script the message out to the best of your ability using a storyboard. That way, you can ensure that your application provider understands what you want your message to look like and what your message is supposed to accomplish.

Delivering your MMS content

After you have your message put together, you can either give your media files to your application provider, or build your MMS message on your own using a do-it-yourself application or partner.

Here are the two ways to set up and deliver your MMS mobile marketing campaign:

- ✔ Use a do-it-yourself (DIY) program to enable you to create your own MMS messages and deliver them to a list of recipients.
- ✔ Use an application provider to execute the program on your behalf.

If you want to give it a go on your own, check out do-it-yourself tools such as Mogreet (www.mogreet.com). With a DIY tool, you can upload your media and have it assembled by the software application into an MMS message. With these applications, all you need are the media files and your story layout, and you are ready to go, as shown in Figures 6-2 and 6-3.

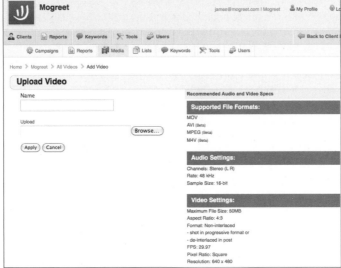

Figure 6-2:
The Mogreet MMS tool enables you to upload your video in standard formats.

Courtesy of Mogreet

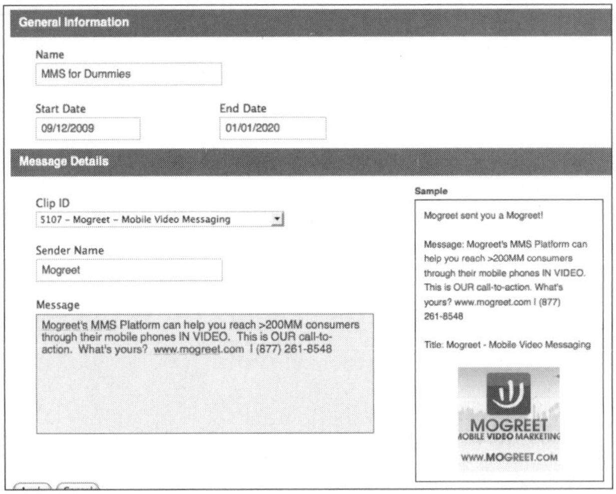

Figure 6-3:
DIY applications let you preview your MMS messages.

Courtesy of Mogreet

Do-it-yourself applications are great for simple MMS messages, and for sending them to small groups of people. DIY-minded small businesses and early adopters looking to take advantage of the benefits of MMS should try the applications from Mogreet or CellySpace (www.cellyspace.com).

Don't want to do it yourself? Given the complexity of actually creating an MMS and the emerging nature of the DIY platforms, hiring an application provider isn't a bad idea, especially when you consider the fact that the application provider typically has expertise to share.

For those creating more customized MMS messages, looking to send out large volumes of MMS messages, or needing some help with the creative work, contacting an MMS application provider is the way to go. The application provider can help you with

- ✔ Obtaining and managing carrier approval processes for your program. (See Chapter 3 for more on the rules and regulations of mobile marketing.)

- ✔ Obtaining the use of a common short code or getting your own if you need to send a lot of MMS messages. (See Chapter 4 for understanding common short codes.)

- ✔ Managing the formatting and delivery of the content and customizing it for the many different types of cellphone carriers and handsets out there. (For example, delivering an MMS message to an Apple iPhone is much different than delivering it to a Motorola RAZR.)

- ✔ Targeting MMS messages for specific subgroups of customers. (For example, your MMS message to your customers with iPhones could include a link to download your iPhone application, which you would want delivered to iPhone customers only. All your other customers could receive a different MMS message.)

- ✔ Tracking the success of your campaign and building a database of your customers' mobile phones.

Because this is pretty complicated stuff, only a handful of companies can help you with your MMS marketing campaign. We recommend using established players such as Mogreet (www.mogreet.com), Hook Mobile (www.hookmobile.com), or Skycore (www.skycore.com).

Make sure you test your MMS before you mass-send it. Keep in mind that an MMS will look different on, say, an iPhone versus a BlackBerry. Make sure that the message you use in your MMS makes sense given how your customers will actually see the message. For example, don't say, "Watch the video" in the text portion of your MMS if your video automatically plays when they open the message before they see the written content. Your MMS provider can help you manage the delivery of MMS to different device platforms.

Sending Common MMS Campaigns

MMS marketing is rather new, so you need to be creative when considering the utility of MMS to drive customers to your business. Some MMS marketing campaigns, however, are tried and tested. Starting with a few "typical" MMS campaigns keeps you from wasting time, energy, and money on messages that don't work. The following sections show you three MMS marketing ideas that have been used by lots of companies with great success so you can see the features and benefits of each and apply them to your business and your future MMS strategy.

Sending MMS greeting cards

Greeting cards, shown in Figure 6-4, are by nature perfectly suited to MMS delivery because they feature animated content and evoke personal emotions. Best of all, they can be delivered instantly to a very personal place — the recipient's phone!

Figure 6-4: MMS greeting cards are a personal and fun way to reach out to customers.

Courtesy of Mogreet

Sending a greeting card is a great way for businesses to connect with their customers in a very thoughtful and unobtrusive way. Many businesses who send out paper greeting cards during the holiday season are switching to mobile because they are cheaper than sending paper cards with $.40 stamps and they are more personal than electronic greeting cards delivered to a shared computer or e-mail inbox. Here are some tips to remember when creating mobile greeting cards:

- ✔ **The content of your greeting cards should be focused on building a relationship, not just selling.** That being said, be sure to include all your company's contact information, including your phone number and your Web site address.

- ✔ **Keep your messages personal, but not too personal.** For simplicity's sake, target the content of your message to a group but make it generic enough to allow you to send the same message to all your customers within that group. For example, you might be able to send the same golf-themed greeting to all the golfers in your customer database without personalizing every single message.

- ✔ **Get the timing right.** Holidays are easy to time, but birthdays, anniversaries, and thank-you cards sent after a purchase must be individually timed. You can schedule reminder greetings using some DIY MMS tools, or you can provide the dates in your database to your MMS application provider.

Remember that including unlicensed content from someone else could get you in trouble. Contact the owner of any footage you plan to use in your mobile greeting cards before using it. You can visit content licensing libraries online, like Creative Commons (`www.creativecommons.org`), to find tons of content to include in your messages.

Be my mobile Valentine

On Valentine's Day, 2010, American Greetings customers sent and received mobile greeting cards to every state in the United States and in Canada! This means that people in every part of the U.S. were sending and receiving mobile greetings!

Running picture-to-screen campaigns

Picture-to-screen campaigns enable your customers to take pictures with their phones and send them into a short code to be instantly posted on a digital screen. That digital screen could be as simple as a single television screen in your store or as complex as multiple digital billboards in sports stadiums all over the country.

Several picture-to-screen applications are being used today because they get audiences excited and engaged in an activity surrounding a promotion, while also having a viral element to them. Some of the more compelling applications of picture-to-screen campaigns include the following:

✔ **Displaying picture messages from the crowd at sporting events, concerts. and nightclubs:** For example, a beverage company might ask people to send a picture of them drinking their product in order to win a prize.

✔ **Displaying pictures from the viewers of TV shows to increase audience participation:** For example, a television show host might ask people to send pictures of themselves using a specific product and the pictures could be displayed at the bottom of the television screen (after someone reviews them, of course).

✔ **Displaying news and information through citizen journalism and live mobile blogging:** For example, consumers could send pictures and videos directly from their phones to Web sites with the latest local news, weather, or traffic. Check out CNN's iReport (www.cnn.com/ireport) or Allvoices (www.allvoices.com) to see examples of citizen journalism in action today!

To set up a picture-to-screen campaign, pick a location where your customers can post and view the pictures they create. This could be a screen in your store or a more public venue. Many retailers now (from Wal-Mart to Nordstrom's to EBGames) have digital screens in their stores, which can showcase the picture-to-screen campaigns.

To get the word out about your picture-to-screen campaign, you can use the digital screen to tell people how to send the pictures. For example, your screen could say "Text a picture of such-and-such product to 21534 to be entered into a contest to win free season tickets!"

Picture-to-screen campaigns are usually best for getting people engaged in an advertising message, but they can also be used to capture mobile phone numbers from people. If you use picture-to-screen campaigns to collect phone numbers, make sure your opt-in message complies with carrier regulations and is part of a joint campaign. You can read more about mobile opt-in regulations in Chapter 3.

The process of receiving pictures in from a mobile phone, filtering them (because some consumers send pictures that you don't want posted on public screens), and posting them on a digital screen is a very technical process. We strongly recommend that you contact an application vendor to have them guide you through it for maximum success.

Companies that can help you set up a picture-to-screen campaign right away include TxtStation (www.txtstation.com), MangoMobile (www.mango mobile.com), Phizzle (www.phizzle.com), Aerva (www.aerva.com), Telescope (www.telescope.tv), and Mogreet (www.mogreet.com).

Creating MMS coupon promotions

Imagine the power of a coupon that includes a full video of the product in action or a testimonial of someone who used the product. Mobile coupons are a fast-growing way to deliver special deals to your loyal customers, and sending mobile coupons with MMS gives your coupons an instant upgrade to interactivity.

Make sure your coupon includes instructions for redeeming the offer and think about how you plan to track the offers before you create the coupon. MMS coupons can be redeemed in any of the following ways:

- ✔ By showing the coupon to the clerk in a store.

- ✔ By including a promotional code in the coupon. This could be a link with special tracking code or a number that needs to be entered into a mobile Web site. If you want your customers to view the entire MMS message, ask them to listen or watch for the secret symbol or word in the message and then use that word or message to redeem the offer.

- ✔ By asking your customers to take the same action shown in the MMS message. For example, the MMS message could teach the viewer a jingle that needs to be sung by the customer in the store in order to receive the offer.

- ✔ By asking the viewer of the message to take action on their mobile phone in response to the message. For example, you might ask them to send a text message or a picture to a short code or call a phone number shared in the message.

 Businesses doing MMS promotions should remember not to over- or under-communicate with your customers on their mobile phones. If your customer has opted in, they expect to receive regular communication from you. Most MMS marketers send out offers one to four times per month and constantly change them to make them fresh and interesting to their customers.

 Because MMS campaigns are affordable relative to other forms of marketing, and because MMS messaging is somewhat new, you should create a few different ideas and test them against one another. That way, you can easily see if one idea has better results than another and apply what you find out from this research to your next promotion.

Chapter 7

Mobile E-Mail Marketing

· ·

· ·

*I*n the early days of mobile e-mail, if you wanted to make sure people on mobile phones could read your company's e-mail newsletter, you had to send some sort of text-only version of the pretty-looking HTML e-mail you sent to your customers' computers. That's changing fast. Mobile phones and the programs that run on them are getting sophisticated enough to display complex HTML and standardized enough to ensure that your e-mails look basically the same on a majority of devices.

Don't relax yet, however. You need to do more than just worry about getting your e-mails to look good. You also need to make sure your e-mail content is accessible on multiple platforms like computer-based e-mail programs, Web-based e-mail programs, and even social media sites. You also need to be able to utilize other forms of mobile communication to build your e-mail list and ensure that your mobile e-mails are actionable through mobile devices so your customers are able to make purchase decisions without waiting until they're in front of a computer.

This chapter shows you how to make changes to your overall e-mail marketing strategy so your e-mails get results when they're viewed on mobile devices. To find out how to build your overall e-mail marketing strategy, get your hands on *E-Mail Marketing For Dummies,* by John Arnold (published by Wiley).

Getting a Grip on Mobile E-Mail

Think of e-mail marketing as one of many forms of mobile communication with certain advantages and disadvantages. Table 7-1 compares the main forms of mobile communication so you can understand where mobile fits into your strategy.

Table 7-1	E-Mail Compared to Other Forms of Mobile Communication			
	Mobile E-Mail	**Text Messages (SMS or MMS)**	**Social Media**	**Really Simple Syndication (RSS)**
Delivery Options	Mass delivery to private inboxes and one-to-one personalization are possible.	Mass delivery to private inboxes and one-to-one personalization are possible.	Mass delivery is public. Personalized delivery to private inboxes is manual.	Mass delivery is public. Personalization is a challenge because opt-in is often anonymous.
Delivery Rates (% of Messages That Are Delivered Correctly)	E-mail delivered by a good e-mail marketing provider can exceed 97%. Filters and changes to e-mail addresses can degrade deliverability.	Assume 100% delivery. Carriers control opt-in and delivery gateways, so filtering is low. People don't change mobile phone numbers as often as e-mail addresses.	Mass messages are posted rather than delivered and anyone can view them. People can easily un-follow and ignore posts.	Mass messages are posted rather than delivered, and anyone with an RSS reader can view them. People can easily unsubscribe and ignore posts.

	Mobile E-Mail	*Text Messages (SMS or MMS)*	*Social Media*	*Really Simple Syndication (RSS)*
Audience	Almost everyone uses e-mail and people can easily make the transition from reading e-mail on a computer to reading e-mail on a mobile phone.	Usage is increasing rapidly for users older than 30 and text messaging is a standard for most people younger than 25. More than 95% of phones on the market can send and receive text messages.	Once popular only with young audiences, social media usage is now widespread. Few people, however, consider social media to be their primary form of communication.	Fewer than 15% of consumers realize they use RSS*, but the technology is used to enable many familiar blogging functions like feeding a blog post to other Web sites or posting someone else's content to your own blog or social media page.
Building a List	Obtaining e-mail addresses and permission is required. Confirmed opt-in is not required, but it's still a good idea.	Obtaining mobile phone numbers and permission is required. Confirmed opt-in is required by all the carriers.	Obtaining personal contact information not required. Permission is inherent in the decision to follow your messages.	Obtaining personal contact information not required. Permission is inherent in the decision to follow your messages.

(continued)

Table 7-1 *(continued)*

	Mobile E-Mail	*Text Messages (SMS or MMS)*	*Social Media*	*Really Simple Syndication (RSS)*
Formatting	Nearly unlimited text and graphic designs are possible. A variety of links and images can be included.	Text limited to 160 characters and graphic design limited to images. Links are subject to character limits.	Text limited on some sites, such as Twitter. Limited graphic design. Links to files and downloads are limited.	Limited text and graphic design unless the reader clicks through to the source of the feed. Links to files and down-loads are limited or not included in the feed.
Cost	E-mail service pro-vider recom-mended. Flat-rate and per-message plans avail-able at fractions of pennies per message.	Service provider required. Per-message plans start at around $.10 per message and go lower based on volume.	Going direct to each social media site is free. Service provider is required to manage multiple sites and audiences. Costs are minimal.	Service provider or program-ming skills required. Most ser-vices are free or very low cost.

*According to a ClickZ report

E-mail is perfect for sending highly personalized, targeted, private, and interest-specific messages to a large number of people at once. You can include links to files, Web pages, and other content, and you can control your brand identity with colors, images, and text formatting. You can also deliver e-mail to personal inboxes on a mass scale. This means you can reach a lot of people efficiently, and your recipients are more likely to pay attention to your e-mails because they sit in an inbox until they're opened or deleted.

The advantages and trade-offs of e-mail don't end with the utility of e-mail as a form of communication. You need to manage several technical issues in order to be effective in mobile e-mail marketing. The next sections show you how to think through the technical challenges and deal with them.

Dealing with devices and browsers

Looking at an e-mail address won't tell you whether the person on the other end is going to be looking at a computer screen or a mobile phone screen when they read your e-mail message. Most people with mobile e-mail can access the same inbox from their phone and their computer.

This poses a challenge to e-mail marketers because some e-mail characteristics are more desirable for a person in front of a computer than for a person in front of a mobile device, and some e-mail characteristics that are possible to view on a computer are impossible to view or interact with on a mobile device.

For example, sending an e-mail newsletter with three columns of text could look great on a big computer screen, but it's really hard to read on a three-inch mobile screen (see Figure 7-1). Similarly, sending an e-mail that contains a link to purchase a product might get an immediate response when recipients are in front of a computer, but cause frustration for those who discover that they can't make the purchase via their phone because the technical capabilities of the phone or the online store are limited.

Here are the four technical issues that affect the ability to interact with e-mails on mobile devices, followed by a few tips for dealing with them (or at least tolerating them):

✔ **The device:** Some native device characteristics make it difficult to interact with e-mail. For example, a device without a touchscreen can make clicking on a link frustrating or even impossible. Even if you know the capabilities of every device used by every one of your customers and you can somehow keep that information updated when your customers change to another device, it's next to impossible to design an e-mail that allows seamless interaction on every device. Besides that, it's not practical to design a different e-mail for every device. That defeats one of the main benefits of e-mail, which is mass delivery.

Figure 7-1:
Some e-mail
designs
are more
friendly
to mobile
devices
than others.

Courtesy of ConstantContact.com

✔ **The operating system or browser on the device:** Device manufacturers install software on their phones so the phones will function. Some phones, like iPhones, Google Android phones, BlackBerry phones, and Palm phones have their own operating systems. Other phones manufactured by companies like HTC and Motorola could be using Windows Mobile or software installed by the carrier who provides service to the customer. To make matters worse, some phones install standard Internet browsers like Safari, Firefox, or Internet Explorer to display HTML designs, whereas other operating systems aren't capable of displaying HTML at all. Every operating system and browser has the potential to display your e-mails differently or disable some functions you build in to your e-mail's HTML.

✔ **The e-mail program being used:** Even if you have a group of people using the same phone and the same operating system, the program they use to read their e-mail might be completely different and cause your e-mail to encounter variations in functionality. For example, some people with an iPhone might check their e-mail using iMail, whereas others using the same device and operating system use Outlook so they can synchronize their corporate e-mails. The programmers who build the e-mail programs we use make decisions based on their perception of usability, and those decisions aren't always good for everyone, let alone based on the same standards. For example, one programmer might decide to limit all incoming e-mails to the first 150 characters until the recipient decides to download the whole message, whereas another decides to allow everything to display as soon as the e-mail is opened. This isn't just a mobile e-mail challenge. E-mail marketers have been struggling with variations in standards among e-mail programs like Outlook, Hotmail, Gmail, Yahoo!, and AOL for as long as HTML e-mail has been around.

✔ **The HTML format of the e-mail:** When building an e-mail for mobile, you can't assume that the HTML will work the same way as the HTML in your Web site works. For example, e-mail programs don't read JavaScript, and they won't display form fields either — even on computers. Your HTML also dictates the width of the e-mail, the placement of links, and the design and formatting of your e-mail, all of which can be wrong or right, depending on the other aforementioned issues. For example, set-ting your e-mail width at 600 pixels wide might work well for a computer, and for mobile devices with zoom capabilities, and e-mail programs that automatically resize HTML pages to match size of the mobile screen. However, phones with 150 pixel screens and no ability to zoom or scroll sideways will hide 450 pixels of your e-mail from view (see Figure 7-2).

The aforementioned technical issues result in an almost unlimited number of possible device, operating system, and e-mail program combinations. Don't worry about designing an e-mail for every combination, however. The geeks (like us) who invent this stuff want consumers to have great experiences when viewing e-mails, and they won't expect the business world to conform to a wide variety of non-standards. Standards are emerging, but it's going to take time. Put the following advice to work while you wait for industry standards to emerge for displaying HTML e-mails on mobile phones (you won't have to wait too long):

✔ **Use an e-mail marketing provider (EMP) to build and deliver your e-mails.** These companies build tools that include the latest standards and give your e-mails the best chance of successful interaction. Many of the top e-mail services are experts in mobile e-mail design and delivery, and some even provide tools that allow recipients to select and view mobile versions of your standard e-mails. You can read more about EMPs in the next section.

Figure 7-2:
E-mails
that are
wider than
the mobile
screen may
hide your
e-mail
content.

Courtesy of ConstantContact.com

✔ **Collect e-mail preferences at sign-up and group your recipients.**
   Grouping recipients by device, operating system, or e-mail program
   gives you too many groups. Instead, use a few groups like iPhone users
   or non-iPhone users. Alternatively, at sign-up, ask your customers if they
   prefer e-mails formatted specifically for mobile phones versus computers and then set them up accordingly. Flip ahead to the section called,
   "Choosing a Mobile E-Mail Design Approach" for more information about
   the challenges of grouping subscribers.

✔ **Be patient and wait for the standards to emerge.** Your customers are
   probably well aware of the limitations of their personal devices. Use
   the tips in the following sections to make things as standard as possible
   until the day when the vast majority of phones can read your e-mails
   with negligible variations in interactivity.

Choosing an e-mail marketing provider (EMP)

Design standards, spam filters, firewalls, junk folders, and consumer distrust are all reasons to turn to professionals for help with your e-mail strategy. *E-mail marketing providers* (EMPs) are companies that provide one or more of the following commercial e-mail services:

- ✔ Improved e-mail deliverability
- ✔ Database and list management
- ✔ E-mail template design
- ✔ E-mail message and content creation
- ✔ Tracking reports
- ✔ Advice and consulting

 EMPs allow you to accomplish much more with your e-mail marketing than you otherwise could on your own. Some EMPs even provide various levels of outsourcing for higher prices if you don't want to do your own e-mail marketing. Here are a few examples of the kinds of benefits that EMPs provide for delivery to mobile phones:

- ✔ **Give your business a professional look:** EMPs can help you create great-looking e-mail communications without programming knowledge. Most EMPs provide templates with consumer-friendly layouts to accommodate any type of message. Some EMPs provide mobile-friendly templates with additional mobile features such as links to mobile versions of your e-mails (see Figure 7-3). Template-creation wizards allow you to control all your own design elements for a low cost, and some EMPs either include professional services to help you with semi-custom designs or allow you to completely outsource and customize your template designs. Here are some of the templates that EMPs usually provide:

  - Newsletters
  - Promotions
  - Announcements
  - Press releases
  - Event invitations
  - Greeting cards
  - Business letters

Many EMPs offer custom templates designed for your specific needs, for an additional fee, of course. Sometimes the templates offered don't suit your needs, but this can be a helpful alternative for you if the price (and the template) is right for you.

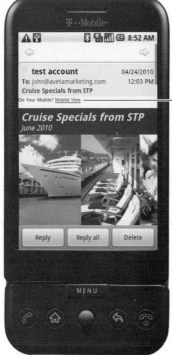

Link to mobile version

Figure 7-3:
EMPs can provide templates with links to mobile-friendly e-mail versions.

Courtesy of ConstantContact.com

✔ **Keep your marketing legal:** EMPs are required to take current e-mail laws into consideration to make sure customers can easily comply. Reputable EMPs take compliance a step further than the basic legal requirements and adhere to more professional standards that reflect consumer preferences. Examples of professional standards include the following (for more information about laws governing e-mails, see Chapter 3):

 • Safe one-click unsubscribe links

 • Privacy statements

 • Physical address added to e-mails

 • Sending from a verified e-mail address

✔ **Help you with logistics and reporting:** EMPs can help you manage the data and feedback associated with executing your e-mail strategy. Here are some examples of ways EMPs can help you manage your information:

- Storage and retrieval of subscriber information
- Reports on deliverability
- Automated handling of subscribe and unsubscribe requests
- Tracking information on blocked and bounced e-mail

✔ **Help with content:** EMPs want you to be successful because if your e-mail messages are effective, you'll likely reward your EMP by being a loyal customer. Many EMPs have resources available that help you develop your content and use best-practices. Examples include

- Online communities
- Webinars
- Tutorials
- Classroom-style training
- Consultation

✔ **Teach you best practices:** EMPs can give you valuable information on consumer preferences that would be too expensive or impossible for you to obtain on your own. EMPs send a lot of e-mails on behalf of their customers, and they're good at staying up-to-date on consumer preferences and professional standards. Some EMPs are willing to share their knowledge to make your e-mails more effective. Some things you might find out include

- Best times and days to send
- How to improve your rate of e-mail actually opened by recipients
- How to avoid spam complaints
- What to do when e-mail is blocked or filtered
- How to design and lay out your content

EMPs come in a variety of do-it-yourself and outsourced models. If you choose to do it yourself, remember that you'll likely need to engage with other services, such as mobile Web site design and text messaging services, to enable the full extent of mobile interaction with your e-mails. If you have the budget to outsource some or all of your e-mail marketing activities, look for an EMP with expanded capabilities or a marketing agency who has an integrated partnership with an EMP and the other services you need.

Collecting E-Mail Addresses through Mobile Devices

A quality e-mail list represents a very personal and direct line of communication with customers and prospects, and mobile devices represent an opportunity to collect e-mail addresses on-location. Building a quality list is also challenging because you need to make sure that everyone on your list wants and appreciates your e-mails. Otherwise, you'll be sending unwanted communications and inspiring all kinds of negative attitudes toward your business. (In other words, people will get mad at you.)

Before focusing on e-mail address collection through mobile devices, make sure you're ready to adhere to legal and professional permission standards. See Chapter 3 for more details on the legalities and standards of mobile communications, including e-mails.

All of the following methods of mobile e-mail address collection are worth employing in your business. They imply gaining permission as an inherent part of the process of exchanging e-mail address information.

Texting in an e-mail address

Use your advertising to ask customers and prospects to text in their e-mail address. Here are two ways to ask for e-mail addresses by text message:

- **Ask people to text their e-mail addresses to your mobile phone number.** If you don't expect a lot of volume or can't afford a short code or text messaging platform, this method allows you to accept e-mail addresses from people on your mobile phone and add them to your address book so you can send them e-mails. It's highly manual, and you have to share or advertise your own mobile phone number, so we don't recommend this method.

- **Ask people to text their e-mail addresses to your short code.** To enable this for your business, make sure your text messaging application is set up to populate your database with e-mail addresses sent by text. If you have a dedicated short code, you can ask people to text their e-mail addresses to your short code. Your platform's database can automatically recognize the e-mail addresses and put that information in the proper database fields for you, as shown in Figure 7-4. If you use a shared short code, you need to ask people to include your keyword along with the e-mail address as in "text *KEYWORD e-mailaddress* to *12345*," where *KEYWORD* is your short code keyword, and *12345* is your shared short code. (You can read more about short codes and keywords in Chapter 4.)

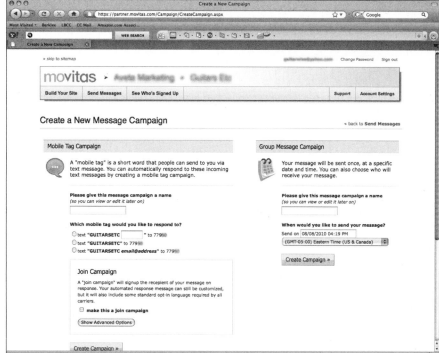

Figure 7-4:
Some text
messaging
databases
can recog-
nize e-mail
addresses.

Providing forms on mobile Web sites

Your mobile Web site should include a sign-up form so people can join your
e-mail list from their mobile phone, as shown in Figure 7-5. List the domain
name of your sign-up form in all your ads (for example, `www.yourcompany.
com/sign-up`). Keep your sign-up form short. Remember that the person
signing up might be typing on a very small keyboard. Ask for an e-mail
address, first name, and allow them to select an appropriate list. You can collect additional information later.

Figure 7-5:
Put an
e-mail list
sign-up
form on your
mobile Web
site.

Courtesy of Movitas.com

Capturing addresses through mobile e-mail

Because e-mail is available on a lot of phones, your advertising can ask people to send any e-mail to a special e-mail address that automatically responds by confirming a subscription. For example, you might ask people to send an e-mail to subscribe@*yourcompany*.com. When you receive the e-mail, you can add that e-mail address to your database.

Make sure your advertising clearly spells out the fact that the e-mail address is used to sign people up for marketing e-mails and sets expectations for content and frequency. You should also set the expectations in a confirmation e-mail sent in reply to the subscription e-mail, as shown in Figure 7-6.

Using mobile applications to collect e-mail addresses

Some e-mail marketing providers have applications for your phone that help you to collect e-mail addresses when you're not in the office. That way, if you have your mobile phone on you, you can add someone directly to your e-mail database when he is standing right in front of you. An example of an e-mail address collection application is shown in Figure 7-7.

Figure 7-6:
Send a
confirmation
e-mail when
someone
signs up for
your list.

Figure 7-7:
Some
mobile
apps allow
you to col-
lect e-mail
addresses
in person.

Courtesy of ConstantContact.com

Protecting your e-mail list

A quality list of permission-based e-mail subscribers segmented by interest and behavior is something to be proud of. Lists and data are assets and represent a significant competitive advantage to your business.

When it comes to e-mail data, protecting your assets is as important as building it in the first place. Don't violate the trust of your e-mail list subscribers by sharing their e-mail addresses

with others who don't have permission to send to your list. Don't abuse your e-mail list subscribers by sending information they didn't ask for or by using their permission as a platform for selling lots of unrelenting banner ads in the body of your e-mail newsletters.

As a general rule, don't do anything with your e-mail list data that isn't explicitly agreed to and expected by your subscribers.

You can use mobile applications to collect e-mail addresses at

- ✔ Networking events, so you don't need to take a business card and type the info in later
- ✔ Tradeshows, when you're walking the floor or working your booth
- ✔ In your store, if you have a physical location and you interact in person
- ✔ In your office, during an appointment

Building and Sending a Mobile E-Mail Campaign

Mobile device adoption has opened up a whole new world of opportunities and challenges for e-mail marketing. The main challenges are

- ✔ Most people access the same e-mail inbox with both mobile devices and computers. So, you shouldn't design e-mails for mobile phones without thinking about how the designs will work on computers and vice versa.
- ✔ Mobile screens are small. Your e-mail designs have to make it easy for people to view the content and click on links when viewing the e-mail on a mobile.
- ✔ Your audience needs to be able to take action on your e-mails using their mobile devices and their computers.

In this section, we show you how to adapt and enhance your e-mail designs and e-mail content for mobile readability and interaction. To discover how to design and send e-mails from scratch, we recommend you read *E-Mail Marketing For Dummies*.

Choosing a mobile e-mail design approach

When sending e-mail marketing messages, you have three basic design choices:

✓ **Build separate e-mails — a mobile-friendly e-mail for mobile users and a computer-friendly e-mail for computer users.** Choose this option when some of your customers tell you they only read e-mails on a mobile devices and they never read e-mails on their computers. To group your subscribers into mobile and computer users, you can use a survey or provide a mobile preferences check box on your e-mail list sign-up form, as shown in Figure 7-8.

Keep in mind that grouping your list subscribers by mobile preference means you're setting the expectation that your e-mails will look great and function correctly on every mobile device. We don't recommend going with this option unless you know that your audience has adopted the exact same standards (for example, you're sending weekly e-mails to 1,000 sales people and every last one of them uses an iPhone with Outlook installed as the e-mail system). If you need a reminder of the challenges with this option, go back to the section called, "Dealing with devices and browsers" earlier in this chapter.

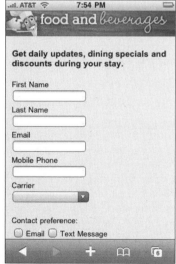

Figure 7-8: Asking for mobile preferences is recommended only when your audience has adopted the same standards.

Courtesy of Movitas.com

✓ **Build all your e-mails for use on a computer and live with the fact that most of your e-mails will have limited capabilities unless your audience is in front of a computer.** Choose this option if your customers tell you they only read e-mails in front of a computer, but they check their e-mail on mobile phones to decide what to read later. If you choose this option, let readers know that your e-mail is best viewed in front of a computer. More on that a little later in this section.

✔ **Build your e-mails for the best possible use on either a computer or a mobile device.** Choose this option when you want your customers to be able to interact with your e-mails on either a computer or a mobile device and you are willing to accept the fact that your e-mails will sacrifice some features you would otherwise include in an e-mail designed specifically for one environment or the other. This option is recommended and requires adapting your regular e-mail content to ensure easy interaction in most environments. This option is also recommended because devices and programmers are beginning to adhere to standards that make adjustments to HTML e-mails to make them easier to navigate on mobile screens. That doesn't mean you won't have any challenges, but it will make your computer-friendly e-mails and mobile friendly e-mails have more in common than not. The next sections show you how to use this option.

Creating a mobile-friendly e-mail design

The most critical factor in mobile e-mail design is the positioning of key content to make sure the e-mail's message is displayed prominently on a computer screen or a smaller mobile screen. Most if not all mobile devices display e-mails beginning with the upper left portion of the e-mail when the e-mail is opened, which means that the most important content should either begin or should be placed entirely in the upper left portion of your e-mail, as shown in Figure 7-9.

A good way to visualize your content positioning is to mentally divide each of your e-mail designs into quadrants and then position the most important content in your e-mail in the upper left quadrant. Although you don't have to divide your content into quadrants visually, you should emphasize important content in the upper left. Here are some examples of the types of content objectives that work well when positioned in the upper-left quadrant:

✔ **Display your brand:** Your audience is more likely to read your e-mail when they recognize the source of the e-mail. Make sure that your business name, logo, and other brand-identifying design elements appear somewhere in the upper left.

✔ **Begin your e-mail message with a main headline:** A main headline doesn't have to reside completely within the upper left, but main headlines get more attention if they begin there. Some e-mail programs automatically fit headlines into the small screen and others allow the reader to scroll sideways or zoom. Either way, keep your headlines to four words or less.

Figure 7-9:
Put the most
important
content in
the upper
left of your
e-mail.

Courtesy of ConstantContact.com

✔ **Include your e-mail's main call to action:** A call to action is a statement that asks your audience to do something specific, such as purchasing a specific item, clicking a link, or pressing a button to dial a phone number. If your e-mail contains valuable offers, make sure your main offer is contained — or at least referenced — in the upper left. If your e-mail's main intent is to get your audience to read a specific section of your e-mail that contains your main call to action along with supporting information, make sure you use the upper left to prompt your audience where to look.

✔ **Place the strongest visual anchors:** Visual anchors — such as images, links, icons, bullets, and graphics — can reinforce your audience's perception of your most important content. Strong visual anchors used in the upper left of the screen help minimize how long your audience spends trying to figure out what content is important enough to read. (Images draw attention, but if you include an image in your e-mail that takes up most of the upper-left quadrant, your audience might miss the text associated with that image. If you decide to use an image in the upper left, use one small enough to allow the inclusion of the first few words of a text headline.)

✔ **Show your audience where to look next:** If your e-mail includes important content below the screen, use navigation links and directions in the
upper left to help your audience navigate the e-mail. For example, the
e-mail's upper-left quadrant might contain a table of contents with navigation links. You can read more about creating a table of contents in the
next section.

Adding navigation links to mobile e-mails

Navigation links are HTML links that allow your audience to jump to different
sections of content within the body of your e-mail. If your e-mails have one or
more headlines or bodies of content that your audience has to scroll to for
viewing, you can include navigation links in your e-mail to

✔ Highlight the content that your audience can't see immediately

✔ Allow your audience to access the information by clicking a link instead
of scrolling

Navigation links are actually anchor links in HTML. *Anchor links* are HTML
tags that reference a specific portion of content within an HTML document
and automatically scroll the browser to the top of the referenced content
when clicked. To create an anchor link, create a name for the anchor using an
anchor tag and place the anchor in your e-mail code at the beginning of the
content you want to link to. Then add a link in your e-mail text that points to
the anchor. Using your HTML or Web site editor of choice, follow these basic
steps (the specifics depend on the editor you're using):

Text only, please

Some mobile phones still convert e-mails into
text automatically because they aren't capable
of displaying HTML. When a device converts an
HTML e-mail into text, the e-mail can become
garbled and confusing for the recipient. Some
conversions result in displaying the entire
HTML code; others show the text along with
long lines of code for links, images, and other
design elements.

Because sending text-only e-mails to everyone eliminates links and tracking altogether,
you might want to use an EMP that allows your
e-mail list subscribers to choose a preformat-
ted, text-only version of your HTML e-mails.
That way, your e-mail is converted and formatted to look good to the recipient before it's sent.
Some services even allow you to create and
edit text-only versions of your HTML e-mails so
you can control the content of the text version
completely.

1. **Use an anchor tag to place your anchor and include the `name` attribute to identify the anchor's name.**

   Use the first word of the headline or section of content for the anchor name so you can remember how to name your anchor link later.

   - *To set the anchor in text,* include an <a> anchor tag with a name attribute within your paragraph tags:

   ```
   <p><a name="anchorname">headline or title</p>
   ```

   - *To name an image as an anchor,* include the name attribute within the image tag:

   ```
   <img name="anchorname" src="http://www.yourcompany.
       com/
       sample/image_file/imagename.jpg">
   ```

   If you're new to HTML, note that you should replace *anchorname* in the preceding examples with whatever name you'd like to use. Also, *headline or title* stands in for the text that actually appears on your site. The URL in the preceding image tag also stands in for the location and filename of the image you actually want to use.

2. **Create your anchor link by inserting the <a> anchor tag in your HTML e-mail text, with the `href` attribute pointing to the anchor name you specify in Step 1, and preceded by a # character.**

   - *To create a TOC link that scrolls to your anchor tag, use the following:*

   ```
   <a href="#anchorname">TOC link text</a>
   ```

   - *To create a navigation link that scrolls to an anchor link on your Web site, use the following:*

   ```
   <a href="http://www.yourwebsite.com/page.
       html#anchorname>
       navigation link text</a>
   ```

HTML can be tricky to master and frustrating for those of you trying to format your newsletter without an EMP. For your own sanity, brush up on your HTML skills first with *HTML 4 For Dummies, 5th Edition*, by Ed Tittel and Mary Burmeister (published by Wiley) before you attempt anchor tags or other bells and whistles in your code.

Most EMPs allow you to create navigation links in your e-mails without knowing anything about HTML, and many include navigation links in basic e-mail template designs.

Navigations links can be combined to create a table of contents for your mobile e-mail. An e-mail *table of contents* (TOC) is a special group of navigation links that lists headlines; each headline is linked to a different section of content within your e-mail. Your e-mail TOC can appear at the top of your e-mail, as shown in Figure 7-10. Alternatively, you can place it at the bottom of your e-mail and include a Skip to Navigation link at the top so your audience can easily get to the TOC and still see some of the content at the beginning of your e-mail as shown in Figure 7-11.

Figure 7-10:
You can place an e-mail TOC at the beginning of your e-mail.

Courtesy of ConstantContact.com

TOCs are necessary only when your e-mail has lots of content that your audience has to scroll to view. If you decide you need a TOC because of the amount of content in your e-mail, take a moment to think about whether you're sending too much information in a single e-mail in the first place. Cutting down on your content and increasing your frequency might be a better solution to making your e-mails easier to scan on a mobile.

If you can't cut down your content, using a TOC is a great way to summarize your content and allow your audience to find and access the content that interests them most. Here are some tips for including a TOC in your e-mails:

Figure 7-11:
Use a
Skip to
Navigation
link to give
your audi-
ence easy
access to
the TOC and
beginning
content.

✔ **Include a heading above your table of contents:** Use wording, such as Quick Links or Find It Fast.

✔ **Keep your link headlines short:** You can use the first few words of the article headlines to which you're linking, or you can repeat short head-lines as your main headlines and then use subheadings in your articles to expand on main headlines.

✔ **Make your link headlines clear:** Links should clearly communicate the content readers will see when they click. Clever links intended to generate curiosity are generally harder to understand than clear link headlines — they might cause disappointment if the linked message doesn't meet the clicker's expectations.

✔ **Keep your TOC above the scroll line:** The *scroll line* is the point at the bottom of your audience's mobile screen where the e-mail content is no longer visible without scrolling. The whole point of a TOC is to keep people from scrolling. If your TOC is so long that it stretches beyond the scroll line, your e-mail probably has too much content.

Writing mobile e-mail content

Creating effective mobile e-mail content begins with placing familiar and motivating information into every e-mail header. The *header* is the portion of your e-mail that contains the following:

- A From line
- A From address
- A Subject line
- Messages and code inserted by e-mail programs

Mobile e-mail programs display portions of your e-mail's header information so users can sort and prioritize their e-mails and decide whether to view and open each e-mail. Figure 7-12 shows how Gmail displays headers on an Android device.

Figure 7-12: The e-mail header helps readers to decide whether to open the e-mail now or later.

When used appropriately, your header information helps your audience to identify you as a trustworthy sender and also helps to determine whether your e-mails are worthy of immediate attention.

Although you can't control all the information in your e-mail headers, you can control three important pieces of information that are most useful to your audience:

- **From line:** Your *From line* is a line of text that tells the recipient of your e-mail whom the e-mail is from. Most e-mail applications and e-mail marketing providers allow you to add a line of text to the header of your e-mail to identify yourself. Ask yourself how your audience is most likely to recognize you and then craft your From line to include that information.

- **From address:** Your *From address* is the e-mail address that is associated with you as the sender of the e-mail. Some e-mail programs display your From e-mail address along with your From line, but others display one or the other. Make sure your e-mail address has your company name in it as in `john@yourcompany.com` or `yourcompany@gmail.com`, for example.

- **Your subject line:** The most effective Subject lines are those that prompt your audience to open your e-mails to look for specific information. Keep your subject line between five and eight words so most or all of it displays on a mobile screen.

After you've determined what your header information should be, you need to write your e-mail content. All e-mails should be concise, and any e-mail that has the potential to be viewed on a mobile device should be as short as possible while still getting your point across.

One way to ensure that your e-mail is going to be well received on a computer and a mobile device is to include a prologue at the beginning of your e-mail. A *prologue* is one or two sentences summarizing the content of your e-mail so that mobile recipients can decide what to do with your e-mail, as shown in Figure 7-13.

Figure 7-13:
Use a
prologue
to tell your
audience
what to do
with your
e-mail.

Courtesy of ConstantContact.com

Your prologue should contain one or more of the following bits of information:

- **A link to a mobile-enhanced Web version of your e-mail content so mobile phone users can see the e-mail:** Point the link to a mobile Web site that can detect the phone and browser and display the e-mail content properly. You can read more about building mobile Web sites in Chapter 8.

- **The main purpose of your e-mail:** People often use their mobile phones to sort and prioritize e-mails before reading them. Use your prologue to sell the value of your e-mail content so people want to read it immediately.

- **What to do with the e-mail:** If the recipients can take action immediately, state that in the e-mail prologue. If they need to be in front of a computer, tell them to save the e-mail for later.

The information you include in your e-mail after the prologue depends on what your e-mail is asking your audience to do. For example, if you want your audience to click away from the e-mail and buy something on a mobile Web site, you need just enough content to make them want to take that action. You should provide the minimum amount of information necessary to entice your audience to take the next step and focus on one call to action for each e-mail. To determine the minimum amount of information, work backward from your goal by writing your goal, the action that leads to the goal, and the minimum amount of content your audience needs to make the decision. Here are two examples:

Example 1:

- ✔ **Goal:** Drive traffic to my store.

- ✔ **Action:** Show coupon to clerk at the store.

- ✔ **Content:** Coupon, product photo, link to more photos, link to store map and directions, one paragraph explaining the items for purchase, and a sentence telling the reader how to take advantage of the offer (by showing the e-mail to the clerk).

Example 2

- ✔ **Goal:** Get 100 people to read an article.

- ✔ **Action:** Read the article on the mobile screen, or click the article to read on a mobile site, or save the article to read later on a computer screen.

- ✔ **Content:** All or part of the article text, a link to the mobile-enhanced Web site containing the article, and a prologue suggesting the three ways to read the article.

Keep in mind that most actions with business value take place outside of the e-mail, so you only need to put enough information in your e-mail to get your audience to take the first step, and then put the rest of the information where that next step takes place. For example, making a purchase on a mobile Web site requires someone to visit the mobile Web site. Use your e-mail content to get people to your Web site, and then put content that entices them to take additional action once they arrive on your Web site.

Including mobile calls to action in your e-mails

If you're interested in using e-mail as an effective marketing tool, you're better off if your e-mails make it easy for your recipients to take immediate action, whether they are in front of a computer or a mobile phone. For example, if the main offer in your e-mail requires someone to print a coupon on their printer and walk into your store to redeem it, computer users can simply print the e-mail, but the recipients who are reading that e-mail on their mobile phones have to go home, log back in to their e-mail account, open the e-mail, print the coupon, get back in the car . . . you get the picture. To address both audiences, your e-mail should invite them to either print the e-mail or simply use their phones to show the coupon in the e-mail to the clerk at the counter.

The following list shows you which goals are appropriate for mobile e-mails and how you can ensure mobile interactions with your e-mails.

- ✔ **Opening and reading the e-mail:** If your main goal is to inform, mobile enables an immediate look and reading on-the-go. Keep your e-mails concise if you expect people to read them immediately.

- ✔ **Linking to a mobile Web site:** The majority of phones have an Internet browser, and mobile Web sites have the ability to automatically change the way they display based on detecting the phone. Mobile Web sites are capable of a lot of interactivity, but you need to make sure the links in your e-mail point to a mobile Web site if you expect mobile interaction. You can read more about mobile Web sites in Chapter 8 and you can find out more about creating mobile links a little later in this chapter.

- ✔ **Using a mobile coupon:** You can ask your audience to use their phones to show the coupon to someone on location as shown in Figure 7-14, or you can send a coupon code that can be used on a mobile Web site.

- ✔ **Replying to the e-mail:** If you're looking for an immediate reply, your recipients can send you a reply e-mail right from the phone.

- ✔ **Calling a phone number:** Some devices allow the recipient to touch a phone number to immediately call that number, so make sure you include phone numbers in your e-mails.

- ✔ **Saving the e-mail:** If your e-mail includes advanced functionality that only works on a computer or if your e-mail has a lot of content and takes time to get through, ask your recipients to save the e-mail by summarizing the benefits contained in the e-mail in the first few sentences.

✔ **Gathering feedback:** You can include a link to a mobile Web site form or ask your recipient to text you to begin an SMS survey.

✔ **Enabling social media sharing:** If you want your audience to share your e-mail message, you can provide a link to your e-mail content by making the e-mail into an archive and posting it to the Web. Your e-mail marketing provider can show you how to archive your e-mails.

Figure 7-14:
Ask your customers to redeem mobile coupons by showing them on the phone.

Courtesy of ConstantContact.com

Linking to an e-mail address

Instead of linking text to a Web page, you might want to link to an e-mail address. An e-mail address included in the body of an e-mail often shows up as a link, and automatically opens a new message in your visitor's default e-mail program.

People on mobile phones are often checking e-mail between other tasks or during short periods of downtime. You should also include calls to action in your e-mails that deter your audience from deleting your e-mail just because they are busy at the moment.

In order to help your audience make decisions while putting the actions off until they have more time, or are in front of their home or work computer, try using these calls to action as guides to create your own (you can put the calls to action in your e-mail body, the prologue, or the subject line):

✔ Save this e-mail — it contains your 50% off coupon.

✔ In this e-mail are three new products and photos from our road show.

✔ On a mobile device? View a text-only summary. (Link to a text-only paragraph at the bottom of your e-mail using an *anchor tag.*)

✔ This e-mail is archived on our Web site (include a link to your archive).

✔ Please call 555-1234 if you're unable to order from this e-mail.

✔ Visit www.companywebsite.com for complete information.

✔ Are you driving right now? Stop reading this! (Okay, we're just kidding on that one.)

Part III
Mobile Media, Publishing, and Advertising

In this part . . .

Perhaps the most exciting thing about mobile marketing is that it gives you the ability to create rich experiences through mobile Internet sites, mobile applications, and mobile advertising.

Chapter 8 tells you how to design mobile Internet sites and avoid the traps that make traditional Web sites dysfunctional on mobile devices. Chapter 9 explains the always-expanding world of mobile applications and gives you tips for building and distributing them.

Chapter 10 shows you how to display advertising on mobile Internet sites and in mobile applications. Chapter 11 helps you understand how to utilize the voice functions of mobile devices so you can launch integrated voice response campaigns. Chapter 12 is all about mobile social media marketing and gives you tips for adapting your social media strategy for mobile fans and followers.

Chapter 8

Designing and Developing Mobile Internet Sites

In This Chapter

▶ Getting acquainted with the mobile Internet

▶ Settling on the purpose of your mobile site

▶ Securing a mobile domain name

▶ Designing, testing, and updating your mobile site

---

*T*he rising tide of mobile device use, especially smartphones and connected devices (see Chapter 1) is the piston driving the mobile Web forward. As billions across the globe grow to rely on their mobile devices to connect and communicate, the mobile Web's importance expands exponentially.

Today, many users are wowed by mobile applications (see Chapter 9) designed to do everything from simply looking like a Zippo lighter, to recognizing songs on the radio, recommending restaurants in the immediate area, buying stuff, or conducting global banking and commerce. The current apps craze, while impressive in its sheer inventiveness, may ultimately be left behind by a richer mobile Web that provides users with the same content and functionality now found on the traditional Web (For the curious, see the sidebar titled, "The mobile Web versus apps and the role of HTML 5" at the end of this chapter for more on this topic.) To ignore or underestimate this natural progression of the mobile Web is to miss a huge marketing opportunity.

Moving forward, many first impressions between companies and consumers will be made on the mobile Web. If you don't have a mobile Web site for mobile users, your first impression could be your last. In fact, if you learn nothing else in this chapter, know that having a mobile Web site is absolutely crucial to your business, whether it's a full-fledged optimized site or a simple default site with your company's address and contact information.

In this chapter, we help you understand the mobile Web's nuances, potential, and limitations, consider the purpose of your mobile site, introduce site development tools, discuss design and site content considerations, and help you choose a domain strategy.

Understanding the Mobile Web

Offering up the same content and experience to mobile users that you provide people in a desktop environment is a huge mistake because mobile devices have a vastly different form of use than computers. The mobile Web implies an intimate one-to-one experience, often with a user that is on-the-go or visiting the mobile Web to perform a specific purpose (like checking sports scores and the weather forecast or looking to buy a specific item). The mobile Web is a completely different animal than the traditional Internet, which was and is developed for stationary consumption.

When building your mobile site, put yourself in the user's mindset. People on the go or with a specific agenda in mind have little time to dig through menus, scroll left or right, or wait for pages to load. They're frequently multi-tasking — walking down the street or drinking a cup of coffee with one free hand while browsing at the same time with the other. Keep in mind that about 90% of the population is right-handed, so you may want to optimize one-hand use with the idea that the right thumb can reach the primary features. It's critical that you think through what people will want to do on your site and make sure that your site lets them perform these actions quickly and easily.

One common mistake is trying to give mobile Web visitors quick access to your entire broadband Web site experience. A more prudent plan is to develop a simple, clean home page that loads quickly on a mobile device over the wide range of mobile networks and puts key information a click or two away. Simplifying makes sense. Creating a short, descriptive page title, using simple language, and providing order to the content you present are all great ways to stay on track.

The next sections show you how to think about the differences between the mobile Web and the traditional Web so you can have a new perspective and incorporate that perspective into your mobile Web site design.

Putting your mobile site in the right context

Context should always be a high priority when developing a mobile Web presence, that is, a mobile Web site. Context simply refers to all the data that helps you understand how to make the site relevant to the user's current situation — that is, location and time are key contextual elements, as are events in the news, the weather, and so on, as well as all the things you may know about this person, like her past behavior, interests, and so on. For example, your customer might be trying to find directions to your store while she is her car. (Hopefully, she's pulled over to the side of the road!) Put yourself in the shoes of people coming to your site. They are usually looking for quick access to actionable information around a specific task. They probably aren't going to be browsing around to find out everything about your business. They usually do that type of browsing on a computer.

The user experience is different on the mobile Internet. A recent Microsoft Advertising study (2010) noted that the average person conducting a search on the mobile Web finishes what she sets out to do, for example, performing a local search, in about an hour, whereas on a PC, this search effort on average takes a month.

Here are some other behaviors you may consider about mobile users. Today, for the majority of mobile users, people visiting your mobile site

- ✔ Won't be planning their vacation, but they *will* be checking their arrival/ departure times, searching for area restaurants, and looking for phone numbers, maps, and recommendations.

- ✔ Won't be looking to compare mortgage or savings rates on their phone, but they *will* be looking for your nearest branch bank office.

- ✔ Won't be reading in-depth news reports (unless they're on an Apple iPad or Cisco Cius), but they *will* be checking headlines, stories, sports scores, and checking the weather.

- ✔ Won't be browsing your entire fall lineup of fall fashions, but *will* be looking for your contact info, special sales, and online coupons. Alternatively, they might buy a specific item like the latest Steve Madden shoe at `http://m.stevemadden.com` or a printer cartridge from Best Buy at `m.bestbuy.com`.

You can help yourself discover the context your customers are most likely to be in by using a survey to ask them how they use your Web site and how they use mobile sites. Go to Chapter 5 to learn how to send out a mobile SMS survey, or consider doing it through e-mail. You can also use location detection and then use this data to determine what is happening around them.

Keeping your focus on the experience

Your approach to the mobile Web can have a direct impact on what customers think of your company. A simple example may prove illuminating. Suppose you're out holiday shopping. You can't find the perfect gift, so you look up a retail Web site to locate a store nearby and browse for gift ideas. One of three things is likely to happen, depending on how the retailer's mobile Web site is designed:

- ✔ **The Web site you go to is Flash-based or has a lot of scripting.** Because most mobile phones don't display Adobe Flash content (the mobile video Web standard supported by Adobe) or scripts, your customers will see only broken links (see Figure 8-1). You move on and unconsciously write off the retailer.

  User experience: Not good. The user can't even see the site.

Figure 8-1: Sites with Flash or other non-mobile formats won't render on most mobile phones.

✔ **The Web site comes up, but the content is not relevant.** Instead of information your customer needs, the site displays company information, press releases, career opportunities, and investor information. Your customer is forced to dig for the information they want, but eventually exit, thinking that the retailer doesn't really understand or value mobile users like them. Figure 8-2 is an example of this type of site.

User experience: Frustrating. The user can't easily find the information he needs.

Figure 8-2: Mobile site content can be difficult to navigate if it's not optimized for mobile devices.

Courtesy of Steve Madden

✔ **The Web site is optimized for mobile users.** Your customer is quickly able to find a phone number, store locator, sale links, and an online purchase path, like the site shown in Figure 8-3. He can browse sale items, call your store, find out that you have exactly what he needs, and spend part of his afternoon in your store buying gifts. He thinks "Cool. This company gets it. I'll be back." In fact, he does go back. Regularly.

User experience: Relevant and memorable. The user can easily view and interact with all aspects of the site.

Figure 8-3:
Mobile site content that is optimized provides the best experience.

Courtesy of Steve Madden

You can find similar examples in most any line of business. When people use a mobile phone to access the Web, they demand three things:

✔ **Speed:** Pages load much slower on most mobile devices than they do on a computer — even on a 3G network. That's because the device's processing power isn't as robust as that of a computer. Because time is of the essence for most mobile users, *abandon rates* (the percentage of people who get impatient and give up waiting for a site to load) on the mobile Web are much higher than on the traditional Internet. Most understand that if your site is slow to load, it probably hasn't been optimized for mobile, so it's a waste of their time to wait. When designing your site, use the minimum amount of content necessary to get your message across and format your images and videos for mobile devices.

✔ **Easy navigation:** Because most mobile devices don't have a mouse and have a really small screen, your navigation links can't be the same as on a computer. Mobile navigation is often placed at the bottom of a site, as shown in Figure 8-4, but a variety of navigation schemes work for the small screen. (We discuss these in the section "Designing and Building Your Mobile Site" later in this chapter.)

✔ **Relevant content:** Probably one of the most important things about a mobile site is the task-oriented nature of its content. People who browse the mobile Web are usually trying to accomplish a specific task — even if that task is just being entertained while killing time. Flip ahead to the "Creating Mobile Site Content" section to discover how to make your content more relevant to task-oriented visitors.

Figure 8-4:
Mobile site navigation should be different from navigation on a computer.

Designing for multiple devices

Why can't the rich, interactive Internet experiences you enjoy on your personal computers be seen on your mobile device? The answer is deceptively simple. Most Web sites aren't created using a language that the mobile Web browser can understand. It's like asking someone who only knows English to read and write in another language. Feature mobile phones, the phones with the largest penetration in the U.S — about 75% as of this writing — simply do not have the capabilities and format of a full computer, which leads to limitations in rendering traditional Web sites on the phone. Smartphones, which account for 25% of the phone penetration in the U.S., have much more capable browsers and can view rich media Web sites. Smartphones are expected to reach 50% market penetration in the U.S. by end of 2011. To compensate for these differences, new browser languages are being developed for the mobile phone.

To make matters more complicated, different mobile browsers, screen sizes, and handset features make it challenging to design your mobile Web site so each user on each handset has an optimal experience. Indeed, the very same handset can react differently depending on which mobile operator network it's running on.

You could build a different mobile site for every type of phone and operating system, but that wouldn't be practical because there are literally thousands of different mobile devices and operating systems. Although standards are emerging, you simply can't design a different site for every one of your customers. You would have to know what phone and operating system every one of your customers has! Fortunately, mobile Web application providers have a way around these rendering problems (the display of your mobile Web site on these different types of phones). First, they can offer you mobile device detection code for your broadband Web site to redirect mobile users to the mobile version of your Web site. Mobile Web app providers can also offer you code that detects which of the many thousands of devices may be requesting your page so that the application provider software can dynamically modify the site (size of images, width, scripts and code) to suit the phone. When someone comes to your mobile site, the code automatically detects the phone, browser, and operating system and renders the mobile site in the format that's best for that phone (see Figure 8-5).

Figure 8-5:
Mobile application providers can detect different phones and render your site properly.

Of course, the code doesn't work by itself. Your application provider's platform has to be able to interact with the code to serve up your site's pages in all kinds of different configurations and it has to keep track of all the new phones, operating systems, and browsers coming on the market. Talk to your application provider to make sure your mobile Web site has the capability to render in all environments, especially to those mobile devices your market research has determined are carried by the majority of your customers. Review your Web site logs or use third-party research services like comScore and Nielsen to find out what devices your customers use.

Until standards are established for a format that works for all mobile devices, many mobile Web developers choose to design their sites based on the top four or five handsets and screens that are used by their target customer base, or by those phones visiting their broadband site. They may create two or three versions of the same mobile site that vary by image size, line breaks, columns, and so on. For example, they may create versions specially designed for the iPhone, Google Android, and BlackBerry. The version served up to the user is based on the detection code we mentioned previously. They then have their application provider's platform automatically render the site for the thousands of other phones. More on this in the section "Designing and Building Your Mobile Site" segment later in this chapter.

Considering the Purpose of Your Mobile Site

A traditional Web site is usually the destination for all your company's information including everything from products for sale to job postings. Mobile sites need to be established with a specific purpose in mind because people who view mobile sites aren't going to dig through hundreds of links to find the task-oriented information they need.

The next sections help you to establish a purpose for your mobile site so you can serve your customers and prospects with only the most relevant information.

Identifying the needs of your mobile audience

Establishing a purpose for your mobile Web site should take the needs of your prospective visitors into account, not the needs of your company. Answering the following key questions can ultimately help lead to a solution that works for you and your customers:

✔ **What are your customers most likely trying to accomplish with your site?** Make a list of all the tasks that your customers need to accomplish on the go. Examples include finding your phone number or directions to your store, looking up in-stock availability of an item, or making a reservation.

✔ **What functionality do you need to give customers on your site?** You can serve up content like text, images, videos, and audio, or you can give them interactive functions such as chatting with customer support.

✔ **Will your audience be buying things through your mobile site?** If so, you need to make sure your site can accommodate payment gateways and security. If not, your site can act as a source of information for making purchases through another means such as on a computer or in a store. Remember that people can phone in a purchase too. After all, it's still a phone!

✔ **Will social media be a consideration?** Social media interaction on mobile devices is getting a lot more popular and familiar to mobile users. Make sure you build social media into your site if you have social media users among your customers and prospects.

These are just a few of the questions you should ask and answer for yourself. You know your business best, so think through them all. To help generate additional thoughts, see Chapter 2.

Choosing from three types of mobile Internet sites

Before you head off to design and develop your mobile Web site, consider that there are many different types of sites, all of which have their uses. Among the many permutations, there are three basic types of mobile Web sites you need to be aware of:

✔ **Basic landing page:** This is generally a simple, one-page site built to deliver basic information fast. Traffic frequently comes from online ads. Restaurants, small retailers, and service companies are often well served by this type of site. Populate the basic site with

- Key contact information

- Operating hours

- Map/locator

- Special events

- Any other information important to people on the go

✔ **Promotional site:** Promotional sites are built around a specific product, event, or limited time promotion. For example, a music festival would likely build a promotional site to provide festival-goers with the lineup/schedule, sponsorship information, maps, special events, and links to local happenings and restaurants. After the event is over, the site might go away.

✔ **Persistent site:** Persistent sites are permanent, evolving sites designed to meet the ongoing needs of mobile Web site visitors. Businesses expecting constant customer traffic — from airlines and banks to social media and on-the-go information portals — build persistent sites to provide easy access to information mobile Web visitors constantly need. An airline company, for example, might create such a site to make it easy for visitors to check departure and arrival status, view reservations, and check in online.

Your mobile Web marketing strategy might involve building and maintaining more than one type of mobile site at a time. To avoid confusing your audience as to which site to visit, choose a domain name strategy that differentiates your mobile sites. We discuss mobile domain strategies in the next section.

Choosing a Mobile Internet Domain Strategy

Getting people to visit your mobile Web site requires them to know the address of that site, for example, `www.mobilemarketingfordummies.com`. Before you decide on a name, you need to know how to spot the different parts of a domain name:

✔ The part of your site's address that includes the letters before the dot is called your site's *domain name*.

✔ The part of your site's address that includes the letters after the dot is called your site's *domain extension*.

Your domain name strategy is critical because your audience needs to know your domain name in order to visit your site. You have several options when it comes to how to create your mobile domain:

✔ **Use a completely different domain for your mobile site.** For example, you could use `abccompany.com` for your traditional site, and `abccompanymobile.com` for your mobile site. This means you are asking customers to remember both your traditional Web site address and your mobile site address. This method is not recommended unless you're creating a special promotional mobile site that is named after your product or your event.

✔ **Create a *subdomain*, such as** m.abcompany.com **or** mobile.abc company.com, **to keep your mobile site as part of your brand.** This method isn't much better than creating two different domains because ultimately you're still asking your customers to remember two different domains.

✔ **Use a .mobi domain extension, as in abcompany.mobi.** The .mobi extension is a top-level domain extension meant specifically for delivering the Web to mobile device users. A .mobi site signals to visitors that your site follows certain style guidelines to optimize it for easy viewing. Still, your customers need to remember to use the .mobi extension when visiting you on the mobile Web.

✔ **Use detection code on your server to parse traffic based on the device being used.** (See the sidebar "How does broadband to mobile redirect work?" elsewhere in this chapter.) Your mobile Web application provider can give you code that automatically detects the device and sends computer users to your traditional Web site and mobile users to your mobile site. This method is often called *user agent detection*. This is a great solution, but keep in mind that your mobile users might sometimes want to see something on your traditional site. If you go with this method, include a link to your traditional site in your mobile site just in case your visitors need to find some content your mobile site doesn't contain (see Figure 8-6).

Whichever naming convention you choose, keep it short. Remember, typing a long URL into your mobile browser can make for the start of a bad user experience.

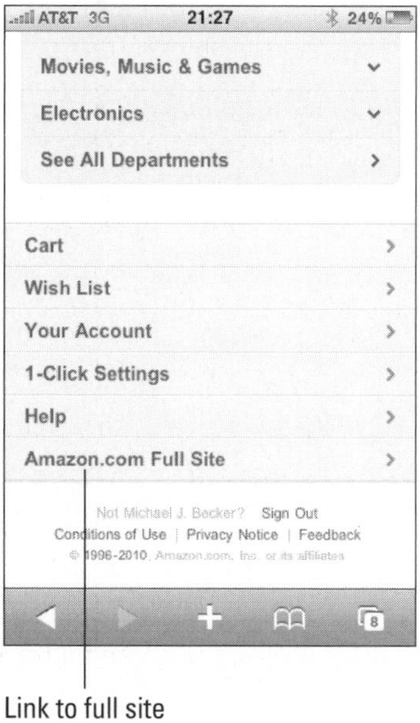

Figure 8-6:
Include a
link from
your mobile
site to your
traditional
site if you
use user
agent
detection.

Movies, Music & Games ⌄
Electronics ⌄
See All Departments ›
Cart ›
Wish List ›
Your Account ›
1-Click Settings ›
Help ›
Amazon.com Full Site ›

Not Michael J. Becker? Sign Out
Conditions of Use | Privacy Notice | Feedback
© 1996-2010 Amazon.com, Inc. or its affiliates

Link to full site

How does broadband to mobile redirect work?

One of the most common questions we hear is, "How do I redirect a user to my mobile Web site if they enter the URL for my traditional Web site on their phones?" There are a lot of ways to do this, but the simplest way is to have your Web designer (or agency, if you had someone build your site for you) add some code to your traditional Web site to detect that your customer is attempting to view your Web site from their mobile phone. After it's detected, the customer's phone can be redirected to the site you've developed specifically for mobile device visitors.

All kinds of different HTML coding standards exist. One of the more popular standards — that is, a standard that is supported by the majority of Web services — is Java/Java Server Pages (JSP). Companies with Java/JSP-based sites can implement the following code example on their main Web site (for example, http://*examplecompanysite*.com) to do some lightweight device detection and automatically redirect mobile browsers to a mobile optimized version of their Web site (http://m.*examplecompanysite*.com or http://*examplecompanysite*.mobi). A leading mobile Web developer, Mad Mobile (www.madmobile.com), shared the following sample code that can be added to a Web site with us. (Remember: This is just a sample. We don't warrant that it will work on your site, so check with your developer before adding it to your site.)

```
JAVA (jsp)
===================== Getting some header values ===================== String
        user_agent = request.getHeader("user-agent"); String accept = request.
        getHeader("accept"); String x_wap_profile = request.getHeader("x-wap-
        profile");
String profile = request.getHeader("profile"); String opera = request.getHeader("X-
        OperaMini-Phone"); String ua_pixels = request.getHeader("ua-pixels");
==================================================================
// Checks the user-agent if (user_agent != null) {
// Checks if its a Windows browser but not a Windows Mobile browser if (user_agent.
        contains("windows") &&! user_agent.contains("windows ce")){
return false;
}
// Checks if it is a mobile browser
Pattern pattern = Pattern.compile("up.browser|up.link|windows ce|iphone|iemobile|mini|m
        mp|symbian|midp|wap|phone|pocket|mobile|pda|psp", Pattern.CASE_INSENSITIVE);
agents
}
Matcher matcher = pattern.matcher(user_agent);
if (matcher.find()){ return true;
}
// Checks if the 4 first chars of the user-agent match any of the most popular user-
String[] ua = {"acs- ","alav","alca","amoi","audi","aste","avan","benq","bird","blac",
        "blaz","brew","cell","cldc","cmd -","dang","doco","eric","hipt","inno","ipaq
        ","java","jigs","kddi","keji","leno","lg-c","lg- d","lg-g","lge-","maui","ma
        xo","midp","mits","mmef","mobi","mot-","moto","mwbp","nec- ","newt","noki","
        opwv","palm","pana","pant","pdxg","phil","play","pluc","port","prox","qtek",
        "qwa p","sage","sams","sany","sch-","sec-","send","seri","sgh-","shar","sie
        ","siem","smal","smar","sony","sph-","symb","t-mo","teli","tim-","tosh","tsm-
        ","upg1","upsi","vk- v","voda","w3c ","wap-","wapa","wapi","wapp","wapr","web
        c","winw","winw","xda","xda-"};
```

```
for(int i = 0; i if (ua[i] == return true;
}
}
// Checks the accept if (accept != null) {
< ua.length; i++ ) { user_agent.substring(0,3)) {
header for wap.wml or wap.xhtml support
if (accept.contains("text/vnd.wap.wml") || accept.contains("application/vnd.wap.
        xhtml+xml")) {
}
}
return true;
// Checks if it has any mobile HTTP headers if (x_wap_profile != null || profile !=
        null || opera != null || ua_pixels != null) {
}
return true;
```

This code checks the `userAgent` string data in the header of requests (that is, when the mobile device pings your Web server, it tells the Web server what type of mobile device it is via its `userAgent`) to determine whether the browser is a mobile device. Here is an example of a `userAgent` string for an iPhone:

```
Mozilla/5.0 (iPhone; U; CPU iPhone OS 2_0_1 like Mac OS X;
en-us) AppleWebKit/525.18.1 (KHTML, like Gecko) Version/3.1.1
Mobile/5B108 Safari/525.20
```

After a user is redirected to a mobile-optimized Web site, more granular device detection takes place. You can utilize deeper device data (for example, video capability, display size, screen resolution) from device data sources such as WURFL (`http://wurfl.sourceforge.net/`) or Device Atlas (`www.deviceatlas.com`) to deliver a truly device specific mobile experience.

Designing and Building Your Mobile Site

Web sites designed to be viewed by PCs are developed in a number of different programming languages, including HTML, Flash, XML, Ajax, PHP, and more. Your browser is designed to read and understand the instructions written in these languages, as well as learn new languages. The same concept holds for your mobile Internet browser. Languages have been developed to improve your experience when viewing the mobile Web — including WAP, XHTML, cHTML, and KHTML — but they are all device- and operator-dependent, meaning they don't work on all phones or networks. Because fewer than 1% of Web sites today can be viewed properly on a mobile phone, we have a long way to go before the mobile Web is a finished product.

One strategic decision sure to have ramifications for how you build your mobile site is what types of handsets you plan to support. Because handsets are not standardized, you need to determine which type of site to build:

✔ A default site that renders the same on all mobile devices

✔ A medium site that increases functionality and design possibilities

✔ A high-end site that provides an optimal experience for people on feature-rich devices

To determine which type of site you need, take a good look at your audience. Who is coming to your site and what do they need to do on it? Site analytics can give you a very clear idea of what type of handsets access your site and what kind of site might be your best bet (see Chapter 14 for more on site analytics).

Default site

A default site should be designed for the lowest common denominator, to render the same on practically all mobile handsets. A default site is generally a basic, low-effort text site free of bells and whistles that gives visitors easy access to key information on your site using simple HTML, CSS, and semantic markup.

When designing a default site

✔ Choose a readable font and size

✔ Use a single-column format

✔ Minimize scrolling

Medium site

If a basic default site isn't enough, the next step up is a site designed to provide more functionality and a richer user experience. Using style sheets, forms, and map integration, for example, you can ensure that visitors can access a professional-looking site to get the information they need and take advantage of advanced handset capabilities. For more details on style sheets, forms, and maps, see *Mobile Web Design For Dummies* by Janine Warner.

When designing this type of site, determine what specific phone capabilities you want to take advantage of or enable before you get started. Testing is very important, as even the same handsets react differently depending on the network.

High-end site

This type of site gives users access to videos, forms, maps, and other features and functionality enabled by iPhones, BlackBerrys and Windows Mobile phones, among others. If you want to ensure an optimal experience for customers on smartphones, this is the way to go. Although it takes more effort to build out your site, but it also provides considerably more benefit and improves usability for more sophisticated mobile users.

Choosing tools to build your mobile site

Building a simple mobile version of a Web site isn't difficult. Building a mobile site that looks good on multiple mobile-phone models and browsers is an entirely different story. Your options depend on your site's complexity, your expertise, and your budget. You have three primary options:

- ✔ **Working with an agency:** If you have a budget, high expectations, a demanding timeline, and little expertise in mobile site building, working with an agency to develop a mobile Web site is a smart approach. Working with an agency offers many advantages, including brand consistency, ease of maintenance, and a single and trusted point of contact for updates. An agency can help you identify and answer all the key issues involved in your mobile site build. Check to be sure the agency you choose has the specific skills you need, plus broad expertise in the mobile space, Web site design and development, as well as the content development, database, and backend IT capacity you require.

- ✔ **Using automatic transcoders:** *Automatic transcoders* are software tools that look at the HTML code in an existing Web site and translate the code into a mobile-friendly version on the fly or in order to produce a static mobile site. Transcoders work well for simple HTML Web sites. Buyer beware, however. Although they're a nice, simple solution, they are far from perfect. Pages are rendered based on templates, which can lead to a far less visually appealing site. DotMobi, the leading mobile domain registrar, offers a great free transcoder with the purchase of a .mobi domain. UsableNet offers high-end transcoding of existing sites at www.usablenet.com.

- ✔ **Using visual editors (see Figure 8-7):** If you are creating a mobile site from scratch, or maybe just using assets from an existing wired site, a visual editor tool is a good choice. Visual editors are usually Web-based, drag-and-drop or WYSIWYG (What You See Is What You Get) site-building tools. They make it fairly simple to create a basic site. You can upload images and create and format pages simply. Some visual editors even have advanced features, such as the ability to pull in dynamic content from an RSS (Really Simple Syndication) feed and populate databases with user information (RSS is the industry standard for converting Web content into data feeds, like news stories, so that the content can be easily shared across the Internet). Visual editors are a great choice if you want to build a basic site that renders correctly on almost all phones and includes some complex features (RSS feeds and so on), but don't want to bother with designer or developer expenses. However, use caution. Aside from a few templates, visual editors give you little freedom to customize your site. Most sites created with a visual editor will be menu-driven, with copy and links stacked on top of each other. Many visual editors don't have the ability to arrange links horizontally, for example, and type, image, and color options are limited. Some of the leading providers include iLoop Mobile (www.iloopmobile.com), Mad Mobile (www.madmobile.com), and Whoop (www.whoop.com).

✔ **Using code editors:** If you understand Web software coding and development, a code editor may make the most sense for you. Code editors allow you to upload your own code into a tool that ensures your site renders correctly on a mobile device. A code editor can solve some of the issues with customization that often arise when using a visual editor. Many visual editing tools have a code editor feature. If you have a large organization and multiple developers with different mobile skill levels, you should probably license a tool that has both a code and visual editor. Because many editors let you switch back and forth between code and visual editors, the visual editor/code editor combination can serve as a learning aid as your developers get comfortable with mobile development.

Figure 8-7:
Visual editors allow you to build your mobile site with a minimum of coding.

Using Web-standard code for your mobile site

Using Web-standard code is always a smart idea: It saves time, simplifies future updates, and makes your pages more consistent across browsers and platforms. Web-standard code includes

✔ HTML was the first standard to emerge and is widely used on the Web.

✔ XML is an enhanced version of HTML. It's much more flexible than HTML and is designed to structure, store, and transport information.

✔ CSS (Cascading Style Sheets) enables HTML and XML elements to be assigned an appearance and position on the page by applying specific styles to them.

Choose a standard that most closely fits the needs of your viewers. The W3C (World Wide Web Consortium) is a tremendous resource for mobile Web standards. For more information, go to their Web site at www.w3.org.

When coding your mobile site, make sure you avoid the following known hazards:

✔ **Frames:** Stay away from frames, which can be problematic and unsupported by many devices.

✔ **Tables:** Using tables for layout can force your viewers to do unnecessary scrolling. Stay away from them and nested tables.

✔ **Pop-ups:** In general, pop-ups are unpredictable, cause confusion, delay users, and add costs.

✔ **Images:** Limit the use of images for navigation and headers. Keep images small and write meaningful alternative text for users who turn images off.

Giving your mobile site good design features

No matter what kind of mobile site you're designing, always keep these guiding principles in mind:

✔ **Make sure key branding elements are in the header.** This helps users find your page.

✔ **Place important content high on the page.** This helps to minimize or eliminate scrolling.

✔ **Use images and other visual elements only when necessary.** If you use images and want to control the user experience, consider designing various versions for different screen sizes.

✔ **Use short phrases and short blocks of text.** If you must use long text, such as an extended article, make sure the page design is clear, that the user is being taken to an extended story, and that the pages are divided in a way that improves readability.

✔ **Design for both high- and low-end users.** Have device detection code serve the appropriate experience to the end user (see the sidebar titled "How does broadband to mobile redirect work?" elsewhere in this chapter).

✔ **Design for search.** Good design creates increased traffic to your mobile Web site. One of the rapidly growing consumer uses of mobile devices is search, meaning that consumers use Google (www.google.com), Where (www.where.com), Yelp (www.yelp.com), and social media tools like Foursquare (www.foursqure.com) to search for things they're interested in. You want to make sure that your site has a good chance of showing up when a consumer conducts a search. You can do this by optimizing your site for organized search by using the design strategies we previously discussed, making sure your site is designed for a mobile phone. You can also contact local search providers like Google, Yelp, Where, and Citysearch (www.citysearch.com) directly to ensure your site is registered in their database.

✔ **Consider using slide-down menus and charts.** If your site detection determines that the customer's phone supports the feature, consider using slide-down menus and charts. When a link is clicked, the menu slides open (see http://m.stevemadden.com for an example). This capability optimizes the phone screen real estate and provides a good user experience for your customer.

✔ **Include a recommendation engine.** A recommendation engine is a Web site tool that automatically suggests products that are similar to the other products your customer is viewing or comparing. If your site is designed for people to buy or choose from a wide range of content, goods, or services, be sure to integrate a product comparison and recommendation engine. (Talk to your Web designer about ways to do this.) A good recommendation engine enhances the overall experience for the customer.

✔ **Add enhanced navigation features.** Be sure to consider adding enhanced navigation features like Sort (sorts the content on the page), Jump-to (links the user to a page deeper into the site), Breadcrumbs (a navigation tool, often on the top of the page, that shows the user the path they've taken through the site such as Home>Products>Printers>HP, so that they don't have to use the Back button as much).

✔ **Leverage location.** When at all possible, leverage the consumer's current location to tailor what content is displayed (talk to your Web designer about how to capture location data).

✔ **Integrate with social media.** Integrate your site with social media elements like Facebook Like, Twitter, LinkedIn, Foursquare, and other services. This drives traffic to your site.

✔ **Be accessible to customers.** Be sure to have links to customer support and care channels. Make it easy for your customer to text you, call you, e-mail you, check your knowledge database, or post a message to you to get help and answers to their questions.

When designing your site, one decision you definitely shouldn't overlook is the need to establish consistency with your wired site in content, design, and voice. If your wired site is predominantly blue and slightly irreverent in tone, your mobile site probably shouldn't be largely green and straightforward. You get the idea. Visitors to your wired site and mobile site should come away with no doubt that the sites are from the same company.

 Another key decision to make is what handsets you're going to support. Alas, no standard screen size exists, so you have to be diligent with your design to avoid a user's worst nightmare: horizontal scrolling. There is no real standard for mobile device screen size, unless you count rectangles and squares as standards. The most common size is 240x320 pixels, though the trend is to larger screens, such as the iPhone's 320x480. Many smaller screens appear to be phasing out as the mobile Web grows. See the Device Atlas Web site (`www.deviceatlas.com`) to get a sense of all the different type of mobile devices that are out there.

In general, keep your style minimal and content linear so it's easy for users to get to the information they want without jumping around the page. In mobile Web design, less is more, so fight the urge to make the site flashy and deep. A site that's simple and uncluttered, with minimal content, is always your best bet.

Creating Mobile Site Content

All phones with Web browsers can handle a variety of different types of content, including

- ✔ Text and data feeds
- ✔ Links
- ✔ Pictures
- ✔ Video
- ✔ Click-to-call phone numbers
- ✔ Social media feeds
- ✔ Maps and directions

Creating the content for your mobile site isn't a big challenge. It works much the same way as creating content for any Web site. The challenge comes when you have to deliver your content to the device because some content, such as video, needs to be formatted for proper display on every type of mobile device, browser, and operating system combination.

You can choose between four different ways to deliver your content through a mobile Web site:

✔ **Creating static content:** Static content is just what it sounds like — site content that rarely, if ever needs to be changed. Your company address, product descriptions, promotional copy, and About Us copy generally falls in this category. Create it once, and you can be done with it. When creating static content, you can format your content once and leave it alone, but you also can't change the content to match a specific user's phone capabilities. For example, if one of your site's visitors has a touchscreen and another doesn't, your site's content won't change to accommodate it.

✔ **Employing dynamic content:** Dynamic content changes each time the site is visited or the site page is refreshed. The advantage of dynamic content is that the content can change according to the type of device and even the context of the site visitor (such as when content is geographically relevant). Content for dynamic pages is typically pulled and updated from a content management system, most often via standard RSS and XML data feeds. If your content is stored in a content management system that doesn't support data-feed access, consider working with a company that can convert your data to standard RSS or XML, which can be streamed to your site.

✔ **Downloadable content:** Downloadable content can be formatted for a variety of standards such as PDF documents or videos that play on the device. Downloadable content can be served up in different formats just like dynamic content, but your system doesn't have to do it on the fly because the user has to click a link to request the download. For example, when a mobile phone requests audio or video files, the content management system sends it the version of the content that's most suitable for the phone (3GPP, a video format defined by the 3rd Generation Partnership Project, or .MOV, the Apple QuickTime video format, for example). The content is fully downloaded to the phone and played on the device's resident player.

✔ **Streaming content:** With streaming content, which is most likely audio and video content, the content isn't fully downloaded to the phone before it's played back; instead, it's streamed to the phone and begins to play back before the downloading is complete. One of the most common applications for video streaming is mobile television; for audio content, the most common applications are radio and sports broadcasts. Audio and video streaming are very specialized services that don't work across all carriers and handsets. Moreover, the data charges for these services can be quite high if a mobile subscriber is not on an unlimited data plan. Take special care in launching these services, and keep in mind that, as of yet, they're not ready for use in mass mobile marketing.

Streaming content requires speed. Most mobile users engage with this type of content only when they are on a smartphone with wireless access and they happen to be able to connect to a wireless source. These requirements limit your reach if you focus on streaming content.

Testing your mobile site content

After you create a site, test it on the top handsets used by your target audiences. Here are several approaches to consider:

- ✔ Study research from comScore M:Metrics (www.comscore.com) and Nielsen (www.niesen.com). These are two commercial mobile research firms that maintain a monthly record of the top handsets used by mobile subscribers throughout North America and Europe.

- ✔ Check reports from leading mobile Web and mobile app providers. AdMob, recently acquired by Google (www.admob.com), provides a free report of top mobile handsets being used on its global network, as does Millennial Media (www.millennialmedia.com), GetJar (www.getjar.com), Netbiscuits (www.netbiscuits.com), and other leading advertising, mobile Web, and mobile application providers.

- ✔ Test your site with the dotMobi (http://mtld.mobi) mobile-site readiness tool, mobi.Ready, which includes a free evaluation of your site for mobile friendliness, checking everything against industry best practices and mobile Web standards.

- ✔ Subscribe to a commercial service such as Mobile Complete's Device Anywhere (www.deviceanywhere.com), which allows you to test your site on real phones via the Internet.

Although the commercial services are great resources, don't skip testing on live handsets, too. Pick a range of devices to test manually, including specific phones you're targeting. An examination of ten phones should get to most of your universe.

Updating your mobile site content

After you've created your mobile site, you need to develop a plan to keep it up to date. Many forget to keep their mobile site consistent with their traditional site. Using tools like RSS feeds help ensure that your mobile site and traditional site stay in sync.

Be sure to reevaluate your mobile site every three to six months. Take a survey of the marketplace, review your mobile Web reports and logs, and determine what types of handsets make up the majority of the traffic to your site. If a new handset is responsible for a large part of the traffic, you may want to create a version of the site customized for that type of handset.

The mobile Web versus apps and the role of HTML 5

While you're grasping all the new and exciting things you can accomplish with a mobile Web site, keep in mind that one of the many moving parts of the mobile Web is the software language that is used to structure, create, and present mobile Web pages on a mobile device. The goal of a mobile Web software language is to provide a good experience for the mobile consumer: to display content in a legible manner, to be fast (loading pages quickly from all the possible data sources, including content management systems, static pages, image repositories, commerce systems, and so on), and to be secure (protecting the consumer's personal information, commerce transactions, and so on from being monitored by someone who shouldn't be monitoring them).

The first software language used for mobile Web was HTML, which stands for HyperText Markup Language. However, computers quickly outgrew the processing power and capability of mobile phones and HTML quickly became too "heavy" for mobile phones, meaning there was too much code to keep the experience fast, readable, and secure. Next came HTML 2.0 and HTML 4.0, both of which were an improvement on HTML, but had many of the same issues. In the late 1990s, WML, or Wireless Markup Language, a lightweight version of HTML, was released. It relied on WAP, or Wireless Application Protocol — network and computer instructions — to deliver Web pages to the phone. WML/WAP was slow, offered little in terms of a rich media experience, and really did not live up to the commercial hype.

However, for many of the old mobile guard, the term *WAP* is synonymous with mobile Web browsing (today, most just call it the mobile Web). After WML/WAP came XML (eXtensible Markup Language), xHTML (a hybrid of HMTL and XML), cHMTL and iHTML (network-specific versions of xHTML), and Flash Lite (Adobe's answer to rich media experiences on a phone).

All of these technologies still exist and are used around the world by developers when needed, based on the design factors that must be considered, including the type of mobile device the consumer is using, the Web browser the phone is using, the capabilities of the mobile network the sites will be delivered over, how much effort is necessary to code and maintain the site, security concerns, back-end content management system interaction, and so on.

However, a new entrant in the Web page software development lingo has recently emerged that should not be ignored: HTML 5.0. It was first developed in 2007 by the W3C (Worldwide Web Consortium, www.w3c.org), the standards body for the Web. Just recently, we're seeing more and more companies launch mobile Web sites based on HTML 5.0. HTML 5.0 offers many advantages. It's fast, provides a good experience, is secure, and, most importantly, can increasingly be used to provide an experience that is more like an application than a traditional Web site. Why? Because it was designed to help a developer access a device's hardware (like the camera on a home), to level location data, to provide a drag-and-drop user experience in the browser, and more. To get a working example of an HTML 5.0 site on your phone, check out www.google.com from your phone and click the My Location link under the search box. Google is using HTML 5.0 to power this user experience.

Chapter 9

Developing Mobile Applications and Content

*W*hat makes a smartphone a "must-have" device? Is it the sleek design, the bright, easy-to-read touch screen with millions of colors, or the fast wireless network that powers it?

Nope. It's the apps. Applications are essentially miniature versions of the software you use on your PC and they are a very popular way to enhance your mobile marketing strategy. Really good mobile Web sites also exist (see Chapter 8), but the apps are where smartphones really shine.

Apps may be cool, but building them doesn't mean your customers will automatically download them, use them, and buy things from your business. A lot of apps are out there, so you had better have a strategy for making your apps stand out among the crowd.

This chapter gives you the information you need to make good decisions about building mobile applications. We show you how to create a strategy for your apps and how to choose the right method for developing your apps. We also show you some best practices for mobile app design and where to go to get your apps listed in app stores, as well as other methods of app distribution.

Choosing a Mobile Application Strategy

You need to make a lot of decisions before you can even start building a mobile application because apps are so customizable. You can develop apps for specific functions, specific phones, and for an almost unlimited variety of tasks. The next sections show you how to think through your mobile app strategy so you have all the information you need to get started building your app.

Deciding whether a mobile app is the best choice

Mobile apps are cool. You can have so many unique and interactive experiences with them. For example, you can create exciting and fun games, entertainment services, social media and community experiences, financial services programs (for example, find the nearest ATM, transfer money, or even deposit checks through Chase's iPhone app), retail storefronts, picture galleries, broadcast media portals (like those offered by CNN) and so much more.

We don't want to discourage you from building a mobile app. An app can be a very powerful consumer engagement medium; however, before you start building a mobile application, it's a good idea to consider that mobile apps are not necessarily the right choice for *every* business or business need. Before you jump into the world of mobile app development just because it seems like everyone else is, ask yourself the following questions about your business and your goals:

✔ **Am I trying to reach the most people possible?** If you're trying to reach as many people as possible, a mobile application may not be the right choice. For example, today in the U.S. market, only about 25% of consumers have a smartphone, so the reach of a mobile app is limited to that audience. By the end of Q3 2011, this number may be closer to 50%; however, this still means that the other 50% of the market can't download your app.

✔ **Do you need a mobile app or mobile Web site?** This is a chapter on apps, but not every business is aided by a mobile app. Some sites, such as the Weather Channel site at www.weather.com, shown in Figure 9-1, develop mobile apps and mobile sites for their customers. If a mobile Web site can meet the needs of most of your customers, you might want to consider starting there before moving up to an app (see Chapter 8 for more on the mobile Web). A mobile Web site will likely cost less than an app, and mobile Web sites are compatible across multiple phones, including the fanciest of smartphones. Mobile Web capabilities are improving, with many companies, primarily Google, focusing serious efforts there. For the most part, if your customers need to use the native device functions (for example, like a device's camera, address book, location-detection capabilities, motion sensors, and so on) of the mobile device in order to accomplish whatever task you want them to accomplish, a mobile app is the right choice. If you just want to deliver content to your customers, a mobile Web site is probably a better choice. You can read more about building mobile Web sites in Chapter 8.

Figure 9-1:
Mobile apps and mobile Web sites can have similar functionality.

✔ **Do you have the time to do the care and feeding of a mobile app?** Successful apps, like popular Web sites, require care and feeding. If you struggle to find time to update your business Web site, you will likely encounter the same challenge in keeping your app fresh and exciting.

✔ **What phones do your customers use?** Different smartphones and related mobile devices like the Apple iPad require different development, have differing screen sizes, and, in some instances, require completely unique development for each. If your customers use a wide variety of phones, you need to develop a variety of apps or you need to justify the fact that you'll only be reaching a portion of your customer base by developing a single app.

You must develop several versions of each app to work with the various operating systems on your customers' mobile phones (the iPhone, the Android, and so on, see Chapter 1), or you need to realize that you'll only be reaching a portion of your customer base if you develop a single app.

Choosing which devices to design for

Ask anyone who is a big fan of their smartphone why they prefer it over other types, and you will get some pretty vocal responses. Smartphones come in a multitude of shapes and sizes. They not only differ physically, but stylistically as well. When deciding what devices you want to design for, consider the type of user each mobile device operating system (OS) tends to attract (see Chapter 1 for more details):

- ✔ **Apple OS (for example, the iPhone/iPod Touch/iPad):** Apple set the app world afire with the launch of its original iPhone in 2007. Since then, it has followed up with the iPod Touch, effectively an iPhone without wireless network connectivity, and the iPad, which could be called an iPhone on steroids with a much larger screen. All of them share the same operating system and development standard, the iPhone OS. Unsurprisingly, they all utilize the same application store, the iTunes app store, which boasts more than 200,000 applications as of this writing. Having enjoyed the best selection of apps from what could be called the start of the "app era," iPhone users have a high standard when it comes to apps, but they are also voracious consumers, downloading new apps, particularly free ones, trying them out, deleting them, and moving on. Because iPhone users are the largest single market of app consumers, you should consider the iPhone environment first and foremost.

- ✔ **Android OS:** Google followed Apple into the app market with its Android operating system in 2008. Android quickly moved into the second position behind iPhone in terms of app variety and availability in its Android Market (see Figure 9-2). Android customers are often more "techie" than their iPhone counterparts, although this is changing somewhat. The Android Market can be found as an application link called Market on the home page of an Android-powered device.

- ✔ **Research in Motion BlackBerry OS:** If the iPhone created the app revolution, BlackBerry empowered the mobile e-mail revolution with the easy-to-use, some would say addictive, keyboards on the company's devices. BlackBerry has long been a smartphone leader internationally and still dominates the business market. While BlackBerry arrived a bit late to the app party, it has plans to catch up and continues to sell its devices faster than McDonald's can bag burgers. To know a BlackBerry fan is to know someone in a mind-meld with their e-mail. Whether a banker, a lawyer, or a doctor, BlackBerry users tend to consider themselves professionals in every meaning of the word.

- ✔ **Microsoft Phone OS:** Microsoft struggled to ignite app interest with its dated operating system, Windows Mobile 6.5. With the arrival of Windows Mobile 7 in late 2010, Microsoft plans to change all that. Although no one can predict the type of users that will take to the new operating system, discounting or ignoring Microsoft would be foolhardy.

Figure 9-2:
The Android
app market
launched
soon after
Apple's
app store
launched.

Access via
a mobile device

Access via
a computer browser

✔ **Others:** Multiple other smartphone operating systems allow app capabilities, including Palm, Symbian, Qualcomm Brew, Java, Linux, and
Samsung's Bada. As an app developer, you must keep your eye on the
market as it evolves. Luckily, some sites do that for you, including
mocoNews (www.moconews.net), Gizmodo (www.gizmodo.com), and
Engadget Mobile (www.engadgetmobile.com).

Choosing which mobile device OS you need to design for isn't necessarily just
a matter of which device your customers use. You also have to take into consideration the capabilities of each device and the behavior of the people who
use those devices. For example, if your customers are mostly corporate executives who use BlackBerrys, they probably aren't as likely to value a gaming
application.

Choosing a Method for Developing Your Application

Just like when you create a traditional Web site, you have several choices
when it comes to methods of developing a mobile application. Because
mobile apps can get pretty technical, you don't have a lot of choices when
it comes to doing it yourself, unless you have an intimate knowledge of the
code required and the intricacies of the operating systems on all the phone
manufacturers.

Unless you're a programmer, or you have a team of app developers who work at your company, we recommend going with an expert app development company to build your apps. Whether you use your own programmers or hire an outside developer, the next sections give you some tips for making the right development decisions based on your financial and human resources.

Going with in-house development

In-house development means you or your team is going to develop the application, soup-to-nuts. You can choose between three ways to build apps in-house:

- ✔ **Coding:** All mobile operating systems have software development kits (SDKs) that empower programmers to code in order to create applications (see Figure 9-3). These applications are often dubbed *native,* meaning they have been coded to the operating system's exact instructions for creating applications. Although this is a sure-fire way to create an application that works well in a given smartphone, it's also frequently the most costly and requires you to have programmers on-hand who are well versed in the targeted mobile operating systems. This may mean that you can afford to target only a single smartphone type, for example, the iPhone, but no others. To find a developer, ask around on your development team, put an ad on Craigslist (www.craigslist.com), or check LinkedIn (www.linkedin.com) or a similar professional network.

- ✔ **Template-based approach:** What if you have a bit of content, say an RSS feed generated by your blog, a logo, and an interest in getting a mobile app up and running ASAP? Template-based providers may be the right route for you to take. These Web-based solution providers empower customers to get a simple, template-based application up and running in minutes. What you lose in design flexibility (you have little control outside of the templates provided), you gain in speed and, potentially, dollars. Many of these providers even embed advertising banners so that you can make money off your app from day one. Providers include Mobile Roadie (www.mobileroadie.com), AppMakr (www.appmakr.com), and Applicable Media (www.applicablemedia.com). Going this route, you may be limited to just a few operating systems, most typically the top app environments — iPhone and Android. You can find a lot developers and providers simply by surfing the Internet.

- ✔ **Design platform:** A design platform allows the creation of mobile apps for multiple operating systems via a design-centric environment (think Powerpoint or Adobe Photoshop) rather than coding. These powerful solutions require some training and expense, but offer extreme flexibility and allow you the peace of mind that your apps can live and breathe in just about any smart device environment, from iPhone to Windows Mobile and everything else in between. If you have come to the conclusion that you don't want to place your bets on one format by hiring a developer (like the coding option) and templates are simply too limiting, a design platform is ideal. Providers of this sort include Whoop (`www.whoop.com`) and Unity Mobile (`www.unitymobile.com`). See Figure 9-4 for a sample design platform.

You know your business and your customers better than any developer or service provider does. Create an outline through visual storyboards or even a creative brief of what you want the app to do and how you want it to look and use it as a design center that is then passed off to the development group you choose. This way, your developer has a place to start and you have the advantage of their know-how on the technical end to make your vision a reality. They can also give you advice on the practicality of your desired app features.

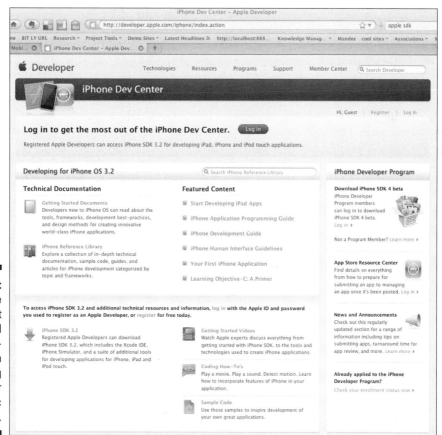

Figure 9-3: Software development kits aid programmers in developing apps for specific devices.

Figure 9-4:
The Whoop mobile application design platform.

Leveraging outside consultants, agencies and partners

It probably won't surprise you to discover, given the billions of dollars that are flowing out of it, that the app world has created a vibrant cottage industry of consultants, typically small one- or several-person shops, and larger traditional agencies, that can happily create your mobile app for you. Before you take this step, however, consider the following:

- **How much app can you afford?** You wouldn't go house- or car-hunting without a budget in mind. The same should be true when you're hunting for a consulting provider. Keep in mind that many providers require upwards of 50% of their total fee upfront before initiating development. Also, additional features may be added during the development process that require more investment than originally planned.

- **What should the mobile app do?** A consultant is only as good as the requirements expected of her. Poor requirements usually result in a poor app. Changes after the initial app's launch can be costly. One of the requirements you need to think about are which smartphones you want them to target: Many consultants specialize in one, maybe two, operating systems at most.

Finding the right resource is a matter of research. This is a critical decision for your business, so you want to take time to find the right partner. Fortunately, there are some easy ways to get started:

✔ **Find out who makes your favorite apps:** If you carry a smartphone and really like a certain application, read the author information in the About section of the app or the store page promoting the application. The app's consultants or developers are often listed there.

✔ **Check out industry sites and awards:** Scan industry sites such as mocoNews.net (www.moconews.net) for word of developers or agencies that have been successful. Review past winners of awards such as the Apple Design Awards (http://developer.apple.com/wwdc/ada/index.html). Some of the leading players include Whoop (www.whoop.com), Trailer Park (www.trailerpark.com), Banzai Labs (www.banzailabs.com), and Teleca (www.teleca.com), to name just a few.

Following Best Practices for Designing Applications

Applications can be built to do almost anything. Instead of showing you in ten thousand pages or more all the best practices for every possibility, the next sections show you what to make sure you include in every app no matter what its function. In the next sections, we also show the most common traps that beset app developers and how to avoid them.

Employing the utility of the touchscreen

A truly useful mobile app is one that keeps the primacy of the screen in mind. Devices that are entirely touchscreen for their interface, the iPhone for example, rely upon navigation that can be manipulated by the touch of a finger. Other devices, such as the BlackBerry Tour or Curve, rely on a keyboard and roller ball/pad for navigation instead. Here are some tips for making sure your app takes full advantage of the touchscreen on the devices that support it and takes into consideration the devices that don't:

✔ **Is it interactive?** If the content of your application is text-heavy (think newspaper rather than TV), it may be better off as a mobile Web page rather than as an app. Apps live to be touched, moved around, and pinched.

✔ **Does it have a lot of A/V?** If your app has a lot of audio or video, it will do well in a touchscreen environment.

✔ **Is it game-like?** The hottest games are targeted to touchscreen devices and for good reason. With all that screen space, manipulation by fingers, whether on-screen or on the side (shaking the device, or moving it to adjust the screen ratio from horizontal to vertical), makes touchscreens the perfect venue for games.

Designing for a platform and hardware

When you have settled on a smart device platform, you have two key pieces of information at your disposal. You know the type of user and the way a user navigates apps on the device. Both are key guideposts for your application's design.

Going further, many smart device platforms have screens of varying size, and this should play a role in your design efforts as well. The iPad, although sharing the same operating system as its smaller cousin the iPhone, has a screen closer to 8x10 inches. An app designed exclusively for an iPad should incorporate that increased real estate, allowing more flexible navigation methods than the iPhone equivalent of the same application.

In all instances, remember that these devices are called *mobile* devices for a reason. Applications on these devices are meant to be used while folks are walking, talking, multi-tasking and, hopefully, not driving. An app that is designed around the mobile experience will see success; the app that feels more at home on a PC won't.

Distributing Mobile Applications

An application, once built, is a lonely one without users to download it. Fortunately, help is ready and available. The only question is which route you choose to take.

Publishing to device app stores

The most popular route for distributing applications is via the app stores of the various smart device companies. The icons of these stores are prominently displayed on most smart device desktops. Although there are other means to distribute apps, think of the app stores as the swankiest department store in the mall with a big, blaring neon sign. They typically carry the endorsement, if not the name, of the smart device manufacturer and enjoy a high level of trust on the part of the device user.

In addition to offering easy, immediate distribution, app stores provide billing flexibility. With device app stores, you can choose to distribute an application for free, a one-time premium charge, or a recurring or subscription-based charge.

Alas, nothing in life is *truly* free. Although most device app stores allow free apps to be made available at no cost (about 80% of all apps are offered for free), they keep a share of any premium charges if and when the application is sold. Known as a *revenue share,* the retail fee of the application kept by the smart device company is generally around 30%. So, even though the app store will help you distribute the application, remember you get to keep only about 70 cents of every dollar charged to your users. Keep in mind, whether your application is sold or offered for free, you can also make money with your application through mobile advertising (see Chapter 10) and through mobile commerce (see Chapter 13) strategies.

Which app store you choose depends on two key qualifiers:

✓ **What environment you developed your app for:** You can't distribute an app to an app store not built for it. The BlackBerry App World doesn't take apps built for Android, for example.

✓ **Which store provides your app the greatest visibility:** You can determine this in a number of ways, including the number of apps in the app store or how many downloads the app store enjoys.

App stores require that you submit your application via a clearance process before an app is posted to the catalog. Keep in mind that some of these approval processes can take months to be completed, so don't go printing flyers with your launch date on them until you know an app has been approved.

The app stores are eager to have your business, so they have made it easy to learn more information about submitting applications. Check out the app store Web sites for more information:

✓ **Android Marketplace (for Google Android devices):** http://market.android.com/publish

✓ **BlackBerry App World:** http://na.blackberry.com/eng/developers/resources/

✓ **iPhone Developer Program (for iPhone, iPod Touch, and iPad):** http://developer.apple.com/programs/iphone/. To get your app into the iPhone apps store, you must go the route of the developer program.

✓ **Windows Marketplace for Mobile:** http://developer.windowsphone.com/Marketplace.aspx

Here are the steps involved in submitting an application to the iTunes app store. The other stores have a similar process:

1. **Open an Apple Developer account at `https://developer.apple.com/programs/iphone`.**

   You have to pay around $100 up front and on an annual, ongoing basis thereafter.

2. **Create a provisioning profile.**

3. **Create appropriate certificates.**

4. **Create app IDs.**

5. **Submit application via iTunes Connect.**

Exact details for each of the preceding steps are explained in the Apple Software Development Kit (SDK) help and forum files. We don't go into detail here because there are a number of different ways of handling each of the steps depending on the strategy you're using to develop, deploy, and maintain your application.

Every application store and every developer network has a different process. You simply have to go to their Web sites and find out what they require.

If all this seems complicated, you might want to have a coder or developer already accomplished in the app store process submit your application on your behalf.

Going on-deck with carrier catalogs

For a long time, you could download applications only from your carrier's app store. If the smart device app stores are the glitziest store in the modern mall, the carrier store was the general store — the only place in town. Known as going *on-deck* because the carrier store front was typically the first and foremost icon in a phone's data menu in the age before smart devices, it provided instant and automatic visibility for an application. To this day, the on-deck approach still does, although mobile carriers have been somewhat eclipsed by their smart device app store brethren.

Spurred on by the smart device app stores, carriers have recently kicked up the marketing of their storefronts. Although it remains to be seen if this effort will amount to *Empire Strikes Back* or *Grease 2,* carrier catalogs are a fine location to present your apps, especially if your app is key for users of a particular network. If, for example, you have built an application destined to be sold to employees of a company that uses Verizon Wireless, you might want to think about submitting your application to Verizon's catalog first.

Allow some lead time for your application to be approved and assume that the carrier will retain some revenue share, typically a third or more. Check out these Web sites for a rundown of carrier app store resources:

- ✔ **AT&T App Center:** `http://developer.att.com/developer`
- ✔ **Sprint:** `http://developer.sprint.com`
- ✔ **T-Mobile:** `http://developer.t-mobile.com`
- ✔ **Verizon Wireless:** `http://developer.verizon.com/`

More than 60 applications stores exist as of March 2010 and the number is growing each month. The Wireless Industry Partnership (`www.wipconnector.com`) maintains an App Store Report that it updates monthly. Check out this report to get the latest and greatest on application stores. Also, another great resource for marketing with applications is the "Sizing up the Global Apps Market" report by Chetan Sharma Consulting (`www.chetansharma.com/`).

Marketing via direct download

Although smart device company app stores are popular, they aren't the only catalogs around. So-called third-party app stores have gained some prominence, especially in Europe. GetJar (`www.getjar.com`) is one of the largest. Remember, there's no wrong way to distribute an app. Stay focused on your target audiences and where they shop, but if you have the time, extra visibility is always good!

Some design platforms, notably Whoop (`www.whoop.com`), allow distribution via a direct download. A direct download means users can simply click a Web address in a text message, browser, or e-mail to download applications to their devices. The mechanism allows you, the app owner, to market and deliver your application however you wish. Even better, direct download mechanisms can work seamlessly with the same apps posted to smart device app stores. At the end of the day, the more visibility your app has, the better!

Creating and Distributing Mobile Content

Mobile content (also referred to as *personalization content*) refers to images and audio files that are used to personalize a mobile subscriber's mobile device, such as the background image on the home screen of a phone (wallpaper), or the phone's ringtone.

Many mobile marketing companies (for example, SendMe, MyThum, and others) specialize in selling mobile content. You may not be in the business of selling content, but you may want to create some to offer it as an incentive for customers to participate in your programs. For example, you may give away your product logo to be used as a wallpaper or provide a popular song as a ringtone to consumers as a form of promotional incentive.

The following provides an overview on how to manage wallpapers and ringtones.

Providing branded wallpapers and screen savers

Mobile wallpapers and screen savers are wonderful ways to personalize mobile phones and are conceptually identical to personal-computer wallpapers and screen savers. A *mobile wallpaper* is the still image displayed on a mobile phone's main screen, and a *mobile screen saver* is the still and/or animated image that's displayed on the mobile phone's screen when the phone is idle. See Figure 9-5 for an example of a wallpaper on the phone.

Figure 9-5:
A phone with branded wallpaper.

The image you use for wallpapers and screen savers can be your company's logo or any other image that represents your business or the objectives of your marketing campaign: a character, artistic scene, cityscape, landscape, and so on.

Finding a graphics application

Creating your own branded wallpapers and screen savers is easy. You just need a graphics application, some artistic talent, a mobile marketing application, and a marketing plan to promote your content or one that uses the content as an incentive to promote another offering.

You can use a variety of graphics applications to create your content, ranging from free and low-cost applications to professional packages such as Adobe Photoshop.

Search the Download.com Web site (www.download.com) for graphics software (available for both Microsoft Windows and Macintosh platforms), or visit a local software store to find an application that suits your needs and skill level.

Creating wallpapers and screen savers

When you create your mobile wallpapers and screen savers, make sure that you create an array of images with the right resolution and file format:

✔ **Image resolution:** You need to configure your images for ten common mobile-phone screen sizes. A screen size typically is measured as number of pixels wide by number of pixels high. The most common screen sizes are

- 96x65
- 101x80
- 120x160
- 128x128
- 132x176
- 175x130
- 176x208
- 176x220
- 240x320 (the size of most BlackBerry devices)
- 480x320 (the size of the Apple iPhone)

Your images should be designed to fit each screen size. Typical phones support 72 dots per square inch *(dpi),* but newer phones like the iPhone support 163 dpi. The higher the dpi, the more detail you can support in an image and the clearer it is.

Both dpi and image dimensions add to the image file size and thereby affect download speeds. You want the files to be as small as possible for quick downloading.

✔ **File format:** Most mobile phones support JPEG, GIF, and PNG file types. Consult your content management system provider about which file type to use.

If you're creating an animated screen saver, you must save it as a GIF file because the other image file formats don't support animation.

Figure 9-6 shows content hosted in a mobile applications provider's mobile content management system. Work with a mobile content provider to help you deliver the content because each mobile carrier network has its own unique requirements.

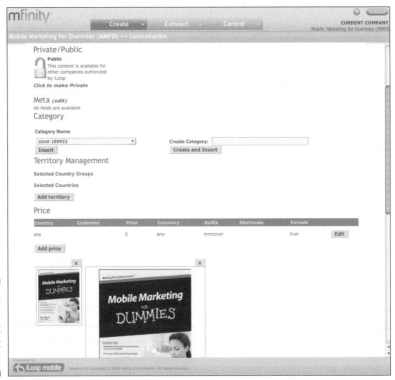

Figure 9-6:
Wallpapers
in a content
management
system.

You may choose to create a single image and rely on the mobile marketing application's content management system to scale it for you automatically. If you use this method, however, the quality of the image may be impaired, especially if the image contains text. Text in an image that looks great on a display 320 pixels wide may be unreadable when automatically resized to 65 pixels wide. A quality mobile content management system uses the appropriate image for the phone and reduces the image size dynamically only as a last resort.

Delivering ringtones and other system sounds

The term *ringtone* refers to the sound a mobile phone makes when it is being called. Ringtones are immensely popular with all consumer segments and can be a great way to offer value to customers. Your subscribers can get ringtones from many places, including their mobile carriers, sounds built into their phones, and third parties like you.

Like wallpapers (which we discuss in the preceding section), ringtones help personalize a user's phone. Unlike wallpapers, however, ringtones are public because everyone around can hear them when the phone rings. Therefore, ringtones are a great way for a mobile subscriber to demonstrate affinity for a brand, campaign, or cause.

During the 2008 presidential campaign, for example, then-candidate for president Barack Obama provided ringtones that let people show their support for his candidacy every time their phones rang. One of the most popular tones was this message: "This is Barack Obama. It's time to change America. Answer the call," which would play when the user's phone rang. All of the Obama campaign's mobile programs, and they were extensive, were envisioned and executed by Scott Goodstein of Revolution Messaging (www. revolutionmessaging.com) along with Douglas Busk, his mobile advisor, two of the leaders in mobile marketing in politics.

Creating a ringtone

A ringtone is simply a properly formatted audio file associated with a mobile phone's ringer preferences so that the audio file plays when the phone rings.

You can use a variety of audio mixing applications to create your ringtones. You can find a free or inexpensive application on the Internet, or you can purchase one. The audio application you use must be able to save your ringtone in an appropriate file format (see the list later in this section).

When you create your audio file, keep the following parameters in mind:

- **Length:** A typical ringtone is 20 to 30 seconds long.

- **File format:** Most modern phones support the MP3 audio-file format, but many older phones don't. Also, some carriers (including Sprint and Verizon Wireless) have special formatting requirements.

   To support the widest range of mobile phones, keep your ringtones to 128 kilobits mono, and produce them in the following formats and sizes:

     • **MP3:** 200 kilobits or less

     • **WAV:** 200 kilobits or less

     • **AMR:** 45 kilobits or less

     • **AMRWB:** 90 kilobits or less

     • **MMF:** 100 kilobits or less

     • **QCP:** 60 kilobits or less

   The files can be bigger, but if they are, they take longer to download and take up more space on consumers' phones.

Distributing a ringtone

After you create your ringtones, you can upload them to your mobile application provider's content management system, as shown in Figure 9-7, which delivers the ringtones when a user requests the tones via text messaging, an application, or a mobile Web site.

You can give your marketing campaign flair by providing unique content for specific events. Before a live concert in 2007, the Black Eyed Peas recorded ringtones and uploaded them to their partner's content management system. When they went onstage, they gave the audience the opportunity to download ringtones that were available only for that night. That's adding value.

If you lack artistic talent and can't create compelling wallpapers, screen savers, or ringtones on your own, don't lose heart. You can always hire someone else to create the content or tap your friends and family members to do it. Outsourcing content development to a third party is common and needn't cost much. A professional marketing agency can help you and will probably provide great service, but you can also go to a local art school college, or high school — or even an elementary school — and ask a student to produce your artwork. You can find a lot of talented people out there!

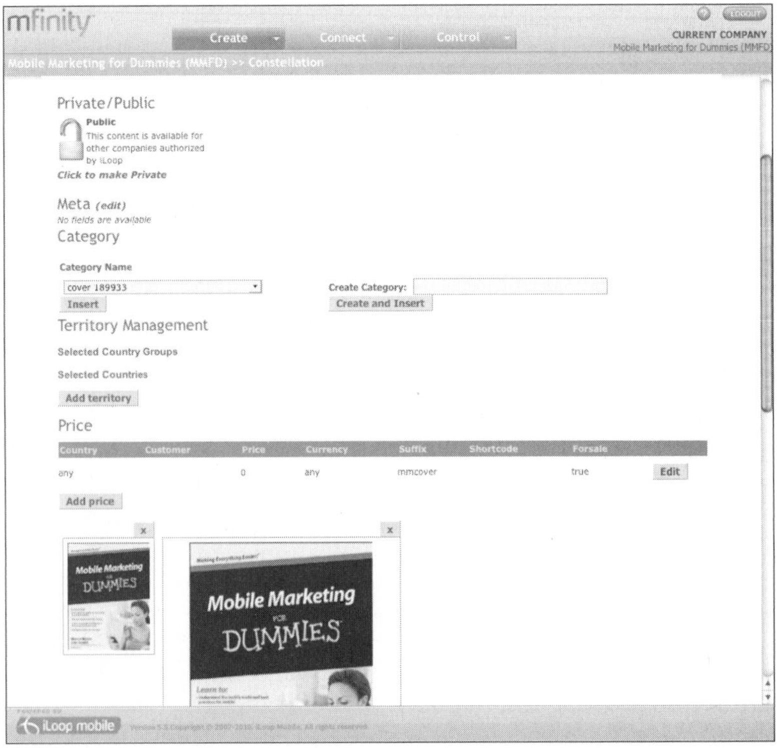

Figure 9-7:
Ringtones
in a content
management
system.

Chapter 10

Displaying Your Advertising on Mobile Devices

In This Chapter

▶ Leveraging buyers, publishers, and networks

▶ Understanding how to buy mobile advertising

▶ Discovering how to monetize your sites with advertising

▶ Placing mobile ads in front of mobile users

*W*ith the proliferation of mobile devices and the increased consumer adoption of services like SMS, mobile Internet and applications marketers like you are turning to mobile advertising, and like them, you can

- ✔ Generate brand awareness. Increase the number of people who know about your company and its products and services.
- ✔ Increase the likelihood that consumers may want to buy your products.
- ✔ Increase sales by driving traffic directly to a transaction.
- ✔ Generate new revenue streams by including advertising in your messaging, mobile Internet sites, and applications.

If you've never bought an advertisement in your life, or even if you're not sure how you can employ mobile advertising, don't worry. You've come to the right place. In this chapter, we teach you all about mobile advertising: what it is, who to work with, and how to buy and sell it.

Squeezing the Advantages Out of Mobile Advertising

Mobile advertising is the practice of a mobile advertiser (also referred to as a buyer) placing paid-for promotional messaging and sponsorship messages within a publisher's mobile media property as supported by a mobile advertising network or search provider (see Figure 10-1). For example:

✔ Text messages, multimedia messages, and e-mail messages

✔ Mobile Internet sites, both your own and others

✔ Mobile applications that people download through application stores

✔ Mobile audio and video content that plays on a mobile device

Mobile advertising is a lot like online advertising, but with three key advantages over traditional online advertising. You should become familiar with each advantage so you can include them in your marketing plans:

✔ **Reach:** Reach is defined as the number of unique individuals seeing an ad at least one time during a specific period. In order to get the best results for the least amount of money, you want your ad exposed to as many people (in other words, to have as broad a reach) as possible.

Mobile has the potential of greater reach than any other medium because the majority of the population is carrying a mobile device and increasingly using mobile media like SMS, mobile Internet, and applications. Research firms like Insight Express (www.insightexpress.com) also point out that mobile generates better brand awareness and overall purchase intent than online media advertising. You can find out more about increasing your reach in the next section.

✔ **Relevancy:** *Relevancy* refers to an ad or advertised product being pertinent to the target audience. If your product or message within your ad campaign is not targeted to a relevant audience, the ad campaign will be ineffective. Increasingly, ad networks are able to adjust the content and type of an ad to take many factors into account, such as the consumers' physical locations, types of phones, their direction of travel (and speed), their stated preferences and interests, their demographic profiles, and past and current behaviors (like what they own or are reading). By taking all this information into account in real time, advertisers are able to ensure that your ad is placed in front of people who are interested in what you have to offer.

✔ **Immediacy:** Mobile offers the best "in the moment" engagement. Given the personal nature, the uncluttered space (most pages have only one or two ads), and the, well, mobile nature of the mobile medium, when they're presented with a relevant ad, mobile users are often inclined to respond immediately. Unlike other forms of advertising, mobile advertising can reach users while they are interacting with a brand or product. For example, an ad for laundry detergent is much more relevant to someone standing in the grocery store than someone sitting at work in front of a computer.

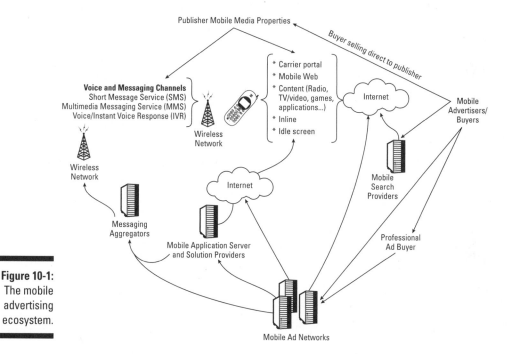

Figure 10-1:
The mobile
advertising
ecosystem.

Leveraging Different Types of Mobile Advertising

Mobile advertising can take a variety of forms. You should be aware of each so you can know your options and think about advertising across multiple channels and formats, which broadens your reach.

Given the rich diversity of mobile media and devices, mobile advertising has a lot of potential. The following sections help you become acquainted with the different types of mobile advertising and their advantages.

Using multiple ad units and placements

The first thing to consider when building a mobile advertising strategy is the type of advertising you want to do. The type of advertising you want to do is known as an *ad unit*. Because each type of mobile advertising space and device supports a different type of advertising, you need to format your advertising using the ad units that make the most sense for each opportunity. Here are the most common types of ad units:

- ✔ **Text:** Text ads consist of alphanumeric text, including mobile Internet URLs and phone numbers.

- ✔ **Banner ads:** Banner ads refer to both static and animated images displayed on mobile Internet pages, in applications, in video, and in animated content (see Figure 10-2).

Chevron sponsorship add in an application

Text link in Mobile Web Page

Mobile Web link in a text message

Figure 10-2: Banner ads are not limited to mobile Internet pages.

Different formats of display advertising

Rich media advertising

✔ **Audio ads:** Audio ads refer to advertisements inserted into audio content, music and radio, directory services, and event text-to-speech services. (For example, when a service reads a mobile Web page to you, advertisements may be interlaced into the content.)

✔ **Rich media ads:** Rich media ads take banner advertising to the next level and are supported on only the latest smartphones and mobile devices. A rich media ad unit may include text, images, video, animation, and audio that may expand to full-screen, float on the screen, or perform any number of other interactive and visual gymnastics. In addition, rich media ad units may leverage the advanced capabilities of the latest mobile devices, like location detection, interaction through the touch-screen, or unique motions of the device (like shaking it).

Almost any mobile advertisement may appear at different places with mobile media, including

✔ **Pre- or post-appended to a text message, MMS message, or mobile Internet site:** That is at the beginning or end of the message or site.

✔ **In-line:** The add is placed in-line within a message, a page, or application.

✔ **Pre- or post-roll:** In this case, the ad is placed at the start and or end of a video or audio clip.

✔ **Interstitial (or bumper ad unit):** The ad is displayed when pages are loading or when applications are downloading.

✔ **Idle screen:** The ad is displayed on the home screen of the device when it sits idle for a period of time, maybe a few seconds or minutes.

Each type of ad unit and placement decision is valuable in and of itself, but advertising is most effective when a variety of messages get in front of the same consumer. Make sure you are familiar with all the aforementioned advertisement types and placements before you come up with your strategy. Consider including three or more ad units and placements in any given advertising campaign.

Placing ads in mobile search

Everyone who browses the Web uses search engines to find Web sites, and advertisers place ads on search engines like Google or Yahoo! in order to attract clicks from the people who are searching for things. Mobile search is a practice similar to Internet search, but with mobile search, people use their mobile phones to conduct the searches.

Most people who engage in mobile search still go to the most familiar search engines, but you should be aware of some key differences in the way that mobile search advertisements work so you can alter any of your search engine advertisements that are targeted at mobile searchers. (If you want to learn the basics of placing search engine ads in general, we suggest you read *Pay Per Click Search Engine Marketing For Dummies* by Peter Kent, published by Wiley.) Here are the key factors to remember about mobile search:

✔ **Mobile searches are usually optimized for location.** Search providers like Google, Yahoo!, oneSearch, and Microsoft with its Bing service have optimized their search programs to take into account a user's location. Local search providers can be very effective as well, such as Yelp (www. yelp.com), Jingle Networks (www.jinglenetworks.com), City Search (www.citysearch.com), Where (www.where.com), and others. For example, if you're in San Jose, California, and you're using your mobile to look for a pizza place, Google starts by showing you the results for pizza places near where you are standing, as shown in Figure 10-3. If you're targeting mobile searchers, make sure your advertisements take the searchers' locations into account.

✔ **Mobile users have access to mobile question and answer services.** These services allow users to post questions to the service. Automated or live agents (meaning real people) answer the questions. Some of the leading providers of this service include Snackable Media (www. snackablemedia.com), ChaCha (www.chacha.com), AskMeNow (www. Askmenow.com), and MobileBits (www.mobilebits.com). These services don't own the whole search market, but it's a good idea to be on one or more of them so your business can be the answer to someone's question about your products or services.

✔ **Mobile directories are more friendly than Web directories.** Mobile directory search, like the local yellow pages, help people find local services nearby. Mobile directories sell listings and are optimized for smaller screens. When listing on a mobile search directory, make sure your listing points to a mobile Web site. (Read Chapter 8 for more information about mobile Web sites.)

Working with mobile search providers to place search engine advertising is pretty easy. For most solutions, you don't have to do anything technically different from your Web-based search advertising to get your search engine advertisements to appear on mobile screens.

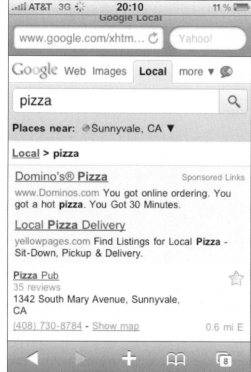

Figure 10-3:
Mobile
search
advertising
reaches
people by
location.

In addition to placing paid search advertisements, you want to make sure your mobile Web sites are optimized for search engines so your site appears in organic search results. To improve your mobile search engine ranking, check out Chapter 8.

Grasping the Basics of Buying and Selling Mobile Advertisements

Mobile advertising involves two primary players — the buyer and the publisher — either or both of which may be your company or another company, depending on the situation. Here's how it works:

✔ The company that pays to place a marketing message in an available mobile space is called the mobile *ad buyer*. For example, you're the ad buyer when you buy an ad on someone else's mobile Web site. Another company is the ad buyer when it buys an ad on your behalf.

✔ The company that provides the space for an ad and takes the money from the buyer is called the *ad publisher*. For example, you're the ad publisher when you sell ad space on your own mobile Web site to an ad buyer, and another company is the ad publisher when you buy advertising space from it.

Buying and publishing mobile advertising requires a combination of technology, connections, and expertise. If you have all three, you might be able to buy and publish your own mobile advertisements. Chances are, however, that you'll need at least one of the companies described in the following sections to be successful with all your mobile advertising.

Partnering with media agencies

If buying mobile advertising is not within your area of expertise, you may choose to work with an outside ad buyer (also called a *media agency*). Media agencies are ad buyers that negotiate and purchase mobile advertising space or inventory on your behalf. Buyers work with you to plan and spend advertising budgets so you can maximize the return on investment for a given ad campaign.

Here are some scenarios where you might want to consider using a professional mobile media buyer:

✔ **You want to advertise on premium sites, such as MTV, CNN, ESPN, the Weather Channel, Disney, and others.** These organizations tend to sell their own ad inventory, or work with a specialty group. Moreover, they often want to work through a media buyer, meaning they don't want to work with you (the buyer) directly, unless your budgets are fairly large and your needs are unique.

✔ **You have a large budget.** When you have a large budget, the buyer can help you draw up a strategy to ensure that your advertisements are spread across all the appropriate mobile media, with the right reach and frequency (the number of times an ad is displayed in a given period). A lot of work goes into this, and you definitely ought to leverage the buyer's expertise.

✔ **You need to place ads across several mobile mediums.** If you want to advertise across mobile mediums, such as SMS, MMS, mobile Internet, applications, and so on, realize that a lot of work goes into understanding how to buy the media as well as deliver it. You shouldn't try to become an expert in all of them — let the buyer do that. If you're buying in only one medium, however, you can go directly to companies like 4INFO (www.4info.com) for text messaging advertising or AdMob, recently acquired by Google (www.admob.com), for display advertising.

✔ **You need several inventory sources.** *Inventory* refers to all the possible locations where your advertisement may be placed in all the different forms of mobile media. Even the biggest media properties such as CNN or ESPN may not be able to get you the reach and the exposure you're looking to achieve with your advertising. You may need to go to many media companies and use many mobile mediums to get the reach you're looking for. A buyer can help you with this.

✔ **You want a discount.** An ad buyer can negotiate discounted rates due to prior relationships and bulk rates. He also knows the best sources of inventory. He saves you time and money and delivers better results by managing the different allocations of spending across inventory sources where the ROI (return on investment) is highest.

✔ **You're short on time.** You should use an ad buyer when you can't dedicate resources to real-time campaign management, monetization, and the negotiations for getting the best price for your advertising buys.

✔ **You need an expert.** For big-spending clients new to the advertising space, buyers can provide more expert industry knowledge and resources to invest in the most relevant products and targeting methods.

Resources such as *Advertising Age* (http://adage.com/datacenter/) can provide lists of the most popular ad buying agencies. The choice of which to use is a personal one and can depend on your product, the size of the ad, and the resources that agency can dedicate to an ad campaign. There is really no easy way to figure out which one is best for you. You simply need to call a few candidates to see whether they know anything about your market and whether their pricing is competitive. If they've been in the industry a long time, you probably can trust that they can do a good job, but be sure to look at smaller firms that may be hungry for your business or have a unique specialty in serving your market. Sometimes the larger firms won't really understand the nuances of your business, in which case a smaller firm may do a better job for you.

Because every ad needs a space in order to be seen by consumers and because advertising generally works better when it's placed in lots of spaces, every ad buyer needs to buy space from *multiple* publishers. If you're working through a formal ad buyer or agency, however, you won't have to interact with mobile publishers directly. The agency will work on your behalf to purchase relevant inventory on placements to obtain the highest ROI.

Another advantage of using media agencies to buy ads for you is that they can also work with multiple publishers to provide data that shows how your ads are performing on their sites in aggregate. Read more about tracking mobile advertising performance in Chapter 14.

Working with mobile advertising networks

Mobile advertising networks aggregate supply and demand for advertisers and publishers by buying inventory from multiple publishers and by providing different types of ad units (see Figure 10-4 for an example). That way, buyers and agencies can reach groups of people who use different mobile sites without needing to work with a different publisher for each site. For example, if an advertiser would like to target females ages 25–54, the ad network can target multiple sites that attract a large number of women within this age range. Women from the category who use different Web sites see the same ads, and the women from the category who use multiple Web sites see the ads multiple times.

Additionally, mobile advertising networks allow an advertiser to target multiple audiences with one or more specific characteristics that span the entire audience. For example, you may want to advertise to people who live in Boston, love sports, and own iPhones. Your advertising network can place your ads on mobile sports sites and display the ads only to people in Boston using an iPhone. Networks can also allow you to target by behavior, so someone who loves the Yankees won't see your ads when they visit a sports site while they happen to be visiting Boston.

If you decide to work with an advertising network, some of these organizations have HTML script (software code) that they'll give to you to paste it into your site. AdMob, shown in Figure 10-5, is one such network.

After the code is in your site, everyone who visits your mobile Web page (or application) sees the ads that your advertising network pulls based on relevancy to the page or application being viewed.

One of the leading advertising networks for do-it-yourself mobile advertising is AdMob (AdMob was recently acquired by Google). AdMob is a major mobile advertising service provider. What follows is an example of how to work through its process to create a mobile ad. Other vendors are available, so make sure to do your research to find out which one is best for your needs.

Figure 10-4:
Millennial
Media, an
industry-
leading
mobile
advertising
network.

To work with AdMob, refer to the following steps (most of the other firms have a similar tool):

1. **Go to www.admob.com and click the Not Registered? Sign Up Now link.**

2. **Complete the registration form and select the Submit button.**

   To fill out the form, you have to supply an e-mail address, password, your first and last name, address, country, city, state, and ZIP code, and you also need to read and confirm the terms and conditions.

   After you click Submit, wait to receive the registration confirmation e-mail. Your account is not active until you've confirmed your e-mail address by clicking the confirmation link in the e-mail from AdMob.

3. **After you've activated your account, return to the AdMob site and log in.**

   You may be asked to verify or update your account information and specify the type of account you want. For example, are you an advertiser, publisher, or both?

Figure 10-5:
Some
advertising
networks
allow you
to cut and
paste code
into your
mobile site.

After you've created your account, you need to create your first ad. Because you're looking to create an advertisement, click the Marketplace link on the top of the page, click the Campaign tab, and then click the Create New Campaign button. Follow the four steps below to create and launch your ad:

1. **Complete the campaign details form.**

   You need to set a start date and optional end date, and specify your daily budget, for example, $50. The daily budget reflects how much money you're willing to spend each day to have your ad served to a publisher's site. If you set the CPM (cost per thousand) bid rate for your ad at $1 (how much you're willing to pay a publisher to serve your ad), your ad will be displayed 50 times a day ($1 X 50 = $50). You also need to specify the delivery method you want: Standard, which spaces ads out evenly throughout the day, or Accelerated, which shows them as fast as the publishers will take them.

2. **Next, specify where you want your ads to go: mobile Web sites, applications, media (like iTunes), or local business search channels.**

3. **Set the targeting parameters for your ad: what type of devices do you want it served to, what geographies (countries, regions, states, cities), what networks (carriers, Wi-Fi), and specific consumer demographics (gender and age groups). Finally, you need to set your bid rate.**

4. **In the final step, specify the type of ad you're running — a text ad or a banner ad. If you select text, you must enter the text and promotional link for the ad. If you select banner, you have to upload the banner image (file size must be 75K or less) and link.**

As soon as you complete the form, your ad is ready to go and will be published on the start date. You'll be advertising your products and services!

AdMob is not the only mobile advertising network provider with a self-administration tool for advertising management. Millennial Media has a very powerful and easy to use solution, too; see Figure 10-6.

Figure 10-6:
The AdMob mobile campaign details form.

Buying ads directly from publishers

If you choose not to buy through a formal publisher or advertising network, you need to reach out directly to the sales staff that sells the space for the publisher in order to buy space for your mobile advertising. You can get a list of top mobile ad sites by looking at Nielsen (www.nielsen.com) — a top data collection and research firm with specific outlets for mobile data. Visit its Web site to find out how to license its data.

Some publishers can also be aggregators that work with several inventory sources at once. These aggregate publishers can help you to simplify what would otherwise be a very complex process of ad placements because mobile handsets, carriers, and diversity in the types of ad space tend to require many different creative and technical capabilities. Strong mobile publishers also have best practices to ensure creative compatibility.

Advertising with crosses

When ad networks target ads, they usually base them on several crosses. *Crosses* are characteristics of the ad and the audience that intersect, such as the intersection of age, interests, location, and gender. Examples include the type of handset, demographics, geography, gender, and so on.

The people at mobile advertising networks use a lot of geek-speak to describe the different programs they offer. Here are some of the ways mobile advertising networks can help you target consumers and the terminology you need to be familiar with if you want to get your point across:

✔ **Run of network:** Your ad runs on sites across the mobile ad network's full list of publisher sites, at a frequency set by you. When placing run-of-network ads, make sure you know your network's reach in terms of number of audience members and audience makeup. Your network should have these numbers, but Nielsen also issues a monthly custom rollup of the mobile advertising networks that indicates the reach capabilities of each ad network. The Nielsen numbers may be licensed for a fee. (See www.nielsen.com.) Sometimes, however, you can find Nielsen summary reports available for free at www.slide share.net and www.marketing charts.com.

✔ **Channel:** You can choose to target your ad by content affinity, such as advertising on all sports sites, or female sites, or automobile enthusiast sites.

When targeting channels, don't be afraid to cross channels to hit an intersection of your target, for example, crossing the female and sports channel to hit only females within sports sites.

✔ **Custom subnet or sub network**: Your mobile ad network sets up a two-tier custom affin-ity site list. Examples include female sports sites or working mothers.

Make sure to tell the network the specifics of your demographics, but do not narrow it down too much or you will ultimately limit the total reach of your campaign. For example, if you are marketing an expensive electronics sale, don't target only users with an annual household income of more than $150,000. Instead, be a bit more broad, say to $100,000. You are advertising your brand to this larger demographic and also hitting users more likely to buy as well, with the specific message of a sale.

✔ **Takeovers or network blocks:** A *takeover* or *network block* is also commonly referred to in the online space as a *roadblock.* Ultimately, these refer to large ad campaigns (in terms of budget and target impressions) delivered in a short time frame (typically less than a day or two). A takeover simply means fully taking over inventory (typically only one mobile site or a segment of one site), owning every ad on that particular target within the specific time. A network block is used only by networks and targets a large amount of impressions within a target audience (based on geographic location, demographics, gender, channel, and so on) across a group of sites.

Typically, any type of block has two goals: reach (to hit as many unique people as possible within your target) and frequency (hit all users as many times as they access the inventory). You can only maximize one of these goals within one campaign because they are inversely related. Given that blocks are not performance geared (driving traffic or having a user complete an action), they are typically only sold on a CPM (cost-per-thousand) or flat-rate basis. These are a "must-buy" component of an advertiser's ad strategy mix.

If you work with a sophisticated ad network, chances are that it can uniquely identify users and therefore create custom audiences based on affinity and behavior. Keep in mind that the more targeted your ads, the more your advertising costs. For a full list of the global mobile ad networks, their attributes, and how they stack up against other similar mobile ad nets, visit mobiThinking at `www.mobithinking.com`.

When you go directly to a publisher to make ad placements, ask your publisher for advice so you can decide how much to spend. Mobile publishers should be able to evaluate the best placement for ads. They do this based on their audience and traffic and by choosing when and how often to show ads in order to optimize the user experience on the site and maximize interactions with ads. If your mobile publisher can't show you lots of useful data, don't buy space from it!

Advertising with mobile carriers

Mobile carriers such as Verizon, AT&T, Sprint, and T-Mobile, offer advertising space on their proprietary mobile sites, also known as *on-deck inventory*. Carrier sites are a good choice when your goal is to reach only the customers using a specific carrier, but keep in mind that you'll need to also consider other characteristics of the people who use that carrier. For example, advertising the availability of an iPhone app to Verizon customers won't work because Verizon doesn't currently carry the iPhone.

Understanding all the carrier's devices, users, geographic coverage, and data plans can become cumbersome, especially when you're trying to run a single ad campaign on more than one carrier's inventory. Unless you really need to reach the customers of a specific carrier, choose a mobile advertising network instead.

Paying publishers and billing buyers for mobile ads

Mobile advertising is purchased on terms that are based on the level of interaction with the ad — just like online advertising. The terms can dictate the cost of each ad displayed or the cost of various actions taken in response to an ad. Here are the most common payment terms for mobile advertising followed by some advice for choosing the right method:

- **Cost-per-thousand (CPM):** CPM means that you pay a fee based on the cost of one thousand *impressions* (every time the ad appears in front of someone). For example, a CPM of $5 means that you pay $5 for every 1,000 times your ad appears. Keep in mind that CPM does not require anyone to click on the ad or even to look at the ad. It just means it was displayed when someone visited the page where the ad is placed. That's why CPM is usually used as a way to compare impressions to clicks or other actions rather than a way to bill you for advertisements.

- **Cost-per-click (CPC):** CPC means that you pay a fee every time someone clicks on an ad (or, in the case of mobile, every time someone touches the ad with her finger). For example, a CPC of $5 means that you'll pay $5 every time someone touches one of your ads. Use this method when your main concern is driving traffic to a mobile Web site and you are trying to convert visitors to customers.

- **Cost-per-action (CPA):** CPA means that you pay a fee every time someone completes a specific action as a result of touching an ad, such as visiting a Web site, filling out a form, or sending a text message with a secret code word found in the ad. Use this method when your agency or another partner is responsible for driving traffic to a mobile Web site and converting visitors to customers for you.

- **Sponsorship:** Sponsorship means that buyers can also simply pay a publisher a lump sum and sponsor the inventory in a media property for a fixed period of time. For example, you may sponsor the development of an application and pay a little extra to have your logo on the *launch screen* (the screen that appears when the app is loading) for a number of months.

You can't have a meaningful discussion about paying your mobile buyer, publisher, or network until you know what actions you want to pay for. Make sure everyone involved understands your goals so you can build a payment strategy that charges you no sooner than the moment you get value in return.

Getting a Return on Your Mobile Ad Buying

If you want to get a return on the money you spend buying mobile advertising, you want to make sure to pay attention to the purpose of your advertising in relation to the costs of your advertising. If you spend too much, it's probably not because you paid too much, but rather because

✔ You failed to effectively target your ads to the right audience.

✔ You paid the agency, network, or publisher for the wrong deliverable.

✔ You failed to invite your audience to take the right action on your ads.

The next sections explain how to target your ads and set them up to invite actions that lead to sales.

Choosing targets and formats for your mobile ads

Before placing any mobile advertisements, you should make sure your ads are going to reach the right people — the people who are most likely to buy from you! Here are three questions you need to answer before you talk to an agency, make any placement decisions, or spend any money:

✔ **Am I trying to reach everyone or a specific group?** If you're targeting a specific group of people, you'll need to know which Web sites, applications, and phones they use. Publishers can give you this information. Make sure you ask for it before placing any ads.

✔ **How do I want people to engage with my ad?** If you just want people to see your ads, you have more choices than if you need people to be able to click through and complete a purchase or share the ad on through social media. You should choose actions that move your audience closer to completing one of your goals. We discuss actions in more detail in the section called, "Inviting action on your mobile ads" later in this chapter.

✔ **How will I know that my ads achieved my goals?** Decide from the onset how you'll measure success and how you'll track and quantify your results. Your publisher or network can give you a variety of data points that demonstrate your advertising performance. Many of the ad networks allow you to create predictive models so you can make your initial placement decisions and make changes afterward if you aren't getting the results you want. You can read more about ad tracking in Chapter 14.

After you have answered these questions, you should have a good idea of your target audience and target goals. The next step is to share these targets and goals with your publisher or agency or apply the goals to your network by including them in your ad parameters. Then you can begin creating your ads.

Creating ads for mobile properties

When creating ads for mobile properties, like mobile Web sites and applications, you need to make sure your ads are sized and formatted correctly. If you're working with an agency or network, they usually have creative services to help you. If you're buying directly from a publisher, you need to do the creative work yourself in some cases. Even if you're outsourcing your creative work on some level, you need to keep the following in mind so you can get the results you need:

✔ **Size:** There are many standards sizes for different screens. The typical standards include X-Large Image Banner (300x50 pixels), Large Image Banner (216x36 pixels), Medium Image Banner (168x28 pixels), Small Image Banner (120x30 pixels), and Text Tagline (text of about 10–24 characters). Make sure you create banners of all sizes so that your advertising network can send the appropriate size for the consumer's phone.

✔ **Format:** The format of the ad depends on the type of phone the ad is being served to and the network it's going over. It's best to work with an expert when deciding on a format because there are so many variations. For example, iPhones don't support Flash (Adobe's multimedia platform used to add video, animation and interactivity to Web pages) and most phones don't support JavaScript or other rich media.

✔ **Analytics:** Make sure you've integrated a mobile analytics package such as Google Analytics (`www.google.com/analytics`), Omniture (`www.omniture.com`), AdMob (`www.admob.com`), or Bango (`www.bango.com`) to track the traffic on your properties and the success of your programs. The data from these tools helps you optimize your strategy. See Chapter 14 for a more detailed review of mobile analytics.

Inviting action on your mobile ads

Whether you use publishers, agencies, or networks to place your mobile ads, you need to decide what you want people to do, if anything, when they see your ads. Making your ads clickable or touchable is not enough. If you want people to take action on your ads, your ads need to suggest or invite those actions, and then those actions need to meet two criteria:

✔ **Your actions must be mobile-friendly.** For example, if your mobile ad asks someone to touch or click the ad in order to visit your Web site, your Web site had better work properly on the mobile phone that person used to touch or click the ad (see Table 10-1).

✔ **Your actions must help you reach your goals.** For example, if your mobile ad asks someone to watch a video, that video had better include enough information and incentives to invite a purchase if you're trying to use the video to help sell a product.

Table 10-1	Mobile Marketing Association Mobile Web Ad Guidelines	
Name	**Technical Specifications**	**Sample Creative**
X-Large Image Banner	**300x75 pixels** **Universal unit:** GIF, PNG, JPEG for still image Less than 5K file size **Supplemental unit:** Animated GIF for animation Less than 7.5K file size	
Large Image Banner	**216x54 pixels** **Universal unit:** GIF, PNG, and JPEG for still image Less than 3K file size **Supplemental unit:** Animated GIF for animation Less than 4.5K file size	
Medium Image Banner	**168x42 pixels** **Universal unit:** GIF, PNG, and JPEG for still image Less than 2K file size **Supplemental unit:** Animated GIF for animation Less than 3K file size	
Small Image Banner	**120x30 pixels** **Universal unit:** GIF, PNG, and JPEG for still image Less than 1K file size **Supplemental unit:** Animated GIF for animation Less than 1.5K file size	
Text Tagline	Up to 24 characters for X-Large Up to 18 characters for Large Up to 12 characters for Medium Up to 10 characters for Small	Show Times Click Here

Mobile audio advertising

We often forget that the mobile phone is just that, a phone, and that voice calls can be made with it. Moreover, with the proliferation of smartphones, more and more users are streaming audio over the data channel (the Internet) over their phones. Recently, a number of companies have emerged to make it possible to serve advertising into these audio channels. Here are a few examples:

- ✔ **Click-to-call audio advertising:** Buyers promote phone numbers in text messages, mobile Web sites, and applications, as shown in the following figure. When the ad is clicked, the phone dials out and the ad plays. The leading provider of this form of advertising is UpSnap (www.upsnap.com/).

- ✔ **Directory services:** Jingle Networks (www.jinglenetworks) deploys a robust advertising-supported directory service. Consumers may receive free directory services and forgo the carrier charges by calling 1-800-Free411. To receive the free directory services, all they need to do is to listen to a few ads. This is a great place for buyers to research.

- ✔ **Internet radio:** As radio and related audio services go mobile, leading firms like TargetSpot (www.targetspot.com) are making it possible to buy advertising within mobile radio broadcasts.

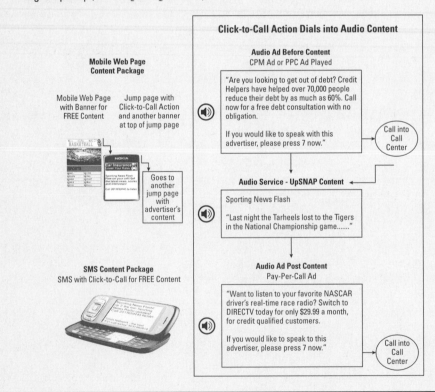

Mobile is a location-aware media. That means your ads can invite location-based actions without requiring a click or touch, such as asking someone to walk into a store and show the ad to the person behind the counter.

Here are some ways you can invite action from people using your mobile ads as the starting point, and some tips to make sure those actions are friendly to mobile users. (Mobile advertisers call these *post-click actions*.)

✔ **Ask them to submit a form:** Use a mobile form to enlarge your mailing lists, take orders, or collect survey information. Mobile forms shouldn't be too long because screens and keyboards are small. The simpler, the better.

✔ **Invite click-to-call:** Click-to-call can happen two ways — directly from an ad, or redirecting to a landing page that customers opt to dial. For an immediate response, click-to-call from the ad is the way to go because it immediately asks a user to touch and automatically dial the phone number. For a secondary opt-in to ensure the user really wants to connect with someone live about the product, redirect the user to the landing page and give him the choice to dial there. This essentially acts like a double opt-in, which could lead to better caller quality, but could lead to drop-off (users getting impatient and moving away from the process before they make the call). In either case, make sure your ad copy asks the caller to mention the ad so you can track the number of calls resulting from your ads.

✔ **Display a coupon:** Use mobile ads as coupons to capture comparison shoppers on-the-go or to enable a discounted purchase on a mobile Web site.

✔ **Promote a store locator or map:** Mobile ads can be set up to utilize GPS so you can direct shoppers to specific locations such as product displays or VIP parking lots.

✔ **Offer an application download:** If you've built an application, mobile ads are a great way to drive people to install the application on their phones.

✔ **Show a video:** Only certain phones are capable of displaying video on the handset. Typically publishers and ad networks are able to tell clients which handsets are mobile-capable. The video must be formatted to fit mobile specifications. The videos can be created by an in-house mobile creative staff, or can be outsourced to mobile creative agencies or ad networks with a creative department. Users have the option to interact with the ad campaign through streaming video either through the ad unit or as a call to action on your mobile site or landing page. (The action could be to watch a movie preview, demo a product, watch an interview, and so on.) If a client doesn't have a video specifically built on his home page, a link to a YouTube video works as well, but is limited in the devices it can play on — at this time, mostly only advanced devices (such as iPhones, BlackBerrys, and so on).

Mobile service providers (like Rhythm Media Networks `www.rhythm newmedia.com`; Smith Micro, `www.smithmicro.com`; Kyte, `www.kyte.com/`; Brightcove, `www.brightcove.com`; and VMIX, `www.vmix.com`) can help with video optimization and help you reach the largest audience able to view a video.

✔ **Make mobile commerce:** Allowing an immediate purchase as part of your call to action requires the consumer to provide credit card or payment information. To enable this action, you need a mobile application or a secure mobile site. You can read more about enabling mobile commerce in Chapter 13.

✔ **Go social:** Direct people to your social media site to become fans or ask people to share your mobile ad with friends. You can read more about mobile social media in Chapter 12.

Of course, if you just want people to see and remember your ads, that's okay too. Lots of companies use mobile advertising to increase recall or loyalty and that doesn't necessarily require a click or touch. Just make sure you are measuring recall and loyalty by taking surveys or doing research before and after you run your advertising campaigns. You can read more about tracking mobile advertising in Chapter 14.

Placing Ads in Your Own Mobile Properties

If you want to be an ad publisher and sell your own space to other ad buyers, or if you want to advertise your own products or services in the mobile properties you already own, you can use the available space in your mobile properties to place advertising as a publisher. For example, you could place advertisements in

✔ Your own mobile Web site

✔ Text messages and multimedia messages you send out

✔ Mobile applications and downloadable content you own

Placing ads on your own mobile properties allows you to make money on those properties or pay for the costs to create them. Either way, mobile advertising is a great way to make money. The following sections show you how to publish ads in the aforementioned three mobile properties.

Placing ads on your own mobile site

If you're placing your own ads on your own site or if you have a simple mobile Web site and only a few advertisers buying space from you, you can simply cut and paste the ads you create into the appropriate space on your mobile site. If you really want to make money selling mobile ads, use an advertising network so you can sell your inventory to multiple buyers and allow them to bid for the price of your space.

If you want to publish with a network, you need to verify that your mobile marketing Web site application is integrated with one or more mobile advertising networks. If it's not, have a member of your technical team or your mobile applications provider contact a mobile advertising network aggregator to ask what it will take to integrate your application(s) with the ad network. After you have verified network integration, you can use either of two methods to include advertising network ads in your mobile Web Internet sites and pages:

✔ **Use a mobile Internet visual editor.** Mobile Internet visual editors make placing ads on your mobile Internet site a snap. These editors are integrated with the leading mobile advertising networks. You simply need to get your account credentials (such as user name and password) from the mobile advertising aggregator, paste this information into the editor, and click Save to insert an ad placeholder into your site. When a mobile subscriber visits your site, the mobile marketing application reaches out to the aggregator's system, requests an ad, places the ad on the site, and displays it to the mobile subscriber — all in a matter of seconds. See Figure 10-7 for an example of a mobile Internet site visual editor, like iLoop Mobile (`www.iloopmobile.com`), Mad Mobile (`www.madmobile.com`), Mobile Card Cast (`www.mobilecardcast.com`), and others.

✔ **Paste ad network code into your pages.** If you're not using a visual editor and are simply working in code, getting an ad onto your mobile Internet site may take a few more steps, but is definitely doable; see the section titled, "Working with mobile advertising networks" earlier in this chapter.

Text advertisements can be inserted into Short Message Service (SMS) messages to advertise products, services, or special offers. The ads are usually placed at the end of standard SMS messages as links or ads can stand as text alone. SMS ads are not display ads because they are made up of text only. SMS ads can be linked to display ads, however, as shown in Figure 10-8.

Figure 10-7: Inserting ads into a mobile Internet site with a visual editor.

Figure 10-8: SMS ads can include links to display ads placed on mobile sites.

MMS (Multimedia Messaging Service) advertising can be formatted with images, text, audio, and video, which makes them great for delivering richer ads, as shown in Figure 10-9.

Format is important here to allow for the greatest number of viewers. Service providers can compress content like videos in your MMS advertising and use their unique applications to make your content work across more carriers and handsets.

Figure 10-9:
MMS ads
can contain
pictures or
videos.

Courtesy of Mogreet

In most cases, MMS and SMS ads need to be sent through an MMS or SMS service as opposed to an advertising network because it's impossible to dynamically insert advertising into MMS and SMS messages through code insertion. To find out how to create an MMS message to send advertisements, read Chapter 6. You can discover how to create SMS messages in Chapter 5.

Not all carriers support MMS messages. Using them may reduce the number of people you are able to reach if rich content is the only communication you offer.

Advertising in applications and downloadable content

In-application or *in-app* refers to advertisements placed in free or paid applications installed on a mobile device. Ads can be sold within applications to make money or to help offset the cost of building and maintaining the applications. Ads can also be placed by the application owner to increase the brand recall or confidence of the people who use the applications. Ads can also be placed in downloadable content, such as videos, ringtones, or podcasts to achieve the same goals as in-app advertising.

Placing ads in mobile applications and downloads requires forethought because you need to include the ability to display advertising when you're building the applications or downloads. Talk to your programmers or application providers about including dynamic ad network servers or static display ads and make sure your agency is aware of your goals and target audience. To find out more about building applications, read Chapter 9.

Chapter 11

Executing Voice-Enabled Mobile Campaigns

In This Chapter

▶ Choosing automated and live agent models and partners

▶ Determining which voice campaigns are best to achieve your goals

▶ Understanding how to configure and launch a voice marketing program

*I*t's easy to forget that a mobile phone enables you to verbally communicate with your customers because you can do so many other exciting things to reach people on their mobile phones and related devices. It is, after all, first and foremost, a phone. The fact is, however, that marketing through voice is just as exciting as any of the other mobile media, not to mention the fact that the ability to talk and listen is the one and only feature that is available on all mobile phones. Because pretty much everybody knows how to talk on the phone, you don't have to worry whether the majority of your customers will be able to interact with your voice campaigns.

Marketing through voice can involve humans, it can be automated, or both. Your marketing can invite calls from people or initiate calls to people. Either way, the mobile phone presents an opportunity to reach literally everyone with a mobile phone in a familiar and useful way.

In this chapter, we show you how to tap into the voice features of phones when designing your mobile marketing campaigns, and we explain how to set up and run voice-enabled mobile campaigns. We also touch briefly on using mobile for engaging with a live person, but the majority of this chapter is about how to set up and run campaigns using automated voice solutions.

Choosing an Approach to Mobile Marketing with Voice

You can hire real live people to answer the phone when people call you from their mobile phones, but it's also possible for people to get an answer, book a flight, or find the local Chinese restaurant by voice even if a human doesn't pick up the phone on the other end.

The following sections help you decide between live agent and automated voice campaigns. We also show you how to choose a partner for the automated methods because you need some technology to enable automated voice campaigns.

 Keep in mind where your customer is most likely to engage with your mobile program. If your customer is more likely to use your service in a public place, think about the environment and tailor your content to that environment. Having your customers speak personal information aloud within earshot of strangers or in a crowded loud venue is not ideal. In those situations, an SMS or mobile Internet-based program might be best.

Choosing a live agent approach

Live agent voice means that a live person — or agent — is answering the phone line. Sometimes it takes a human to do a human's job, despite our best attempts to automate things. Some things are too important or too difficult to automate, or you simply may not be allowed to. For example, financial services companies don't allow you to leave voice mail messages with your broker to make a trade — you must speak to them live. Examples of jobs that humans are likely to be called up to do include

- ✔ Roadside assistances services, like those offered by the American Automobile Association
- ✔ Opting in to a sweepstakes entry
- ✔ Getting or requesting a product sample
- ✔ Fulfilling a transaction triggered from a mobile Web site or application

Even if your circumstances don't require a live agent, you may choose a live agent approach if it makes it easier for your customers to place orders or get technical support. For example, you may choose to link your mobile Web site to a call center so that customers may place their orders over the phone by talking to a live agent, as shown in Figure 11-1.

Figure 11-1:
Linking your
Web site to
a call center
can enable
voice
ordering for
customers.

Click to initiate a call
to the call center

You should employ a live agent approach when it makes more money than an automated response. Try testing one against the other to find your return on investment. For example, you might find that people won't give their credit card numbers over the phone unless they're talking to a live person, whereas other businesses find that people feel more secure sharing a credit card with an automated system. Each business is different. Sometimes people simply need or want the human touch.

Voice is great for multi-tasking

When it comes to marketing by voice, you have a lot of opportunity to effectively engage your audience during other activities. For example, it's easier for your audience to talk on the phone than to stare at a screen and type while watching the kids play soccer, standing in line, or walking down the street. People can use their voice to

✔ Take a survey or leave a comment or opinion without using their hands to type

✔ Check on the status of something they need to pick up without visiting a Web site

✔ Securely leave information such as an e-mail address or a credit card number and securely receive information such as recorded messages or order confirmations

✔ Listen to music, a podcast, a broadcast, or recorded announcement

✔ Request turn by turn directions while trying to find a store, hotel, or other location

Just remember that some contexts, such as driving, are inappropriate for voice if your customer has to look at the screen or push any buttons at all.

Choosing an interactive voice response (IVR) approach

Automating your voice communications is known in the industry as *interactive voice response* (IVR). IVR isn't just listening to a recording prompting you to press 1 for support. These days, IVR can provide very rich and interactive experiences.

IVR offers a lot of possibilities, so choosing an IVR approach is usually a matter of looking at some examples of what other businesses are doing and applying the basic idea of that approach to your business. Here are some examples you may want to consider to see if there is a basic approach that applies to your business:

- ✔ **Location-based sales assistance:** In a store, you call the phone number on a sign next to a product to check whether any store locations offer a model in a different color.

- ✔ **Location-based search:** You call the bank's phone number and request a list of the nearest ATM locations sent to your phone by text message.

- ✔ **Instructions or directions:** You call a toll-free number and enter your ZIP code or phone number to receive detailed information on voter registration and polling instructions for your area.

- ✔ **Directory search:** You call a toll-free or directory service to find a shoe store near your office and the IVR system asks you what you're looking for using voice recognition.

- ✔ **Options-on-hold:** Instead of getting music on hold while waiting to talk to a live agent, the IVR system gives you multiple options so you can leave a message, subscribe to a text message club, or listen to program promotions.

- ✔ **Promotional engagement:** You call a phone number to enter a sweepstakes or participate in a survey. A few years ago, Sony Pictures promoted their movie *Vacancy,* a thriller, by advertising a 1-800 number on television. When viewers called the number, they could hear the sounds of the movie and choose from options to interact with the promotion.

- ✔ **Content delivery:** You call a phone number to hear an audio announcement or to request a wake-up call while you're staying at a hotel.

- ✔ **Information requests:** You call and leave your e-mail address or physical address and the system sends you a brochure via e-mail or regular mail.

- ✔ **Automated ordering:** A mobile Web site's banner ad contains a phone number that connects to an order system.

Mobile-enabling Web sites and text

Many people suffer from reading disabilities or simply want to listen to content rather than read it. With the advent of smartphones, advancements in mobile Web sites, and the speeding of mobile networks, you can now provide your customers with the capability to listen to your content, or, if they wish, they can download and listen to it later. Services like these are powered by companies like VoiceCorp (www.voice-corp.com), which translate text from numerous languages into a dialect-appropriate voice, meaning they read a Web site or mobile Web site page or article to you (see the following figure).

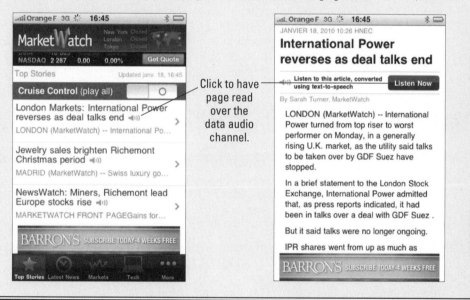

Click to have page read over the data audio channel.

IVR is the cornerstone to voice-enabled mobile marketing programs and the preceding are just a handful of leading examples. We show you how to plan IVR campaigns a bit later on in this chapter.

Finding a voice services provider

If you opt for a live agent approach, search the Internet for companies that offer customer care and support outsourcing services. These companies are also often referred to as *call center* service providers.

Three types of IVR providers exist:

- ✔ **Full-service agencies:** They can manage the entire process for you.

- ✔ **Online applications:** Online apps allow you to log into an application and manage your programs yourself.

- ✔ **Software:** Software solutions can be installed on your computer network so you can manage IVR within your company's data network (this later option is for a highly advanced organization).

A few of the leading IVR solution providers include CommerceTel (www. commercetel.com), SmartReply (www.smartreply.com), Angel.com (www. angel.com), and Nuance (www.nuance.com). These are just a few of the stellar organizations that can help you get up and running with mobile marketing and IVR. Do a search on the Web and you can find a number of others.

Setting Up IVR Programs

IVR programs require a bit of setup. You need to plan out your goals, write scripts, and record your voice-overs and options so that people who call you have options to select. The next sections show you the steps in the process of setting up an IVR program. We show you how to launch different kinds of campaigns in the next section.

Planning your campaign

You want to make sure you think through and make decisions about a number of items before you launch your voice program:

- ✔ **What is the purpose of the campaign?** Is the goal of the campaign primarily customer care, marketing outreach, or direct revenue? Don't mix multiple objectives together unless you are sure that your primary objective is being met.

- ✔ **Who or what is behind your message?** You can choose a live person, a recorded voice, or a computer generated text-to-voice message. Make sure your customers are comfortable with your choice. If you decide to go with a live person, you can choose a professional voice talent or a regular person. Again, your customers should be the judges of what to use.

- ✔ **What is your time frame?** It takes time to identify and select a partner and set up your campaign, but you also need to consider the duration of your campaign and your ability to make changes to the voice program over time.

> ✔ **How will you measure the results of your voice campaign?** Tracking the impact of your campaign gives you the ability to make changes to future campaigns. Make sure you or your voice program partner has the ability to track responses and results. (See Chapter 14 for more information about tracking and analyzing mobile marketing programs.)

With voice and "live people," keep in mind the time zone variations if you are working across a large geographical area. You need to decide if you want to pay for 24-hour service. Alternatively, you can state specific hours when the operators are on duty in a recorded message and in any print ads.

Scripting the interaction

A *voice script* is a word-for-word document of your voice prompts that helps you to determine what to say and allows you to make changes to one variable at a time, such as a sentence or a few words. One voice script may generate the results you're looking for, whereas another doesn't, even if you think you're basically saying the same thing conceptually.

Scripting your voice interactions entails writing down what your customers hear and what steps your voice prompts will walk them through when they connect with your IVR program. For example, the following depicts a very simple script:

Customer: Dials toll or toll-free number. IVR system picks up.

IVR system: "Hi there, welcome to our mobile marketing program. To opt-in to the sweepstakes, press 1 when prompted and state your e-mail address. To leave us a voice message, press 2 and follow the prompts."

Customer: Presses 1 and vocalizes e-mail address.

IVR system: "Thank you. Your sweepstakes entry has been received. We'll send you a follow-up text message and e-mail message shortly."

This script is pretty dull, but you get the idea. You want to write down exactly what the IVR system will say and how your customer will interact with it. Keep in mind, as in the preceding example, when writing your IVR script, you want to think through the following:

> ✔ **What are you trying to accomplish?** What is your goal for the call? For example, do you want the caller to leave an e-mail address to opt-in for your sweepstakes program, as in the preceding example?

> ✔ **What is the first thing your customer will hear when the call starts?** Will he hear a voice, or maybe some music? Then what? When will the optional prompts start?

✔ **What option prompts will you play during the call?** For example, "Press 1 for this and press 2 for that," is common, but rephrasing the prompts as "When you press 1, you can get assistance from a live agent — when you press 2, you can search by ZIP code for a nearby location or receive a text message" gets better results.

✔ **What happens when the IVR system does not understand the user's entries into the IVR system, or if the user calls in from a landline phone versus a mobile phone?** If the person calls in from a landline, maybe you tell them they can't participate in the program because your program is focused on deriving a text message at the end of the call.

✔ **What does the IVR system do if the user presses 3 or any other number as an option when 1 or 2 are the only valid options in the program?** In this case, you want to create an error message for the script. Have the system say something like "I'm sorry, that option is not available," and then have it return the user to the previous step. Table 11-1 highlights key examples you'll find in a script. Figure 11-2 is a visual example of a call flow.

Table 11-1	Voice Script Elements
Item	*Description*
Introduction	The audio recording(s) that play when the call first picks up. You may have multiple audio files, such as one recording saying hello, and another with music. Individual files can be strung together to complete a script or experience.
Option prompt string	To *X*, say or press 1. To *Y*, say or press 2. To *Z*, say or press 3 (with *X*, *Y*, and *Z* referring to the actions you'd like to offer the caller).
Individual option prompt responses, for example, when someone says or presses 1	Each audio response when the consumer selects an option. For example, thank you for selecting *X*. Your request is being processed.
Error	We're sorry. We did not understand your selection. (Or your selection is not available. Please try again.) Press 1 to return to the main menu or 2 to return to the previous menu.
Thank you	Thank you.
Conclusion	Goodbye.
Unsupported carrier	We're sorry. Your mobile carrier does not support this program. Thank you for contacting us.

JUMP TO: Other IVR	9	[Jump to IVR# / Name / or Other IVR InBound800ID]
Secondary IVR Greeting (Opt Out Greeting)	1, 2, 9	We're sorry to see you go. At ABC Company, we honor and respect your right to choose the forms of communication you receive from us. If you would like for us to stop sending special sale and offer notifications to you by prerecorded telephone calls, please press 1 now. If you are a member of our mobile marketing program and would like to opt-out of all future text message savings alerts, please press 2 now. If you would like to register a phone number and opt-in to be notified of future sales and savings offers from us, please press 9 now, or to end this call, simply hang up.
Custom Repeating Menu (Secondary IVR)	1, 2, 9	Press 1 to stop receiving prerecorded savings calls. Press 2 to opt out of text message savings notifications. Press 9 if you would like to be notified of future sales and savings offers from us, or to end this call, simply hang up.
Voice Custom Get Phone (Opt Out)	1	To be removed from future prerecorded calls announcing special savings and news, please enter your 10-digit phone number on your keypad, beginning with the area code first. Please enter it now.
Voice Custom Done (Opt Out)	2, 9	Thank you. Your number will be removed from receipt of future prerecorded telephone calls.
Text Custom Get Phone (Opt Out)	2	To be removed from future text messages featuring special savings and news, please enter your 10-digit phone number on your keypad, beginning with the area code first. Please enter it now.
Text Custom Done (Opt Out)	1, 9	Thank you. Your number will be removed from our mobile marketing program. You will receive a text message confirming your opt-out shortly.
SMS MT Confirmation (Opt Out SMS Message)	n/a	You will no longer receive text messages from ABC Company. Thanks for being a great customer.
JUMP TO: Other IVR	9	[Jump to IVR# / Name / or Other IVR InBound800ID]
Goodbye Menu (Opt Out)	n/a	Thank you for calling ABC Company Customer Preference line. Goodbye.

Figure 11-2:
A sample
IVR call
flow.

The key to any script is to

✔ Keep it simple and instructional.

✔ Put the action at the end of the audio recording (for example, "To receive a text message, press 1" instead of "Press 1 to receive a text message.")

✔ Use professional voice talent whenever you can. It's relatively inexpensive and makes the user experience much more positive.

The customer care script for American Airlines

American Airlines has an exceptional IVR system that recognizes the customer. The first time a customer calls the number, he gets a simple prompt: "Would you like for me to recognize you next time you call this number?" After he opts in to be recognized, the next time he calls in, the phone recognizes him, looks up his current flight status, and gives him the information that he is most likely calling about:

"Hello Eric and welcome back. It looks like you are in Dallas connecting to New York. Your flight to New York is scheduled to depart on

time at 1:15 p.m. from gate D23. If I can help you with more information, please say a command, for example, 'Upgrade'."

This system is exceptional at helping customers solve problems and get information. The information is accurate and actionable, exclusive to the caller, and clear. The systems that deliver these kinds of messages are largely delivered by value-added developers of the Nuance platform, a leading enterprise IVR solution that can be set up and installed within your business to power your IVR offerings.

Recording IVR audio prompts

After you have prepared your voice script, the next step in getting ready for your IVR mobile marketing program is to record your voice prompts. In addition to creating the audio recordings for each part of your script, you need to create all the recordings for errors, help messages, and thank you messages that you may want to include. This process is often referred to as creating the *voiceover*. There are all kinds of ways to record your IVR prompts, including

- ✔ **Online recorder:** Your IVR provider may have an online tool you can use to record your files right into its system.

- ✔ **Your computer:** You can use an audio recording application installed on your computer such as GoldWave, Mixcraft, or StepVoice Recorder. For creative audio effects, use the Easy Hi-Q Recorder.

- ✔ **Professional services:** If you don't want to use your own or an employee's voice, hire a professional actor or service to record your audio files. Many of these services have actors that can impersonate a leading celebrity, like Jack Nicolson or Samuel L. Jackson, or maybe Lady Gaga. If you go the impersonator route, you can have a lot of fun with this because your audience will be surprised when they hear the celebrity's voice, and using an impersonator can be a lot cheaper than actually having the real deal record the voice-over for you. Take a look at the athlete endorsements at `www.brandaffinity.net`, a firm that provides celebrity impersonator voices. Other companies provide similar services — just browse the Internet to find them.

If you go the do-it-yourself route, do not skimp on the microphone you use to record your voice-overs! Microphone quality has a direct impact on audio capture quality. Use the best microphone you can afford.

The voice of an IVR system becomes your brand's voice to your customer, in the same manner that voice-overs on television and radio commercials tell you something about the personality and integrity of the company represented by the voice-over. Test different voices and see which ones generate the best responses for your company.

Configuring and preparing program responses

If you're going to have your IVR application provider set up your program for you, you can skip this next step. However, if you've licensed access to your provider's software, you need to follow the steps below. Every application is different, but they all follow the same general principles:

1. **Give your campaign a name, for example, February Sweepstakes, so that you can track it in your reporting. Specify a start and end date.**

2. **Assign a phone number to your campaign.**

   The phone number is the number that people call to engage in your programs or the number that is triggered by an SMS callback or mobile Web click-to-call link.

3. **Specify the parameters of your campaign.**

   For example, one parameter you have to set is the number of times a user can participate in the program in a specific period of time or whether a voice mail can be left if a call is not picked up.

4. **Organize the IVR menu tree, which is the visual representation of your menu options, and upload your audio files for each menu prompt, as shown in Figure 11-3.**

   Your software needs to be able to guide you through the upload process so your customers don't hear the wrong audio message at the wrong time.

5. **Organize the actions that will be initiated by the IVR system when an option prompt is selected.**

   For example, when someone presses 1 on the keypad, a specific action is selected. Possible actions will vary by IVR provider, but the most common are

   - **SMS or MMS trigger:** Send the user a specific SMS or MMS message.

   - **Voice mail:** Capture a voice mail and e-mail to an address or post it to an FTP site to be retrieved later.

   - **Call transfer:** Transfer the call to another number.

   - **Play audio:** Play another audio file in the menu tree.

   - **Web service trigger:** Post the user's phone number and specified campaign parameters to a third-party service, such as your next messaging or mobile Web provider, so that it can pick up the call and take some action on it, like send a text message.

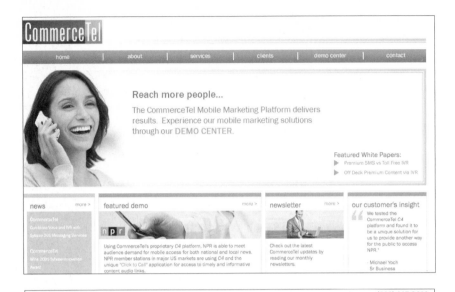

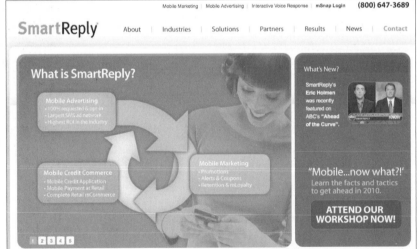

Figure 11-3:
IVR applications allow you to configure IVR options.

Executing Different Kinds of Voice Campaigns

The great thing about mobile voice campaigns is that you can incorporate more features than traditional landline phones allow. The following sections show you how to execute the most common voice campaigns using the capabilities of today's mobile phones.

Plain old dialing

The simplest and most common voice call to action is to invite a customer to pull out her phone and dial a toll or toll-free number. After people place a call, you can put them in a queue to speak with a live agent or direct the number to interact with your IVR program.

Dialing is easy for your customers to understand and every phone is capable of interacting with a dialing campaign. Enabling a dialing campaign is simple. Just put your phone number in your advertising and ask people to call.

Click-to-call

Just like clicking a hyperlink takes you to a Web page, in most phones, clicking or touching a properly formatted phone number in a mobile Web site or application instantly calls that phone number, as shown in Figure 11-4. This is known as *click-to-call*. In fact, the link doesn't necessarily have to look like a phone number. It can be a graphic or any text such as "Listen Now!" linked to a phone number.

Figure 11-4: A mobile Web template — phone numbers listed on Web sites can be formatted to instantly call the number.

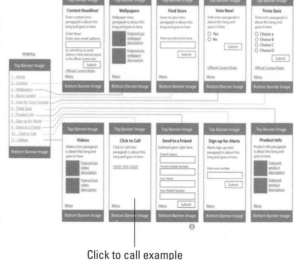

Click to call example

Click-to-call also works in search results when people search on mobile phones using sites like Google Maps and Yelp. Make sure your phone number is listed on every local Internet search page. If you aren't sure you're listed, Google yourself and see what shows up.

Text-to-voice

Text-to-voice returns a voice call for a text message sent by your prospect or customer. For example, a user may see a request to text HEARUS to 472XX. When she does, her phone rings and she hears an automated call with voice options to select from (see Figure 11-5). Some common examples of text-to-voice programs include

- ✔ **Entertainment programs:** For example, at TheLiveLine (www.the liveline.com), users can send a text message to a selected celebrity. Within seconds, the user receives back a prerecorded message from that very celebrity; it's great for advertising and deepening customer engagements.

- ✔ **Retail:** Intel ran a program in Argentina and Peru, powered by SmartReply, a leading IVR provider. When a potential buyer of a product with Intel Inside was browsing a retail store, the consumer could get more product information via text message (advertised on merchandise shelves). When the consumer asked more technical questions, the consumer would receive a call back with greatly expanded product knowledge by IVR and the ability to navigate to similar topics, all by phone. This substituted for having sophisticated in-store representative training and exhaustive signage.

- ✔ **Visa Ad Olympics 2008:** Consumers could text in to receive a call back to listen to the story of an Olympic athlete. For example, "Text PHELPS to 234XX." The phone would ring with the prerecorded audio of the athlete's Olympic story sponsored by Visa.

- ✔ **Sports highlights:** Receive a text message with a sports update and have a phone number to call at the end to listen to highlights. For example, "NFL Update: End of third Quarter: Chargers 31 Broncos 10. To listen to third quarter highlights, call 212-555-1234" or reply NFL. See Figure 11-5.

- ✔ **Social media programs:** Voice can also be used in a social media context, where consumers can leave a voice recording to participate in a marketing promotion like providing input on a new jingle or even superimposing their voices over product images, like the services powered by Beema, shown in Figure 11-6 (www.beema.com).

Figure 11-5:
Text mes-
sages can
trigger
callbacks.

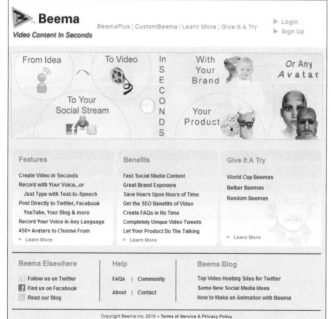

Figure 11-6:
Beema
social
media voice
marketing
services.

Text messages are not a secure information system. When you need to deliver sensitive information, IVR can take a text message conversation and make it secure to capture credit card information or other sensitive data.

Callback and live chat

Callback or *live chat* is also another popular voice service. A user is invited to enter his phone number in a form on a Web page, mobile Web site, or application. After the user submits the form, the IVR system calls the user back.

Voice broadcast

You can use prerecorded messages to deliver a voice broadcast, which is also referred to as a *push* or *shout-out message.* It's just like making a lot of phone calls, but it can happen automatically.

Your IVR system makes the calls, and, if the call is answered, the user immediately hears a recorded or automated message. After the person who answers the call hears the message, you can give him an option to interact with an automated system or be transferred to a live agent.

If the message is delivered to a voice mail box, the system delivers an alternative message without the interactive features. These types of calls are very popular for airline flight notifications, retail sale and loyalty program alerts, and service notifications from utilities.

 The regulations around delivering a prerecorded message to a phone — especially a mobile phone — are vast and complex. Promotional messages require express consent signature-level opt-in, and what state or country you are calling from or to affects the regulatory requirements. See Chapter 3 for more on regulatory issues. Also, don't forget about time zones: You don't want to wake people up in the middle of the night with your alerts.

NPR via IVR

IVR can enable your customers to listen to the radio or other broadcasts. NPR (National Public Radio) has done a fantastic job of using IVR to augment its radio, iPhone app, and mobile Web site (see www.npr.org/services/mobile/). As a consumer, you can quickly navigate to top stories and stories by category from your mobile phone. You can then read the article, or simply click-to-call: Click on the phone number next to the story. Your phone calls the number, and the story as it played on the radio is broadcast over your phone. This is a trend that has the potential to replace podcasts because it is on-demand and equivalent to streaming. Imagine NPR taking the next step and sending the top stories every morning to your voice mail with voice broadcasting. Each morning, you could simply listen to your voice mail to get the news.

Chapter 12

Mobile Social Media Marketing

Social media mobile marketing is all about successfully encouraging your customers to participate in your marketing programs by contributing comments and content or, even better, by starting their own independent conversations about your products and services. Things really start to get exciting when your customers take the initiative to interact with your business in the moment through a mobile device, or even build their own self-sustaining mobile social communities around your products or services.

The very nature of mobile devices allows people to participate more conveniently because they can make contributions anytime and anywhere. The potential of a mobile social community is tremendous because the ability to use mobile technology can be built into your community.

In this chapter, we provide you an overview of how to integrate mobile into your social media marketing activities. We start by showing you how to leverage online communities and create your own mobile-friendly social offerings. Then, we show you how to engage your customers with your offerings through their mobile devices.

Integrating Mobile with Your Social Media Strategy

Your customers aren't going to carry their computers around with them all day and open them up every fifteen minutes to follow your company's latest news and announcements. Instead, they want to stay engaged by quickly checking in with you every so often.

According to Facebook, more than 100 million Facebook users access their pages through mobile devices, and those users are 50% more active on Facebook than computer users. If you want to reach them, your social media strategy had better be active too!

Facebook is just one example of how mobile users participate in social networks and communities. Because social media content can be easily created through mobile devices — and people want to use their mobile devices that way — you need to be thinking about how to include mobile components in your social media strategy and tactics.

Whether you already have a social media marketing strategy or you need to create one, the following sections show you how to make your social media strategy more mobile friendly.

Identifying mobile communities and social networks

Mobile social media is a term that is used to describe content that is created by users and shared using mobile devices. For example, when you use your mobile phone to post a comment to an article you see on the site of *The Wall Street Journal* (www.wsj.com), you are contributing to mobile social media.

A *mobile social network* is any group of people who are drawn together to interact through their mobile phones around a common interest or community. Keep in mind that there are few if any mobile-only social networks. Instead, most networks start online and provide access to the network via one or more forms of social media (see Chapter 1). For example, when you create your own account on Facebook and access it through your mobile phone, you are part of a mobile social network, and the content that is created or shared through mobile devices is considered mobile social media. A number of social networks are increasingly being accessed via mobile. They include

- **Facebook** (www.facebook.com): Facebook is a social community with more than 500 million users.

- **Foursquare** (www.foursquare.com): Foursquare is a location-aware social network and game. Users participate in the community by visiting physical locations and are awarded badges for their interaction in the community.

✔ **Gowalla** (www.gowalla.com/): Gowalla is similar to Foursquare. Users check into locations and interact with their friends.

✔ **Twitter** (www.twitter.com): Twitter is a real-time network where people share their thoughts and ideas (often through text messaging, mobile Web, and mobile applications) in messages no longer than 160 characters.

✔ **Google Latitude** (www.google.com/latitude): Latitude users are able to share their locations and see their nearby friends on a map and contact them.

✔ **Yelp** (www.yelp.com): Yelp is a user review and local search community. Members review everything — restaurants, nightclubs, health and medical services, and more.

✔ **Loopt** (www.loopt.com). Loopt is a social community that helps you find out who is around you, what to do, and where to go.

✔ **Buzzd** (www.buzzd.com): Buzzd is a social community providing up-to-the minute rates of restaurants, nightlife, and venues in cities throughout the U.S.

✔ **Brightkite** (www.brightkite.com/): Brightkite is a mobile social community service that helps friends keep up-to-date with each other.

✔ **MocoSpace** (www.mocospace.com): MocoSpace is a youth-oriented social community with massive mobile traffic.

Not all social media sites are alike. Although many have similar capabilities, in the end, it is the community and networking that really matter. For example, as of July 2010, Foursquare has five times as many users as Gowalla, and the demographic profile of the users differ. For example, men outnumber women two to one on Foursquare.

In order to enable meaningful interactions with a high number of mobile users, you should determine which social networks the majority of your customers already use (the preceding list highlights just a few), and then apply your mobile strategy to those networks. Here are some ways you can poke around to find out which networks your customers are already using while identifying mobile users at the same time:

✔ Ask your current customers which social networks they use and go with the majority or the top two or three. If you do this through a mobile survey or text message campaign, you'll be targeting your mobile users. You can read more about creating mobile surveys via SMS in Chapter 5. You can also create them using forms in mobile Web sites (see Chapter 8) and mobile applications (see Chapter 9).

✔ Provide social sharing links, such as Facebook Like, as shown in Figure 12-1, which depicts Steve Madden, a leading American shoe designer and retailer leveraging the integration of Facebook Like features with its mobile Web site (`http://m.stevemadden.com`). Social sharing links allow your customers to share the content of a Web page with other people through e-mail or social networks. You can place social sharing links on your Web site, in an e-mail, or on your mobile Web site and track how your customers share your content with their friends. Use a service such as `www.sharethis.com` to create the links for you. Services provide the share links and track the details on which networks your customers used to share content.

Figure 12-1: Steven Madden integrates Facebook Like with every roduct.

Courtesy of Steve Madden

Don't be limited by just what you see with existing mobile social networks. If you have a good idea on how to integrate your business with an existing social network, see if that network has application interfaces that you can use to link your services together. Alternatively, you can simply call them and build out a program. In February 2010, Bravo, a leading U.S. television network, announced a partnership with Foursquare to create marketing promotions that encouraged its viewers to visit and check in at upwards of 500 Bravo-tagged locations to receive Bravo badges and a chance to win prizes.

✔ Use a social media monitoring tool to search social networks and communities for keywords related to your business. Check the posts to see if they were created using a mobile device.

✔ Use general demographic data that is available from each social network or service to find out if people using a particular network match the demographics of your prospects or customers. You can find general data at the following pages:

- Facebook Statistics: `www.facebook.com/press/info.php?statistics`

- Twitter 101 for Businesses: `http://business.twitter.com/twitter101/`

- YouTube Fact Sheet: `www.youtube.com/t/fact_sheet` (see Figure 12-2)

- MySpace Fact Sheet: `www.myspace.com/pressroom?url=/fact+sheet/`

- LinkedIn About Page: `http://press.linkedin.com/about`

✔ If you have e-mail addresses for your customers, you can use the major social networks or other services to match those e-mail addresses to customer profiles on social networks to get reliable data on which social networks are used by your customers.

Figure 12-2:
Social sites such as YouTube provide demographic data to users.

If you run a niche business, you shouldn't be surprised to find your best prospects and customers networking on niche social networking sites you haven't heard of and using less popular tools and applications for sharing with mobile. If you run a niche business, use a search engine like Google or Bing to search for social networks and applications related to your niche products or services. For example, pet supply retailer PetSmart runs Pets.com, a social network for people who are parents of dogs and cats. If you can't find a network for your niche, maybe you should create your own! The next section helps you to do just that.

Creating your own mobile communities

Social networks like Facebook or social services like Twitter are so large that they might be all your business needs to engage with the vast majority of your customers and prospects. They also have built-in tools to enable people to share things from their mobile phones. However, large networks and services also provide an opportunity to entice large numbers of people to actively participate in your own mobile social community.

Some possible advantages of your own mobile social community could be to

✔ Create local areas or groups of users within your community based on common interests, such as location or mobile device preference.

✔ Control the messages better by keeping closer tabs on the content and being able to remove unruly customers.

✔ Control access to the network with password protection or by approving members.

✔ Avoid relying on third-party software for such a critical part of your business. After all, this is a new medium and social networks may change, close down or merge with others.

✔ Provide a specific service only to your customers or a subset of your customers. For example, maybe you want to enable your customers to ask questions when they have trouble assembling your products, and you want to allow other customers who have encountered the same issues help you out by answering those questions from a customer's perspective.

✔ Provide special incentives only to your customers within the community that can be used through mobile — such as music or video downloads.

Your community does not have to be a persistent community that lasts forever. You can also run campaign-based communities, where you rally people together for a specific purpose and for a limited period of time. For example, in 2009, the fast food chain Hardees (www.hardees.com/mobile) ran a fantastic program called "Name Our Holes" to support the launch of a new product. They invited the community to name the new product, which consisted of small, round, frosted balls of pastry. Many of the recommendations were hilarious. The program got both customers and the press engaged with the product launch.

MySpace evolution

The MySpace community (www.myspace.com) began in 2004. Starting out as the place for younger audiences, it rapidly gained acceptance by adults and by big brands alike. Whereas brands started to invest in Facebook as its popularity increased, the MySpace community in 2010 is focused on sharing of content and highlights its music community, the largest on the Web. If a non-music company invested heavily in MySpace in 2008 or 2009, they might need to make new investments in a different community now if their customers have moved on to another network.

Groups like the Direct Marketing Association also create social communities around events. Consumers create ad hoc social networks through applications like Bleam, a mobile app that supports the creation of temporary local networks through Bluetooth and Wi-Fi. (You can download Bleam from the iPhone App Store for a fee).

If you don't want to build out the infrastructure to run your own social community, you can license the capability from a number of companies, including ShoutEm (www.shoutem.com), Socialight (www.socialight.com), and INgage Networks (www.ingagenetworks.com). These companies set up, host, and maintain a community that can run using your brand.

If you are going to have a presence in the social networking arena, make sure you monitor the content frequently. The unsupervised nature of the content posted by the public is both a pro and con of social networking. Misleading, incorrect, or negative content can pop up and go viral if you don't keep a handle on it. Find out more about automated activity alerts later in this chapter.

Creating your own mobile social community or application is no easy task. First, you need to create the social network on a platform. For advice on social media strategy and community building from scratch, we recommend that you read *Social Media Marketing For Dummies* by Shiv Singh (published by Wiley). The following steps walk you through the decisions you need to make in order to include mobile users in your overall social networking community plans:

1. **Determine what your customers should be able to do in your mobile community.**

   For example, customers could find other customers by location, tell the community when they're out-and-about, or create groups of people with similar phones.

2. **Determine what mobile devices your customers use.**

If you are currently running text campaigns to your customers, you can get your customer's mobile device data from your application provider. Otherwise, you need to collect data through a poll or survey.

3. **Plan for the capabilities installed on the majority of your customer's phones.**

You should take advantage of all the phone's built-in capabilities, while excluding functions that are difficult for your customers to use. For example, if the majority of your customers use smartphones, you can build your social community to take advantage of all the phone's built-in capabilities, like GPS, cameras, video, and even motion detection. If your customers don't use smartphones, you should build functions that rely on text messaging, mobile Internet, and cameras.

4. **Choose a platform on which to create your own social network.**

Some community-building services are built exclusively for mobile Web users, such as MocoSpace (`www.mocospace.com`) or peperonity (`www. peperonity.com`). Other communities are built for computer users and may or may not include mobile-enhanced features.

5. **Decide how to measure the community or the application.**

Ultimately someone will want to see a return on investment — even if it's increased customer satisfaction scores rather than higher sales. Make sure your community can keep track of new users, returning users, numbers of uploads and downloads, and other metrics that show that users are engaging with the community.

Engaging with Mobile Social Media Users

People aren't going to participate in your social media strategy unless you invite them and give them ongoing reasons to interact and engage on increasingly deeper levels. You have the advantage in a mobile community rather than a Web-based community because of all the great ways that the mobile device can enable engagement.

This section shows you how to invite participation and engage people in discussions and other interactions through text, pictures, videos, and applications so you can encourage them to buy or take other actions in support of your business goals.

Encouraging people to join your community via mobile

People are more likely to share things about your business in the moment than hours, days, or weeks later. For example, imagine that some of your customers are in the crowd at a really exciting football game and they see a funny and entertaining ad for your business on the big screen. If they like the ad, they might make a positive comment about your business to someone sitting next to them at the game. They probably aren't likely to post comments about the ad from a computer when they get home. A lot of time has passed and other events — like the exciting comeback victory by the home team — are at the forefront of their minds instead of the more easily forgotten 30 seconds of advertising comedy.

You'll get more interactions if you encourage people to post comments on their mobile devices in the moment. For example, if the ad shown to the customers attending the aforementioned football game asks the viewers to post a photo of themselves at the game to a social network in order to enter to win a prize, the ad can be shared immediately even if it's forgotten later.

Try these tips for increasing social participation and engagement with your company through mobile devices:

- ✔ Add a text call to action to all your existing marketing efforts as a way to ask people to join your mobile social community. For example, ask people to text "Join" to 12345 for an invitation to your community.

- ✔ Advertise your community on other mobile Web sites; an example of mobile advertising is shown in Figure 12-3. See Chapter 10 for more information on mobile advertising.

- ✔ Make sure your mobile community site is optimized for mobile search engines. That way, when someone looks for you via their phone, they find your new community. You can read more about mobile search in Chapter 10.

- ✔ Invite thought-leaders from other mobile communities to join your community. Encourage them to share by providing incentives such as group leadership privileges or by featuring their expertise on the front page of your community.

- ✔ Encourage your customers to interact with you while they are in your store or office — put up signs asking them to upload photos or contribute their ideas through their mobile devices. Figure 12-4 shows what the user experience might look like.

Figure 12-3: Advertise your mobile community on mobile Web sites to attract mobile users.

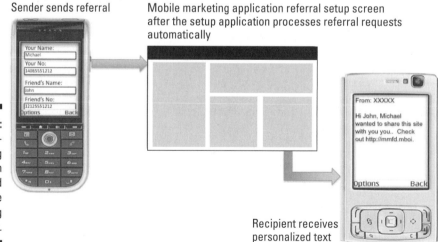

Sender sends referral

Mobile marketing application referral setup screen after the setup application processes referral requests automatically

Figure 12-4: Peer-to-peer sharing between phones and a mobile marketing application.

Recipient receives personalized text

✔ Use Facebook or Twitter as a customer service destination and then tell people they can ask you questions on those networks whenever they need help. For example, Best Buy advertises their "Twelpforce" (employees who answer customers' questions on Twitter) in their stores, by saying "If you need us, Tweet us."

✔ Advertise across TV, radio, and outdoor venues, asking customers to text or use their mobile devices to come to your mobile social site while they are watching, listening, or reading.

Enabling mobile social media interactions

It doesn't do any good to encourage mobile sharing if the people you're encouraging don't have the ability to share from their mobile devices. Most major social networks offer mobile applications to access their sites, so if the majority of your customers use a major network, that network is probably already mobile friendly. For example, lots of mobile Twitter applications are available, and Twitter has a mobile-friendly Web site for phones with mobile Internet capabilities. If your customers use Twitter, you can simply encourage them to download the existing apps or recommend one that best supports your business.

If, however, your customers use a niche network or you are sharing on a network you built yourself, you may need to create your own mobile application or make some adjustments to your own software platform to enable mobile sharing.

Social media applications are sometimes called *MoSoSo* or *mobile social software*. Applications are being created for specific mobile phones and niche networks by independent developers all the time. In some cases, they are creating applications that allow people to share information with lots of different social networks big and small. For example, iSkoot has a mobile and Web application that provides access to Twitter, Facebook, and lots of other networks simultaneously (see Figure 12-5 for the interface on a phone). iSkoot also has branded products for mobile providers and services, such as AT&T, T-Mobile, Verizon, and Skype. These combined applications are getting better and easier to use all the time. To find existing applications, search for them online or on your mobile device's app store. You can learn how to create your own branded apps in Chapter 9.

Figure 12-5:
Mobile
applications
allow your
customers
to share
across
multiple
networks.

If you can't find an application or mobile-ready community to enable mobile social sharing for your prospects and customers, you can use text messaging and e-mail as a way to enable sharing. Some networks allow users to send text messages or e-mails that turn into posts. Check with your social media software provider for information about enabling text messaging posts.

Listening and responding to social sharing

People, especially consumers, like to have their voices heard. These days, those voices take the form of words, pictures, and videos shared through social networks. It's important for your business to listen to what's being shared so you can respond and initiate meaningful interactions. Listening involves one part tracking the things people are saying about you and one part providing different ways for dialogue and engagement to happen.

Social sharing is sometimes very formal, such as when someone writes an opinion or review, and it is sometimes very informal, such as when someone tells a story about an experience. Here are three ways that people typically make their voices heard:

✔ **Sharing with you directly:** For example, someone may send a text-message or e-mail directly to you, or she might send a direct message to your social media inbox.

✔ **Sharing with others directly:** Sometimes people leave you out of the loop and share directly with an individual or a group of people without you knowing about it. For example, a member of a private Facebook group might share a story with the members of the group without your knowledge.

✔ **Sharing with you and others publicly:** Sometimes people direct their messages at the public by posting messages to public forums or they reference your business when making their messages public. For example, a Twitter post is publicly viewable and could also be directed at a company or individual, as shown in Figure 12-6.

Figure 12-6:
Public messages are often directed at a particular business, person, or group.

Content related to Chick-fil-A

When people send you direct messages, it's easy to figure out what they're saying and to reply because the messages are usually in your inbox or posted to your own social page. When someone shares something publicly, however, it's not always right under your nose, so you'll have to go looking for it.

You can find out what people are publicly saying about your business by searching through millions of social media posts on the Internet until you find a related discussion going on, or you can do it automatically by using a social media monitoring service. *Social media monitoring* is available at the enterprise level for a high cost, or you can use free services with fewer features if you're on a budget.

Google Alerts (www.google.com/alerts) is a good tool to get you started if you're new to social media. You can move on to something with more features after you gain some experience and have a need for more in-depth analysis.

Social media monitoring helps you become aware of your customers' perceptions so you can decide how to approach your social media strategy. For example, you may want your monitoring tool to find every instance of your company name that appears in social network postings and then

- ✔ Look for patterns in the types of networks and the types of people involved when your brand is the topic of discussion, and go with the majority.
- ✔ Look for patterns in the things people say about your brand, products, or services.
- ✔ Try to determine how frequently your customers engage in discussions about your brand, products, or services.

The trick in responding to the social interactions you monitor is to remember that people who share in the moment are more likely to expect a response in the moment too. If you're going to respond effectively, you should be prepared to respond to mobile users at all times during your normal business hours or customer support hours.

Use mobile applications to enable mobile responses if you or your staff members are not in front of a computer all day. Here are some of the ways you can interact and engage with the members of your community in a timely manner:

- ✔ Allow customers to sign up to receive text message alerts from your community when updates happen. Most major networks allow you to enable text message sharing from your customers.
- ✔ Make sure you have the ability to type directly into your social network page through a mobile site or application. If your social network's Web site is already mobile-friendly, you only need a phone with a good mobile browser. If your social network's Web site isn't mobile-friendly, you need to use an mobile application distributed by the social media network (if one is available) or text messaging to post content (if it enables it).
- ✔ Create mobile polls and surveys and report the results on your social page. That way, you can aggregate attitudes and opinions from multiple members and respond once to many voices.

✔ Encourage your employees to respond, provided they disclose their relationship to your company and understand how to respond.

✔ Post your availability through a terms and conditions statement, and provide your customer service phone numbers, if available. This helps manage expectations of a timely response.

You need to respond and contribute, but often the other community members will respond to posts before you can. Give your community a chance to respond before you do on networks like Facebook, where everyone can see the question. Make sure you thank people for helping you when they post responses that help your business and have a plan for responding to people who are unfriendly toward your business or your customers.

Engaging with pictures, videos, and other media

One of the most compelling reasons to join a mobile social community is the ability to easily upload media. A lot of phones can take pictures, and an increasing number of phones are capable of recording video and audio.

The major social networks allow people to post photos and videos through special e-mail addresses they provide, and they also provide applications and mobile-friendly Web sites for the same purpose. Here are some tips for engaging your mobile social community members using media:

✔ Remind your customers that they should take photos and upload them while they are shopping or interacting with your business. For example, ask them to take photos of your products in action.

✔ Create video and photo contests, asking community members to create your next commercial or advertisement from their phones.

✔ Encourage event coverage when you are sponsoring an event or attending one, and ask everyone to take photos or video and upload to the site or application.

✔ Ask your customers to submit video or audio as their way of recommending your product to other customers

Photos and videos may be more difficult to monitor than text, which can be scanned for malicious content or profanity. If you are concerned about potential content that users may upload, you should adjust your community's privacy settings so you can visually review all uploads.

Part IV
Mobile Commerce and Analytics

The 5th Wave   By Rich Tennant

"Let's play with that headline."

In this part . . .

Mobile devices are capable of enabling a variety of financial transactions including point-of-sale purchases, subscriptions, and Internet commerce. Mobile devices also give you the ability to track and analyze a variety of financial and behavioral data points when people interact with your mobile marketing campaigns.

Chapter 13 shows you how to enable mobile transactions and set up mobile merchant accounts so your customers can place orders through mobile devices. Chapter 14 guides you through mobile analytics and tracking so you can determine your effectiveness and improve your mobile marketing results.

Chapter 13

Engaging in Mobile Commerce

- -

In This Chapter

▶ Selling stuff through mobile devices

▶ Setting up mobile billing and commerce

▶ Billing through mobile carriers and PSMS

▶ Taking advantage of mobile wallets

- -

Mobile commerce, also known as *m-commerce,* means selling things through a mobile device. It usually involves a monetary transaction as opposed to simply messaging someone who buys something at a later time. You have two basic ways to make money through mobile commerce. First, you can sell content and services that can be consumed on mobile devices, such as ringtones, applications, games, content subscriptions (everything from joke and horoscope of the day to newspaper content), non-profit donations, and more.

The second way to make money through mobile commerce is to sell physical goods and services, like t-shirts, taxi rides, parking meters, hamburgers, computers, tractors, and more, and bill for these items through non-carrier billing channels; for example, credit card, PayPal, or similar billing services.

Charging customers through mobile devices is governed by a select handful of global carriers and paymasters with whom you need a close relationship if you want to collect money from your customers' mobile phones. In fact, every aspect of mobile commerce has its own set of gatekeepers and processes.

This chapter shows you what you need to know about the basics of mobile commerce, how to set things up, and how to bill your customers when you sell content, services, and physical goods through mobile phones.

Deciding Where to Sell Your Stuff

You have three basic choices for selling through mobile, but not all of them support the sale of every type of product or service. The following list shows you which outlets are available for different types of products and services so you can decide where to sell your stuff:

- ✔ **Third-party outlets:** Many independent aggregators of mobile content and products can be found online — just go to your favorite search engine and search for ringtones. You can find hundreds of Web sites devoted to selling that type of mobile content. These sites work by either paying a commission to the sellers or by buying products and content outright and reselling them. The benefit of third-party outlets is that they might have higher numbers of visitors than you could attract on your own. These outlets usually charge a commission of 30% or more for the service of selling your stuff. If the commission is less than what you would spend to drive your own traffic to your own store, a third-party outlet could be for you. Of course, you want to look for those sites with the most traffic representing your ideal customers; in other words, keep in mind that customers gravitate to services that align with their profiles. Use a service that matches up with your ideal customer.

- ✔ **Carrier stores:** Mobile carriers have their own "stores" for selling mobile content (these are often referred to as the carrier's *on-deck* presence). The difference between payment from third-party sites and carrier sites is the fact that carrier sites enable the consumer to purchase content through a credit on their monthly phone bill. That adds a measure of convenience for your buyer, but it also means you have to share most of the revenue with the carrier (see the section titled, "Collecting Payment through Carrier Billing: PSMS and the Mobile Web" later in this chapter.) You should approach all major carriers with your content to increase your chances of pickup; however, this can be a long and involved process. Carriers either buy the rights to mobile content or pay a commission on sales. Neither of these options generates a margin quite as large as selling mobile content yourself. For example, when selling content via Premium SMS (PSMS), carriers often take as much as 60% of the revenue.

- ✔ **Your own mobile store:** This can involve either setting up a mobile Web site or offering content for download onto a mobile device through text messaging. On the plus side, you keep all the proceeds from the sale of your mobile content when you sell it yourself. The downside is that you have to get the word out. If you have an existing online presence with established traffic, this could work as a sales platform for your mobile content.

Setting Up Your Mobile Billing Infrastructure

In order to sell something and facilitate a transaction through a mobile device, you must first have a mobile property, such as

✔ A text messaging program (see Chapters 4 and 5)

✔ An MMS program (see Chapter 6)

✔ A voice service (see Chapter 11)

✔ A mobile Internet site (see Chapter 8)

✔ A mobile application (see Chapter 9)

✔ A tie-in with contactless payment services via Near Field Communications (see Chapter 1)

✔ Something to sell, such as mobile content or a physical product

Whatever mobile property you're using to facilitate the transaction must be capable of setting the billing process in motion upon user initiation. This means plugging a billing initiation process into the flow of whatever mobile property your customers are interacting with.

The following sections tell you what you need to know and who you need to partner with to get started with mobile commerce and billing.

Setting up a merchant account

The first step toward enabling mobile payment is to set up a merchant account. Merchant accounts are available from banks, credit card companies, and third-party services such as PayPal (www.paypal.com).

A merchant account connects your customers' mobile payments to your business and enables the companies behind the scenes of every transaction to identify which transactions belong in your bank account funds.

A typical merchant account usually requires your business to be legitimate and established, so you should expect an application process that asks you for detailed information about your company's financial condition, ownership, and history.

Many, many companies out there would like to provide you with merchant services, and they all negotiate their rates. If you're a small business, we recommend starting with PayPal or your small business bank. If you have a more sizeable business, go with an enterprise solution.

Setting up mobile billing systems and accounts

An m-commerce system has two components, each of which must be established to enable your customers to pay and your business to receive the funds:

✓ **Commercial relationships** with everyone in the transaction process, including

- Mobile commerce application providers that provide the software and user interface to enable payment collection

- Paymasters who control the payment authorization and fund transfer gateways

- Fulfillment houses, if you plan to sell physical goods

- Content providers, if you plan to sell downloads

✓ **Check-out functionality** in your mobile property. For example, your mobile Web site might have a Buy It Now button that is linked to a mobile order form, as shown in Figure 13-1, so your customers can input their order information.

Figure 13-1: Mobile check-out enables customers to pay via their mobile devices.

When you're using a third-party payment option, building these relationships can be as simple as linking your customers to a third-party interface or incorporating some code into your mobile properties that points customers to the payment system. Third-party billing systems typically have all the necessary behind-the-scenes relationships in place for you, adding a level of convenience. Those services aren't free, however, so if you're planning on doing a lot of business on mobile, you're going to save a lot of money if you set up your own accounts and payment gateways.

Here are the four main partners you need to enable mobile commerce on your own:

✔ **Carriers:** Nearly every aspect of mobile commerce on a mobile device is managed by the major carriers; that is, unless consumers are buying content through third-party mobile application stores. Billing for any type of mobile content is generally subject to carrier review. Some payments can actually be billed and collected by the carriers on your behalf after a customer confirms payment by replying to a PSMS message or by confirming payment on a mobile Web site. (We discuss carrier billing through PSMS and mobile Web later in this chapter in the section "Collecting Payment through Carrier Billing: PSMS and the Mobile Web.")

✔ **m-commerce application providers:** M-commerce application providers are companies that specialize in managing the technical details of financial transactions via the mobile device. They work with and through mobile carriers, credit card companies, and related billing services companies to help you sell your goods and services via the mobile device. You have many choices of companies to work with. Here are just a few that can help develop an end-to-end mobile commerce solution. Leading m-commerce paymasters and application providers include PayPal (www.paypal.com), Mocapay (www.mocapay.com), Obopay (www.obopay.com), Usablenet (www.usablenet.com), Digby (www.digby.com), DeCare Systems Ireland (www.decaresystems.ie/), Spotlight Mobile (www.spotlightmobile.com/), Bango (www.bango.com), ShopText (www.shoptext.com/), mFoundry (www.mfoundry.com/), Billing Revolution (www.billingrevolution.com), Branding Brand Communications (www.brandingbrand.com, see Figure 13-2) and Square (https://squareup.com/).

✔ **Content providers:** If you're going to charge people for content such as ringtones, apps, games, or periodic messages, you need content providers to create this content for you. If you are selling products or services through the mobile Internet, content providers are usually the companies who develop the content in your Web site and maintain it. If your company develops and maintains your own content, *you* are the content provider. You can also work with companies that aggregate mobile content from other developers so you can sell it to your customers.

✔ **Aggregators:** Aggregators (discussed in Chapter 2) provide connectivity between an application or content provider and the carriers' wireless networks. Without them, you wouldn't be able to deliver any content to a person who buys from you through their mobile phone. Aggregators typically have agreements with most or all of the major carriers, so you won't have to develop a separate billing system for each carrier. Most of the time, you won't be working directly with an aggregator; more than likely, you'll work with your application provider.

Figure 13-2:
A leading
mobile
commerce
enabler,
Branding
Brand
Communi-
cations.

Making It Easy for Customers to Pay by Mobile

If you launch an e-commerce site, such as a traditional computer-accessed Web site that takes credit cards, you can assume that people who visit your site have a full keyboard, a mouse, and a color display with which to view, select, and purchase your products. With m-commerce, you can't assume that every consumer you want to reach has that same functionality on their mobile device.

Even the most advanced mobile phones differ in the types of hardware and software they support. Here are the key differences and what you can do about them to make sure it's easy for your customers to pay on mobile phones:

✔ **Keyboards:** Some mobile devices have full keyboards; some don't. To reach the widest audience — which is the goal of a mobile commerce program — you need to develop content and user interfaces that are not overly dependent on extensive typing. Some retailers, for instance, include payment forms that require a user to enter his name, address, phone, e-mail address, credit card information, a user name, and a password. You want to collect only the information you absolutely *need* to complete the transaction; otherwise, you run the risk of the customer not completing the transaction because he finds the process too tedious.

✔ **Navigation:** Some mobile devices offer mouse-like cursors, whereas some others rely on scroll-through lists. There are two ways to deal with this aspect of user interface: create separate versions of your mobile site, one optimized for smartphones, like the iPhone, and a streamlined version for less capable mobile devices; or create a single mobile site that is both inviting on the screen (for smartphones) and simple to navigate (for other phones).

The Steve Madden mobile commerce site is a good example of a streamlined interface featuring description, purchase and similar product links, optimized images, and social media integration (see Figure 13-3).

Figure 13-3:
Mobile commerce sites should provide easy navigation on any phone.

✔ **Uniformity in data plans:** No one pays for broadband Internet access at his home or office by the minute or the kilobyte anymore, yet some people pay for mobile Internet access that way. Keep the number of screens that customers must use to make a payment to a minimum. Also, make sure your payment screens load quickly and don't have too many images. Unlimited data plans are becoming more popular, but you still don't want your customers waiting while an overabundance of payment screens download.

✔ **Display size:** Putting tablet computers and iPads aside for a moment, mobile devices always have a smaller display than their computer cousins, no matter how powerful they are. One thing an m-commerce site developer can always count on is having to tailor the size of the site's visible area to accommodate the display limitations of a mobile device. Use a mobile site development program (or establish parameters for your mobile site developer) that keeps payment pages properly sized so that no aspect of the selection or payment process is overlooked by the user.

✔ **Security:** The mobile channel is not inherently less secure than the online channel, but consumers tend to be more wary about their personal information when conducting transactions in the mobile space than they do online. Partly, this is because of the relative youth of the mobile channel compared to online. But both the portability of the mobile device and the personal nature of mobile communications make consumers naturally more mindful of security vulnerability. The trick is to keep things streamlined and easy-to-use without compromising security and privacy protocols. Amazon (www.amazon.com) does a good job of enabling users to perform single-click payments after an initial setup — this is a good example of safe yet streamlined consumer interaction.

Selling Content through Carrier Portals

A carrier portal is a mobile Web site owned by a carrier that offers products and content downloads to the customers of that specific carrier (see Figure 13-4).

Every mobile carrier offers its own branded portal on the mobile phone. This portal features content and services created by the carrier and its partners. You too can offer content through a carrier portal, but the process isn't as easy as you may think. To offer your content and services for sale through a carrier's portal and ensure that you ultimately get paid, you must follow one or more of the paths described in the following sections.

Figure 13-4: Carrier portals can enable you to sell content to the customers of that carrier.

Developing a direct relationship with carriers

Many companies establish a direct relationship with each individual carrier for the purposes of promoting their content and services directly on the carrier's portal. The deals that you can strike can vary greatly, but here are some common ways to develop revenue opportunities with a carrier:

✔ The carrier gives you a lump-sum payment for access to your content for a certain period.

✔ The carrier provides you minimum sales guarantees.

✔ You and the carrier enter into a revenue-sharing relationship in which you share the revenue (often not equally).

Direct carrier relationships take time to develop and negotiate — often, 12 to 18 months or more. This time frame assumes that you already have a head start and generally know who to talk to.

Entering into a channel relationship

Many carriers offer developer and content-channel relationship portals that you can sign up for on the Internet. The channel relationship business model differs from the direct carrier relationship discussed in the preceding section in that you're not negotiating a direct deal. Instead, with a channel relationship, you get access to the carrier portal, business terms that are easy to adopt and employ, royalty payments for the sale of your content, access to the carrier's marketing education materials, and more. Table 13-1 lists various carrier content and developer programs.

Table 13-1	Carrier Developer Programs
Name of Carrier	*Contact Information*
Sprint	`http://developer.sprint.com`
Verizon	`www.vzwdevelopers.com/aims`
T-Mobile	`http://developer.t-mobile.com`
AT&T Wireless	`http://developer.att.com`

Here's how to get started with channel relationships:

1. **Go to the carrier's Web site and sign up for a standard third-party service program.**

2. **Have your content or service certified.**

You *must* be certified before the carrier puts your content on its portal. Every carrier's certification process is different, based on the type of content or service you're offering. Review the details of the process on the carrier's Web site.

3. **Accept the terms and conditions of the program.**

The terms include how much and when you get paid for your services. In very rare situations, you may be able to obtain minor adjustments in the standard program terms.

Contracting with an intermediary company

Some intermediary companies have direct relationships with mobile carriers that have been forged over many years. The intermediary firms sublicense your content to get it on a mobile carrier's portal.

Intermediaries are great channels because they enjoy economies of scale and greater reach than you could get on your own by going to each carrier individually.

Examples of intermediaries include Airborne Mobile (`www.airbornemobile. com`), Thumbplay (`www.thumbplay.com`), Zed (formerly 9 Squared; `www. 9squared.com`), and Mobile Streams (`www.mobilestreams.com`). Each company has its own business model, but you make money from every sale of your content and service, minus any revenue splits, transaction fees, setup fees, and maintenance fees charged by the intermediary.

Collecting Payment through Carrier Billing: PSMS and the Mobile Web

Sometimes it's more convenient for your customers and for your business if you allow the mobile carriers to collect payments from your customers on your behalf. With *carrier billing,* the mobile carrier collects payments from your customers by placing the charges on their mobile phone bills, as shown in Figure 13-5.

Figure 13-5:
Carrier billing
via PSMS
shows up
on your
customers'
mobile
phone bills.

Description	Date	Time	Usage Type	Application Price	Total
Prem_sms 76278 Papa ver 2	06/11	02:58P	Q2	$.99	$.99

When your customers pay their mobile phone bills, the mobile carriers send the payments to your business minus a fee for the service.

Carrier billing is primarily used to sell content, rather than physical products. These days, you can use carrier billing to collect payment from customers who want to

✔ Receive text alert content such as jokes and horoscopes

✔ Participate in voting and contests

✔ Download games, ringtones, and images

✔ Receive MMS messages

✔ Donate to a charity though mobile giving

Carrier billing eliminates the need to collect credit card numbers, send out paper bills, and many of the other hassles that go along with accepting payments directly. Of course, just when you think something sounds simple or too good to be true, there's a catch. Wireless carriers recognized this opportunity early on and established very clear guidelines, processes, and fees for marketers who want to bill customers through their carriers. The following sections show you how to set up carrier billing through premium SMS campaigns and mobile Web sites.

Billing with premium SMS (PSMS)

One of the most pervasive methods of carrier billing is payment via premium SMS. *Premium SMS* (PSMS) refers to the practice of charging a consumer for content, like ringtones, games, applications, and alerts via MMS or SMS messaging. Even though premium SMS includes MMS messages, people in the industry often refer to it as PSMS, so that's what we do in this book.

Before you think about how you're going to bill your customers through PSMS, you have to remember that your customers are the mobile carriers' customers first. Because mobile carriers want to protect their customers and keep them from being unhappy, you have to go through many steps to set up PSMS. Here are the steps involved:

1. **Identify the content you want to sell.**

   Music (including ringtones and full tracks), videos (especially behind-the-scenes and hard-to-find content), graphics and wallpapers to personalize your device, and cellphone games are great things to sell via Premium SMS. Although you can bill people for physical goods, PSMS pricing can make that very expensive because a portion of the sale price goes to the wireless carrier. (Skip ahead to the section called, "Understanding premium messaging payout" for more information on billing details.)

2. Choose a price point for your products.

Your customers are the best judge of what your premium content is worth, so it's often helpful to do a quick focus group and ask people what they would pay for your products. Think of this as getting help from the audience on the game show *Who Wants to be a Millionaire?* — usually, the crowd is right!

3. Get a short code or use a shared one provided by your application provider.

You can read more about obtaining and renting short codes in Chapter 4. This short code is the billing mechanism that enables you to start making money from your content.

4. Because it's not easy to do PSMS entirely on your own, we recommend that you choose an application provider to help you through this process.

Most importantly, your service provider is going to help you write an application (called a *campaign brief*) that the carriers must approve before you can start making money through PSMS (see Figure 13-6). With PSMS, the carriers are very careful about who can charge their subscribers for content. Each carrier has different rules and regulations — this is why a partner can help to simplify this process for you.

CAMPAIGN APPROVAL FORM

Salesperson Information	
Contact Name	
Contact Number	
Email Address	

SHORT CODE AND BILLING			
Will Service Provider Secure Your Code(s)	Short Code Type	Short Code(s)	Premium Charge($) Indicate if Trans/Sub
☐ Yes ☐ No	☐ Random ☐ Vanity	• Requested short code(s): • Nuestar CSC App ID (optional):	

Shared Short Code Needed?	Will this be a premium Campaign?	Will this be a migration?
☐ Yes ☐ No	☐ Yes ☐ No	☐ Yes ☐ No

If a shared code is needed, please explain how long this will particular code will be used. Also what price points are needed.

Figure 13-6: Carriers require approval of a campaign brief before PSMS can be enabled.

Lean on your aggregator to help you fill out the brief. You can to refer to the Industry Standard Best Practices on the MMA Web site at www. mmaglobal.org. The leading wireless aggregators include OpenMarket (www.openmarket.com), mBlox (www.mblox.com), Sybase (www. sybase365.com), and Ericsson IPX (www.ericsson.com/ourport folio/ipx).

5. Prepare a demonstration Web site for your short code application.

This Web site should show exactly the type of content that you will be selling and how a customer might buy the content and get it on his phone. It also must comply with the carrier's guidelines. This is basically a demo of your new business! This is purely to get through the approval process with your campaign brief. The wireless carriers, aggregators, and audit houses need to see a working demo of your service before they approve it to go live.

You should definitely make sure to have your Web site demonstration ready on the heels of submitting your campaign approval form (see Chapter 3) to the carriers. You don't want to move to the back of the line for approval, if you're not ready when your time at the front of the line has come! Getting a campaign brief approved can take up to six months.

6. After your program brief has been submitted, start thinking about marketing your service.

Whether you're an Internet novice or veteran, there are some great ways to use affiliates to drive traffic to your Web site. Check out Commission Junction (www.cj.com), LinkShare (www.linkshare.com), or Amazon Associates (affiliate-program.amazon.com) for a few of the most popular ones. You should also think about using Google AdWords, doing strategic partnerships with other mobile companies and getting your PSMS short code everywhere (from your e-mail signature to your print, television, and radio advertisements), so that any potential new customer hears about your service!

Remember that all PSMS messages require double opt-in by the recipient of your message. To read more about opt-in regulations and attracting people to your messaging campaigns, read Chapters 3 and 4.

Partnering with PSMS stores

If you've got some incredibly unique content for sale, you should think about working with some other companies that would like to resell your products through their Web sites and stores. Several large PSMS stores on the Web and on mobile phones will pay you a commission for your products sold to their customers. Some of these companies include Jamster, PlayPhone, and Myxer. If you're really lucky, some of the wireless carriers also may want to resell their customers too! You can meet with them at the annual CTIA (Cellular Telecommunications Industry Association) conferences bi-annually and see if they want to resell your products.

Understanding premium messaging payout

If you decide to bill your customers $5.00 for a PSMS message, you aren't going to receive the full $5.00 because the carriers charge you a fee for billing the customer and collecting the money for you.

A *PSMS payout* refers to the amount of money you receive from the mobile carriers upon selling your content via PSMS. In return for processing the transaction, billing the customer, and using the carrier infrastructure to manage the PSMS transaction, wireless carriers typically take between 30 percent and 60 percent of the price charged to each consumer's phone bill.

The payout schedule is based on total sales by price point and the payouts can be different for every carrier. For example, if you sell a PSMS piece of content for $1.99, the carriers take roughly $0.60–$1.00 of the $1.99, and your payout is the amount that is left over ($1.00–$1.40).

Although this revenue share is higher than other payment processing platforms (PayPal, Visa, or MasterCard, for example) and it may sound high to you based on your experience outside of the mobile industry, PSMS and the wireless carriers eliminate a lot of pain and challenges encountered during this process in return for their revenue share. They take care of the customer service, billing operations, and billing verification issues, while empowering companies like yours to get into PSMS quickly and inexpensively!

The revenue share typically increases on more expensive consumer price plans. For example, a $9.99 plan will likely generate $7 in gross payout from the carriers (70% payout), compared to a $.99 plan that will net a payout of $.45 (45% payout ratio).

Reconciling PSMS reports

Logging each transaction that your campaign sends is very important for the final step in collecting revenue from your PSMS campaign. This process is known as *reconciliation.*

At the end of each month, you and your aggregator discuss the exact total of PSMS transactions generated over the prior month to ensure that you, the carriers, and the wireless aggregators agree on the revenue that has been collected. Discrepancies do happen, so make sure to have your logging system in place and come prepared to demonstrate your case, in the case that there is a discrepancy between the various transactions records.

When your report comes from the carrier or the aggregator, check the numbers against your sales records and calculate your expected payout to ensure you aren't surprised by unforeseen charges or fees.

Giving goes mobile

In 2007, an industry-leading entrepreneur, Jim Manis, and his team at the Mobile Giving Foundation (www.mobilegiving.org) worked closely with the mobile carriers in the United States to establish the practice of mobile giving. With mobile giving, consumers are able to make micro-donations via premium SMS. The donations are usually in $5 and $10 increments. However, unlike typical PSMS payouts, which are reduced by carrier fees, 100% of the donated proceeds are given to the charity by the carriers and the Mobile Giving Foundation. The charity pays only some nominal transaction and application services provider fees to set up and maintain their mobile giving programs (fees vary by provider).

Mobile giving came into its own in response to the January 2010 Haiti earthquake. Leading charities, including UNICEF and the Red Cross, raised more than $40 million in a little more than a week through mobile giving. For example, the Red Cross, via all its traditional and new media channels (for example, television, e-mail, social media, and related channels), invited people to donate by texting *Haiti* to a short code to donate $10 to Haiti relief, as shown in the following figure. (See www.mobilegiving.org for terms and conditions for this and related programs.)

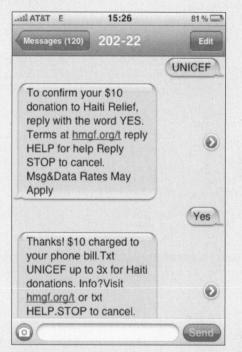

To participate in mobile giving programs, you must be a 501(c)3 and meet the Mobile Giving Foundation qualifications. See the Mobile Giving Foundation Guidelines for details (http://mobilegiving.org/Files/MGFGuidelines.pdf).

Keep in mind that your reconciliation report is not sent with a payment from the carrier. The wireless carriers and aggregators typically pay between 90 to 120 days *after* the billing event happened, which means that businesses should not expect to be paid any earlier from their PSMS businesses. This is vitally important to ensure that you don't get in a cash flow crunch while operating your business. Despite some of these long payment windows, several companies have built very significant PSMS businesses in the U.S. and around the world. We hope yours is the next success story!

Carrier billing via the mobile Web

Carrier billing through the mobile Web is much simpler than PSMS because you won't have to go through the process of obtaining short codes and obtaining opt-in permission through SMS. If you're selling mobile content via the mobile Internet browser, some paymaster application providers, like Bango (www.bango.com), already have relationships with mobile carriers so you can sell content by using a confirmation link on a mobile Web page instead of a PSMS message (see Figure 13-7).

This billing method is much more convenient for consumers and typically generates much higher participation rates (meaning you'll sell more stuff) than other billing methods such as PSMS and credit cards.

Check with your mobile billing application provider to see if it supports carrier billing via mobile Web browser in the country you're looking to sell content. Not every carrier in every country supports this capability.

Figure 13-7: Bango enables customers to confirm carrier-facilitated payments via mobile Web sites.

Actually, selling items through the mobile Web isn't very much different from selling things through the regular Web. (Well, it's better, obviously, but not too different.) The first step is setting up a billing system. To do this, you must

1. **Determine your billing needs.**

   Are you willing to work with an established billing service, like PayPal, that may take a percentage of each sale, or do you want to set up a proprietary billing system? Using a third party like PayPal leads to fewer headaches, but also slightly lower margins. If you're striking out on your own, you need to create software to accept credit card numbers and interface with paymasters (like Visa). That software also has to be integrated, at least on the back end, with any other sales channels (for example, online or in-store) for tracking and repeat customer purchases.

2. **Implement a billing service.**

   Third-party billing services like PayPal plug right into your existing mobile site, but if you're starting from the ground up, you have to create a program that works with your mobile site. Proprietary systems and Web services that allow you to create a billing system that can be incorporated into your mobile site are available. The best bet to avoid PayPal (if that's your goal) is to seek assistance from a mobile payment specialist, like Billing Revolution (`www.billingrevolution.com`), who can work with you through every phase of the billing implementation process.

Leveraging the Mobile Wallet

Here's a vision of utopia for your business: a world where everyone carries a single device, capable of direct communication, Web access, payment, identification, and entertainment, and everything and everyone they interact with can read that device. No more bulky wallets stuffed with credit cards, no more of that foldable green paper with dead white presidents on it. No more being turned away at the sales counter for not having the right credit card and no more guessing at account balances. Every payment is secure, and every transaction is basically at your fingertips.

Mobile commerce is a growing field that enables consumers to use their mobile devices for payment in a physical retail environment, thus turning the mobile device into a mobile wallet. Yes, people carry traditional wallets around too, so they are just as mobile, but not nearly as convenient as having all your purchasing power available in your phone. Some of the leading mobile wallet players in the market include Western Union (`www.western union.com`), Gold Mobile with its GoMo Wallet offering (`www.gomowallet.com/`), mFoundry (`www.mfoundry.com`), and Alcatel-Lucent Mobile Wallet Service (`www.alcatel-lucent.com`), to name just a few.

In the relatively near future, more and more payments will be made through the mobile wallet. Anyone wishing to engage in mobile commerce (this means you) needs to begin searching for ways to make the mobile wallet welcome wherever you sell goods or services.

The following sections show you the features of mobile wallets so you can adjust your marketing campaigns and terms of payment to allow your customers to take advantage of the convenience of paying for your products and services through their mobile wallets.

Accepting mobile integrated payments

At its core, mobile integrated payment is simply the payment for goods or services using the mobile device:

✔ It can be a numeric code, which a cashier can accept as payment. Generating a numeric code can be as simple as concocting a number (4 to 6 digits, for security) and assigning that number as a coupon code at the point of sale (POS). When the cashier or customer enters this code, the POS system recognizes this as payment — just as it might a gift card or a house account.

✔ It can be an encrypted bar code that enables a money transfer, as shown in Figure 13-8. A bar code performs the same function as a numeric code, except it can be scanned by an optical reader at the point of sale. Special Web services and dedicated software programs can create bar codes. Any mobile commerce company is capable of creating a bar code, and incorporating a bar code into a mobile display is the same as incorporating any other data.

Figure 13-8:
Bar codes can enable POS systems to accept payment on mobile devices.

Offering mobile loyalty programs

A typical loyalty program involves going to a retail store that hands you a punch card or asks for your phone number in order to track your purchases so the store can reward you with a discount or freebie when you have reached a certain level of purchases. For example, if you buy twelve lunches at the local Chinese restaurant and get your card punched accordingly, you get the thirteenth for free.

A mobile loyalty program is similar to a traditional loyalty program, except that loyalty points or purchase units are collected on the mobile phone. Loyalty units can also be redeemed through the mobile device, using a form of mobile integrated payment or through an auxiliary system such as a Web site.

Setting up a loyalty program is just like implementing a mobile marketing program. Here are the steps:

1. **Build a mobile database of willing customers (in this case, loyal customers).**

   Databases can (and should) be created from multiple data sources, including online information forms connected to your Web site, in-store collections, and direct SMS opt-in.

2. **Establish a unit/reward system and set up a system that allows your customer to accrue points on the mobile phone.**

   This is best accomplished by setting up an app — see the sidebar titled, "The Starbucks 'loyalty card' on the iPhone" elsewhere in this chapter — or it can also be done through unique customer codes delivered through SMS. (This process would work within your POS or application provider's systems because they keep track of a customer's account and transactions.)

3. **Distribute rewards based on consumer activity.**

   Tracking consumer behavior can be accomplished through a capable POS system, and incorporating that to the mobile channel is a function of database management.

Loyalty programs, like many of the programs covered in this book, aren't unique to mobile. Mobile just made them better.

The Starbucks "loyalty card" on the iPhone

Starbucks provides an excellent example of how a mobile app can be leveraged for mobile commerce. The Starbucks Card Mobile App functions as a loyalty program and a mobile integrated payment system, and it relies on the 2D bar code technology. As of this publication, the Starbucks app allows for mobile payment at all of its Target locations (more than 1,000 in-store cafes across the U.S.).

Built on its existing physical Starbucks Card program, the mobile app allows consumers to load money into their Starbucks Card account through a credit card, and then pay for their purchases by having a bar code on their iPhone screen scanned at the point of sale. The app is effectively a replacement for the physical card. Because the payment technology that powers it is built on an existing payment scheme, the infrastructure investment for Starbucks was minimal.

Selling mobile gift cards

Mobile gift cards function like regular gift cards, except without the physical plastic card. Using aspects of both mobile integrated payment and a system akin to mobile banking, mobile gift cards allow consumers to make gift card payments and check balances through the mobile device.

Mobile gift cards can be sold just as physical gift cards are sold, or they can be sold online or through the mobile device itself. Apps can facilitate the gift card distribution and redemption process (in fact, there are gift card apps available in the iTunes Store). One such app, developed by Wildcard, uses bar code technology for redemption. Other companies, like Target, accept the gift card mobile simply by making gift card information available on the Web, and thus accessible through smartphones. In this sense, the only technology needed to enable the sale of mobile gift cards is the technology needed to implement and redeem mobile coupons.

Mobile gift cards can also be reloaded easily, through mobile banking or at the point of sale, and can be transferred or shared.

The gift card is accomplished through a bar code or a numeric code — for example, the Visa and Neustar's 2D bar code program is based in gift cards — and is powered by a platform that links the two functions. The process of creating mobile gift cards also allows retailers and gift card providers to streamline their gift card development and distribution systems. Fifth Third, an electronic payments and credit, debit, and gift card processing services provider, is using Transaction Wireless's wGiftCard suite of products to target national retailers and restaurants, as well as local and regional merchants. The mobile channel allows for such cross-brand aggregation.

Chapter 14

Evaluating the ROI on Mobile Marketing

*M*easuring and tracking the results of your marketing programs, including both your direct and mobile-enabled traditional marketing programs, is an essential part of your job as a marketer. Over the last few years, marketers have been put under a significant amount of pressure to demonstrate a return on investment for the organizational resources they consume. *Return on investment (ROI)* is the measurement of dollars received for every dollar invested. In other words, you need to show the value of your effort and how those efforts contribute to meeting the company's goals and objectives.

Mobile analytics provide valuable insights into the performance of your mobile campaigns. *Mobile analytics* refer to the process of measuring, monitoring, and tracking your mobile marketing campaigns. With mobile marketing analytics, you can

✔ Track individual user participation in all your programs by time, frequency, location, and other measurements

✔ Measure and compare all your mobile marketing campaigns, in some cases in real time, so that you can make immediate adjustments to your programs

✔ Use data to calculate your ROI to see if you're making more than you spend (a positive ROI) or if you're losing money on your programs (a negative ROI)

This chapter shows you a number of ways you can collect information and analyze it to improve your mobile marketing programs.

Determining What to Track and Analyze

Mobile analytics is the process of collecting data from your mobile marketing efforts so that you can compare a change in a single metric over time and compare multiple sets of data to each other. Mobile analytics impact your mobile strategy in two ways:

- ✔ Analytics help you plan your mobile campaign strategy
- ✔ Analytics help you evaluate the success of your strategy

To gauge your mobile marketing success, you need to analyze which parts of your strategy work and which parts don't. Measurable data collected for the purpose of analysis are often called *metrics*. A *metric* is any number expressed in a scale, used to quantify how much you have of something. (Think temperature in degrees Fahrenheit, or speed limits in miles per hour, for example.)

Marketers use metrics all the time in other media, especially digital, direct, and retail. Although you could track literally hundreds of metrics, Table 14-1 shows you a list of the main mobile campaign interactions and the metrics you should be prepared to track and analyze.

Table 14-1	Mobile Interactions and Associated Metrics
Interaction	*Metrics Worth Paying Attention To*
SMS	Unique participants in a campaign
	Number of respondents, opt-ins, opt-outs, total churn (% of people who opt out compared to the total list)
	Successfully and unsuccessfully delivered messages
	Carrier participation and which mobile carriers drove the most participation
	Participation by geography
	Count of embedded URL visited
	Average revenue per user (ARPU)
	Total revenue per campaign
MMS	All the SMS metrics listed previously
	Number of unsupported devices
	Mobile operator MMS policy rejections
Content downloads	Unique downloads
	Total downloads
	Failed downloads
	Total revenue

Interaction	Metrics Worth Paying Attention To
Mobile Web sites	Unique visitors
	Repeat visitors
	Entry and exit points
	Bounce rates (number of visitors who see only one page)
	Number of page views
	Geographic location of visitors
	Devices used by visitors
	Mobile operators used by visitors
	Average time spent on a site, on a page
	Conversion rate
Mobile advertising	Cost per impression (CPI)
	Cost per click (CPC)
	Cost per conversion (CPC) or cost per acquisition (CPA)
	Total number of click-throughs (the number of times an ad is clicked on)
Voice campaigns	Date and time of incoming calls
	Number of calls
	Total minutes per call
	Billable minutes
	Average call length
	Number of transactions per call
	Revenue per call
	Error messages processed
Mobile applications	Number of downloads
	Download count by handset type
	Unique active users
	Failed downloads
	Time to download
	Total revenue
	Location of download
	User reviews of your application
	Time spent using application
Mobile e-mail	Click-through rate (CTR)
	Conversion rate

(continued)

Table 14-1 (continued)

Interaction	Metrics Worth Paying Attention To
	Opt-ins and opt-outs
	Open rate
	Unsubscribe rate
	Forwards and shares
Bluetooth and Wi-Fi	Total delivered sessions
	Total content downloads
	Frequency and time spent per location
	The type of phone interacting with the system
	The mobile carrier used
	Location access point by location

The metrics in Table 14-1 are by no means an exhaustive list; they simply highlight some of the more prominent measures tracked.

 Metrics aren't just about measuring success. In fact, just as often, metrics help you recognize that parts of your mobile marketing are *not* working, so you can fix them.

Preparing Your Database to Collect Information

A *mobile marketing database* (see Figure 14-1) is simply a database that houses all the information about each and every mobile customer you have and all the campaigns and programs you run. A mobile marketing database allows you to link your mobile marketing campaign interactions with the people in your database and apply metrics to individuals and groups of individuals.

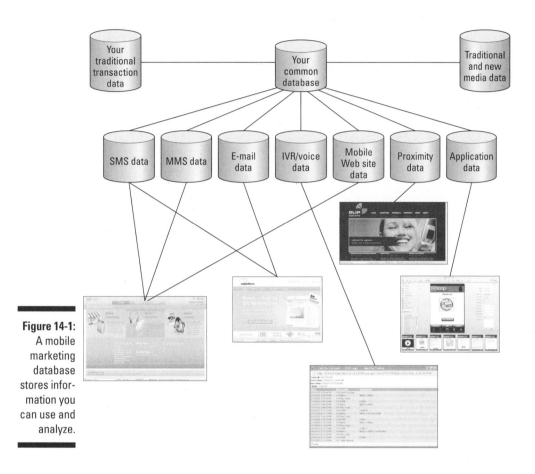

Figure 14-1:
A mobile
marketing
database
stores infor-
mation you
can use and
analyze.

You'll probably end up working with a number of databases, depending on
how many mobile marketing companies you work with. Many companies support multiple mobile media paths (see Chapter 1), but no one supports them
all. For a specific setup of programs, a database is typically built and hosted
by your mobile marketing application provider. Or, you may already have
your own customer relationship management (CRM) system or database that
you work with.

In any event, whether your mobile marketing database is hosted by your
application provider, integrated with your CRM solution, or is some hybrid
model, you need to set up your database files to accept the data you need to
collect and analyze from each type of interaction.

The following sections show you the types of information to consider adding to your database for each customer or prospect who interacts with your mobile marketing campaigns.

Outlining demographic data

Demography is all about studying populations; consequently, demographic data are the data points that detail a population's characteristics. You want to think about the various demographic data points you'll find helpful for your business (every business is different). Data you might consider including in your database include

- ✔ Age (either in the form of a birth date or age range, for example, 14–24, and so on)

- ✔ Sex (male/female)

- ✔ Marital status (single, married, divorced, domestic partnership, and so on)

- ✔ Number of children (zero, one, two, three, more than you can handle)

- ✔ Level of education (high school, some college, college graduate, doctorate, life experience)

- ✔ Occupation (there simply are too many to list — isn't that a great thing?)

- ✔ Income (typically presented in monetary ranges, for example, $50,000–$75,000 per year)

- ✔ Nationality (American, French, British, Chinese, and so on)

- ✔ Geography (residence, place of work, or, if you're a road warrior, American Airlines, seat B17)

In tech speak, all this data is commonly referred to as _metadata,_ or "data about" something. When your engineer asks you, "What kind of metadata do you want to capture?" You can say, "I need demographic metadata — age, geography, and psychographic data (that is, information about your preferences, attitude, intention, and so on)." Now you're cooking!

Organizing psychographic data

You may wish to capture and organize psychographic data about members of your audience. _Psychographic data_ is qualitative data used to measure an individual's lifestyle. Examples could include

- ✔ Behaviors such as frequent travel
- ✔ Attitudes, interests, and beliefs
- ✔ Values and opinions
- ✔ Personality
- ✔ Purchasing motivation
- ✔ Usage behavior

You can include psychographic information in your database to help you describe and identify customers and prospective customers in more detail and to aid in developing promotion strategies designed to appeal to specific psychographic segments of the market for a product or service.

Planning for preferences data

Preference data is data volunteered by members of your audience regarding their preferences, for example, their likes and dislikes (favorite food, music, and so on). Other preference criteria may include the days of the week and times the consumers prefer to be messaged or called, how many times the consumers are willing to let you contact them within a particular time frame (for example, ten times a month, but no more than three times per week).

By setting up your database to include preferences information and using it appropriately, you have a much better chance of pleasing the customers and prospects who interact with your mobile marketing campaigns.

Planning for behavioral data

Behavioral data includes information about past behavior or expected behavior based on past interactions or predictions based on other data. Including behavioral data in your database can tell you whether someone is likely or unlikely to respond to a specific campaign. For example, a person with a behavioral profile that indicates procrastination may not respond to a limited time offer.

You can get some great mobile subscriber behavior data from comScore (www.comscore.com) and Nielsen (www.nielsen.com), two research firms that track user behavior on mobile phones.

Behavioral data is an emerging field in marketing. Talk to your application provider and connection aggregator to get a sense of what they're doing in this area or with whom they're working.

Looking out for location data

Location is a dynamic data point that can be used to adjust your interaction with members of your audience so that those interactions are contextually relevant to their location. For example, if they're browsing mobile Internet sites and your database knows their location, you can display location-relevant advertising or guide them to the nearest location. You can also track location in real time and use that information to deliver location-based messages when your customers give you permission to use their location data.

Mining syndicated data

Syndicated data is consumer purchasing data compiled from individually scanned consumer transactions from thousands of purchase locations. The data is collected by market research firms, cleansed, and put into aggregate to protect the privacy of individuals. It's then used by marketers to better understand the purchasing behavior of their target audience. Marketers use syndicated to data to

✔ Improve sales tracking of their products and their competitors.

✔ Monitor marketing promotions and merchandising for both their own products as well as those of their competitors.

✔ Determine which distributors are using their products.

✔ Segment customers effectively, identifying their best and worse prospects.

✔ Perform market basket analysis, understanding what other products are typically purchased at the same time as theirs.

Syndicated data can be very useful; in fact, it can often be better than data you collect yourself because it amasses information not just about your own client interactions but those of your competitors as well.

Although data and information collection may give you knowledge and power, with this knowledge and power comes great responsibility and liability. You must protect the data you collect. If you don't protect it (if you misuse it, or it gets in the hands of someone else), you may face many commercial and legal challenges. Seriously think through all the liabilities before you collect and use data. Be sure to consult your legal counsel. You can read more about the laws governing mobile marketing in Chapter 3.

Populating a Mobile Database

After you've identified the types of customer and prospect data that you're going to collect and you've worked with your own internal team or mobile marketing application provider to build a database, you're ready to start populating the database, that is, loading it up with all the information about your campaigns and your customers.

The following sections show you how to collect profile information about your customers when they interact with your campaigns. We show you how to track the details of each interaction with your campaigns in the next section.

Collecting data through SMS

With SMS, you can collect some data automatically as well as request that participants of your campaigns provide the data. When a consumer opts into your campaign via SMS, the mobile marketing application captures the participant's mobile phone number. From this mobile phone number, your application provider can identify the following:

- **Previous participation in other programs you've run:** You can match the number to see if the number has been used in other campaigns.

- **Wireless carrier:** Discover which wireless carrier the subscriber is using.

- **Crude location:** Using the country code and area code of the number, you can make a crude estimate of location (country, state, city, and time zone). This method should not be used for real-time location detection because it does not tell you where the person is, just where his phone was registered.

- **Porting history:** Find out if the number has ever been moved from one wireless carrier to another.

- **Technical bits:** Discover if the phone supports binary data (for example, pictures and video), text messaging, or WAP push. (*WAP push* is a method of delivering content and mobile Internet sites. Ask your mobile marketing application provider about this.)

 Your mobile marketing application provider, connection aggregator, or even Neustar's Wireless Message Routing Service (WMRS) service (`www.neustar.biz/interoperability/wmrs.cfm`) can help you collect the preceding information.

In addition to the preceding data, the marketer can request the user to submit any number of different types of data points, including demographic, physiographic, and preference data via SMS. For example, you may ask the user to submit her birth date as an opt-in challenge if you're marketing a program not suitable for children. You simply need to make sure that your text messaging application supports the ability to collect the data you are asking for and in the manner you're asking for it.

Collecting through the mobile Internet and installed applications

You can use Internet and mobile Internet browser forms or forms in an installed application to collect information from your prospects and customers by requesting that the visitor to the site complete the form. Upon submission, you capture the requested data.

For example, a leading marketer to youth retail markets, Access 360 Media, uses Web forms that can capture different consumer preference attributes, as shown in Figure 14-2.

Figure 14-2: A consumer retail-focused preference opt-in form via the Internet.

You can use forms on mobile Internet sites, but be sure to keep them short. Mobile subscribers do not have the patience to complete long forms via their phones, so ask only the basics. If you need more info, augment the experience with another mobile (for example, voice) or traditional path (for example, the

Internet). But be careful. Make sure you understand your audience. For example, not all demographics use all mobile technology, like the mobile Internet, so take care to understand your audience.

Be sure to ask your application provider if you'll be able to create your data schema and forms. Companies like iLoop Mobile have robust mobile customer relationship management elements that give you this capability.

Integrating CRM with mobile campaigns

There may come a time when you want to merge your mobile campaign data with that data stored in your company's customer relationship management (CRM) system. This is easy to do and typically can be handled in one of three ways:

- ✔ **Manually**: You can ask your mobile marketing application provider to provide you a manual report (in Microsoft Excel or in an XML data structure) so that you can combine your data with that of the mobile marketing campaign database manually.

- ✔ **Via data feed:** Your mobile marketing application provider should be able to give you access to an XML data feed that you can pull from on a regular basis (once a day, every five minutes — the timing depends on your application needs) so that you can combine your data with that of the mobile marketing campaign database automatically per the set schedule.

- ✔ **In real time:** You can also ask your mobile marking application provider if it can pass you data in real time as your participants interact with the system (see Figure 14-3). For example, maybe you need to know immediately if someone opts out of your mobile marketing campaign so that you can update the other permission marketing management system in other parts of your company.

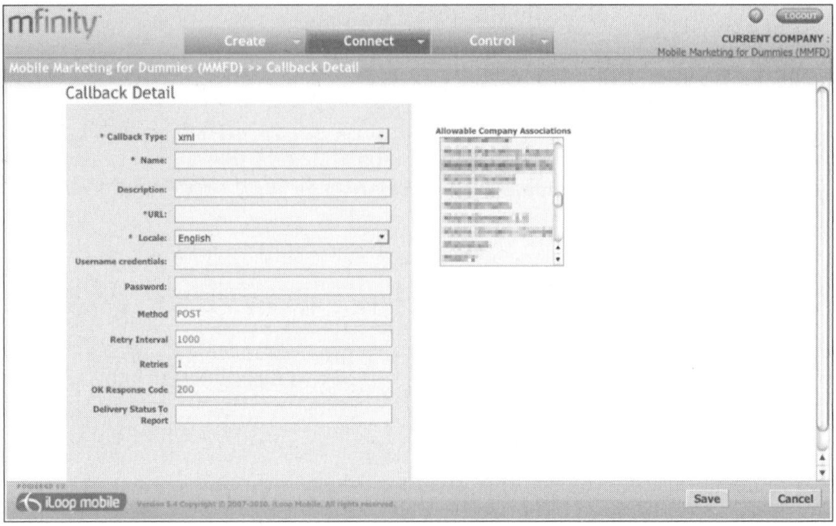

Figure 14-3:
The real-
time data
transfer
configura-
tion screen
in the iLoop
Mobile mfin-
ity platform.

Courtesy of iLoop Mobile, Inc.

Tracking Interactions: Clicks, Calls, Votes, and More

Your mobile marketing application is capable of tracking most, if not all, interactions a mobile subscriber has with it. That includes any calls, text clicks, snaps, scans, StarStars (**), pounds (#), presses, pictures taken, acceptances, submits, votes, requests, replies, and more.

How this information is tracked and reported on, however, varies significantly by the type of mobile method you're using; moreover, you should consult with your mobile application provider prior to running your campaigns(s) to ensure the data you need (that is, the data you want to use to measure and report on the efficacy of your program(s)) is being tracked and retained.

Using third-party tracking tools

You have your choice of a number of mobile analytics providers to track consumer interactions on your mobile Web sites and applications. For example, if you want to track interactions on your mobile Web sites, you can consider using Google Analytics (`www.google.com/analytics`). Google Analytics allows users get rich Web site information, and the account creation process is simple:

1. **Go to `www.google.com/analytics/`.**

2. **Sign up for a new account (or use your existing account credentials).**

3. Add a Web site profile.

You need to enter the URL of your Web site, give the profile an account name, and specify the time zone of your site. Also, provide the first and last name for the primary site contact person and agree to the terms and conditions.

4. After you've completed the preceding steps, you are asked to follow the tracking instructions.

After you've completed the preceding steps, you are asked to follow the tracking instructions, which basically means you copy a bunch of HTML code from Google. This code can then be pasted into your mobile Web site's code. The code acts as a sort of tag that Google can use to track the user's behavior on the site. You can ask your site designer or partner for help at this point. Google sends you an e-mail with the necessary information that you can simply copy and send to your designer — they really make it easy for you.

5. Click Save and you're done.

After you have the tracking code successfully copied, pasted, and saved into your mobile Web site's code, Google immediately starts tracking and monitoring your site. You can then log in to Google Analytics as often as you'd like to see how your site traffic is doing.

Bango has a similar process. See Figure 14-4 for a sample Bango mobile Web report.

Figure 14-4:
A Bango mobile behavior multi-channel meeting report.

Courtesy of Bango

You can choose between a number of application provider reporting tools, including Flurry (www.flurry.com), Medialets (www.medialets.com), Motally (www.motally.com), Bango (www.bango.com), Omniture's SiteCatalyst (www.omniture.com/en/products/online_analytics/sitecatalyst), Mobile Behavior (www.mobilebehavior.com), and others. See Figure 14-5 for an example of Mobile Behavior's reporting tool.

If your mobile application provider won't let you integrate a third-party reporting tool, go find another vendor. Third-party validation is incredibly important.

Obtaining metrics from partners and service providers

You should be able to obtain from your mobile application service provider a wealth of operational and business metrics from your campaigns. In general, obtaining metrics is a straightforward process, and as a marketer, you have to assess what mobile metrics are appropriate for you to measure.

Here is a list of the common metrics, tools, and questions you should be asking your provider about so that you can develop your mobile analytics strategy:

- **Frequency of data available:** How often are the reports updated? (Many providers only provide previous day snapshots, not real-time data.)

- **Summary levels of data (in addition to detailed transactional data from the mobile campaign):** For example, do they provide you with a total SMS message count or mobile Web page view count in a summary report?

- **Specific data elements available**: Ask your provider what data elements they can provide you, like those listed in Table 14-1.

- **Sorting and selecting data capability:** Can you sort and filter the data online, or do you need to export it and do it in a spreadsheet program like Microsoft Excel?

- **Availability of campaign dashboard tools:** Campaign dashboards are graphical Web-based tools provided to marketers for manipulating and visualizing data.

- **Charts and graphs availability:** Similar to summary level data, can you get bar charts, pie charts, time line graphs, and other visual representations of your campaign data?

✔ **Customization options (alarms, triggers, views):** In other words, can the system send you an e-mail notifying you if your opt-out rate exceeds a threshold that concerns you, or if your text message campaigns hit previously unreached heights?

✔ **Integration capability:** Do you have the ability to integrate with databases or other proprietary tools for data delivery?

✔ **Help support availability:** Is both business and technical help available?

✔ **Privacy controls:** Can you administer privacy controls, such as masking a user's phone number out of reports?

✔ **Process analysis (for user flows and consumer acquisition):** Can you evaluate consumer engagement across different types of campaigns, such as moving from initial acquisition and into a loyalty or customer service program?

If your mobile service provider cannot comply or provide the majority of these items, either as a standard offering or by developing a customer report or tools for you, you may want to consider finding another vendor who can help you.

Before you set up a customer report with a service provider or agency, make sure you are clear about who owns the information gathered. Also, be sure you understand and are comfortable with its process for data security. You want to make sure you own the data and that you can take the information with you if you choose to move on to another service, even if the information is collected through its platform. You can revisit more related to this and code of conduct and ethics in mobile marketing in Chapter 3 of this book.

Understanding analytics reports

An *analytics report* is a collection of mobile metrics presented to you in a single report so that you can see all your data as a whole and begin to gather insights from it. You can then use these insights to make decisions on how to best move forward with your business (see Figure 14-5). In other words, reporting and analyzing the data generated from your programs are absolutely critical components of your mobile marketing efforts. What good is the best mobile marketing campaign if you do not have strong insights into exactly how it performed or is performing?

Figure 14-5:
Analytics
reports
quantify the
interactions
with your
mobile
campaigns.

Many of the companies in the mobile marketing space today can provide a
high level of reporting sophistication. Campaign dashboards are often
configurable so that you can see the metrics that matter to you and see them
in a variety of formats.

Reports typically are summary views of a mobile campaign on a daily,
weekly, or monthly basis, but they can also be unprocessed and unformatted
data files, which require additional work to arrange and present the data.

Every mobile application provider has a different user interface for pulling
its reports. Ask about the reporting feature in the application as well as the
mobile Web site reports available when you're selecting a mobile service
provider.

You'd be amazed by how quickly data can be amassed as mobile subscribers
interact with a mobile marketing application. Every click, snap, and call can
be, for the most part, tracked.

From log files to readable reports

In addition to all the reports your application provider shares with you, you should keep in mind that more information may be stored in an application provider's server log files. Application providers capture a lot of data within their systems; however, due to time constraints, technical challenges, or their own failure to realize that the information is valuable, they may not immediately share it with you. All you need to do is ask for it. They may be able to provide you with custom reports and data access or start tracking additional information that they were not tracking before. For example, during an SMS interaction, the mobile marketing application may record the following transaction: abcvote yes 4085551212 543221. In this example,

- ✔ abcvote is the keyword to be associated with a particular text messaging voting campaign.

- ✔ Yes is the vote response.

- ✔ 4085551212 is the mobile subscriber's phone number.

- ✔ 543221 is the wireless carrier's carrier ID, which is a number that tells the mobile marketing application that the phone number is on Verizon Wireless, T-Mobile, or Sprint, for example.

It takes a lot of computer power to analyze data, so often a mobile marketing application processes the data externally to its core applications and/or late or early in the day, say, every morning at 4:00 a.m.. Be sure to ask your mobile marketing application provider to show you what data is available in real time versus what data is processed later. You should also find out what data is available upon request, that is, in the log files, but not readily available in the system for general consumption.

The preceding example is very simple. Log files include lots of other data, including success and error codes, server IDs, time stamps, and so on. Converting the log file data, data that is often unintelligible to the common reader (log files are written in another language, engineering-speak), into actionable results is another matter entirely. Your mobile marketing application provider needs to map the log file codes to a series of database tables that help translate the numbers in the log file; for example, 543221 equals AT&T Wireless. The provider then maps this data to reports.

Transaction reports can come in two flavors: raw data dumps and analyzed reports. With raw data dumps, you receive a report that provides a line item for every transaction. You can use tools like Microsoft Excel to analyze the data and report on it. For analyzed reports, the mobile application provider gives you calculated statistics in an analysis report; for this example, the report provider displays not just the votes, but how many votes there were and which option received the most.

Your application provider(s) no doubt has a lot of experience with collecting and analyzing transaction data; however, more often than not, the application provider is not in your business and doesn't know exactly how you want to look at the data or what analysis of the data is meaningful. Rather than assuming it knows what you need, tell it the type of results and data you want to see in the transaction reports. Have this discussion before your campaign launches; otherwise, you may have some late nights slogging through log files to get the answers you need. If you plan and coordinate with your application provider prior to the launch of your program(s), the application provider can give you the answers you seek in a perfectly packaged report, often in real time.

Often mobile marketing reports can contain both graphs and data for the metrics and be made available in a variety of formats (such as Microsoft Excel spreadsheets, Adobe Acrobat PDFs, or other). A current trend is to provide visual representation, typically in graph form, so a user can quickly see how his campaign is doing.

Figure 14-6 shows a sample trend graph on the effectiveness of mobile advertising.

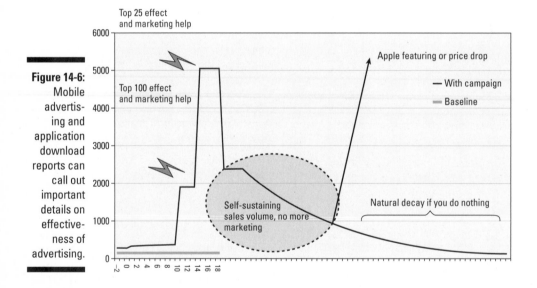

Figure 14-6:
Mobile advertising and application download reports can call out important details on effectiveness of advertising.

Calculating Your Return on Mobile Marketing Investment

Return on mobile marketing investment (ROMMI) is an important measure to keep track of because it lets you know whether you're achieving your objectives and getting more out of your mobile marketing than you're putting into it. There are two basic ROMMI measures: a ROMMI against direct revenue generating programs and a ROMMI against indirect revenue generating programs. Both are discussed in the following sections.

Calculating expected ROMMI for direct revenue programs

Calculating your ROMMI for revenue generating mobile marketing programs is a simple math exercise. The ROMMI for revenue generating programs compares the sales you generated, or expect to generate, in revenue terms against your mobile marketing spending, or expected spending, that helped generate those revenues.

Here's the formula:

Return on mobile marketing investment (ROMMI) = [incremental revenue attributed to mobile marketing (in dollars) * sales contribution margin – mobile marketing spending (in dollars)] / mobile marketing spending (in dollars)

Here's an explanation for each variable:

- **Incremental revenue attributed to mobile marketing (IRAMM),** is the total additional revenue, in monetary terms (for example, in dollars) you generate by running the mobile marketing program as opposed to the revenue you'd receive if you did not run the mobile marketing program. For example, if your revenues were going to be $22,000 before running the mobile marketing program and you estimate they'll be $30,000 by adding the mobile marketing element to your marketing program, your IRAMM is the difference, $8,000.

- **Marketing spending** is the total cost for running the mobile marketing program, including all strategy, creative, tactical execution, and technology elements. See Chapter 2 for details on estimating the cost of your mobile marketing programs.

- **Contribution margin** is the calculation of the marginal profit (a percentage) generated from the product or service being sold. To calculate this, you need to know the selling price of the product(s) or service(s) that is contributing to the revenues being tracked and the variable cost it takes to produce it. With this information, you can use the following formulas to calculate your contribution margin. The calculation is a two-step process. You first must calculate the contribution per unit and then you can calculate the contribution margin:

  - **Contribution per unit (in dollars)** = Selling price per unit (in dollars) – variable cost per unit (in dollars)

  - **Contribution margin (percentage)** = contribution per unit (in dollars) / selling price per unit (in dollars)

Here is an example: Say you're selling T-shirts. The shirt sells for $10 and it costs you $1.50 to make it.

The contribution per unit (in dollars) is $10.00 – $1.50, which equals $8.50. The contribution margin is $8.50/$10.00, which equals 85%.

If you plan to use mobile marketing for the promotion and sales of multiple products, you can use the same model. You simply have to run the math for each product and add things up.

For example, say you own a chain of retail outlets and you want to use mobile marketing to drive traffic to your store to generate T-shirt sales. You're already spending money on a direct mail campaign and you want to mobile enhance the program by adding a mobile coupon call to action. The total cost of the mobile marketing element to enhance your existing marketing campaign is $5,000. You expect the mobile marketing element of the campaign to increase revenues from $22,000–$30,000. You previously calculated that the contribution margin of the T-shirts sales averages out at 85%.

In this case, your ROMMI would be

ROMMI = [incremental revenue attributed to mobile marketing (in dollars) * contribution margin percentage – marketing spending (in dollars)]/marketing spending (in dollars)

The ROMMI for this example = [$8,000 * 85% - $5,000]/$5,000 = 36%

In this case, your mobile marketing program is estimated to generate $0.36 per every dollar of spending. Not bad!

Leveraging industry data as a baseline

As a keen mobile marketer, you should read industry reports, Web sites, and blogs that denote trending or typical mobile marketing statistics. Several of these services have mountains of data and reports readily available. These include Keynote Systems (www.keynote.com), comScore (www.comscore.com), Nielsen (www.nielsen.com), eMarketer (www.emarketer.com), Marketing Charts (www.marketingcharts.com), and other third-party data sources. These services can be used to establish performance baselines for better understanding the relative performance of a mobile marketing campaign.

Leading mobile marketing case studies highlighting campaign results and best practices can also be pulled from free sources like Mobile Marketer (www.mobilemarketer.com) and other companies by doing a Web search for mobile marketing case studies.

Calculating expected ROMMI for indirect revenue programs

Calculating your ROMMI for indirect revenue programs can be a bit harder than doing so from direct programs, but it is not impossible. The same premise applies as for direct revenue programs: You want to estimate the overall value of the mobile market program to your achievement of the company's objectives.

Your goal for indirect revenue objectives is not sales, but rather some other trackable measure (opt-ins, impressions, clicks, traffic, redemptions, and so on). For example, maybe you want to measure the number of new leads in the opt-in database (opt-ins), total mobile advertising impressions generated (impressions), increased traffic in the store or on Internet or mobile Internet sites (traffic), the number of loyalty points redeemed by customers (redemptions), or whatever. In order to calculate your ROMMI, you need to know what each of these measures means to you. Look at your historical data and calculate how much additional revenue an opt-in, impression, redemption, or traffic means to you in terms of real revenue. You can then compare the value of an indirect measure, like an impression, against the estimated/actual costs of running the marketing program to estimate your indirect ROMMI and see if the program is worth doing.

Here's the formula:

ROMMI for indirect programs = [estimated value of measure – mobile marketing spending (in dollars)] / mobile marketing spending (in dollars)

Here's an explanation for each variable:

- **Estimated value of measure** is the total revenue you'd expect from the metric. For example, say historically that you've calculated that every new impression on your Web site, on average, is worth $0.20 in expected revenue.

- **Mobile marketing spending** is the total cost for running the mobile marketing program, including all strategy, creative, tactical execution, and technology elements. See Chapter 2 for details on estimating the cost of mobile marketing programs.

As an example, say that a travel agency wants to sponsor a live event. The sponsorship costs $35,000 (including the mobile marketing program costs). The agency assumes the sponsorships will generate 250,000 impressions, which results in a cost of $0.14/impression ($35,000/250,000). The agency knows that historically an impression is worth, on average, $0.20 in future revenues.

The ROMMI for these indirect programs = [$0.20-$0.14] / $0.14 = 43%

Based on these estimates, the sponsorship is worth the expense.

Part V
The Part of Tens

The 5th Wave — By Rich Tennant

"Snappy ad copy. And it really got my attention."

In this part . . .

Mobile marketing strategies and tactics are always changing and adapting because mobile technology is advancing so rapidly. That's not likely to change for a while, so this Part gives you a snapshot of the things to remember now and where to look ahead to the future.

Chapter 15 shows you ten ways your marketing can reach people now on their mobile devices. Chapter 16 lists ten mobile marketing resource centers you can follow for updates on future technology and the marketing tactics that go along with new technology.

We also include a mobile marketing Glossary so that you can quickly look up the definition of any new mobile marketing terms that you come across.

Chapter 15

Ten Ways to Reach Your Customers on Their Mobile Devices

In This Chapter

▶ Understanding the power of the mobile media paths

▶ Connecting with ads, commerce, and location

▶ Engaging your customer through mobile-enhanced traditional media

*E*ven the most personal and powerful marketing message doesn't help your business if it never reaches a person who can absorb the message and respond with a decision in favor of your business objectives. The great thing about mobile devices, like feature phones, smartphones, and tablets (see Chapter 1) is that they are connected to a single person and they offer lots of different ways to get your marketing messages delivered and noticed by the people who use them.

This chapter discusses ten ways for you to reach your customers on their mobile phones today. Technology is always changing, so make sure you also read Chapter 16 so you know where to look for even more ways to reach your customers as the future of mobile marketing unfolds.

Text Messaging (SMS)

Almost every mobile phone being produced today has the ability to send and receive text messages, also known as Short Message Service (SMS) messages. SMS is limited to 140 characters of plain text, but that's a good thing because short messages are a quick read that save your customers time reading through the stuff that isn't important. SMS is perfect for sending alerts, reminders, coupons, and other messages that get to the point quickly. You can also include links to mobile Web sites, downloads, and phone numbers. You can read about sending text messaging campaigns in Chapters 4 and 5.

Multimedia Messaging Service (MMS)

MMS messages are text messages with the ability to include more text as well as multimedia enhancements such as pictures, video, and sound. Think of MMS messages as e-mails that get delivered directly to a phone's message inbox via a phone number instead of an inbox in an e-mail service via an e-mail address. MMS messages are perfect for sending product brochures, greeting cards, audio messages, and videos that show your products or services in action. We show you how to create and send MMS messages in Chapter 6.

Mobile E-Mail

People check their e-mail at home, at work, in bed, in the bathroom, on the sidelines at the kids' soccer games, and even while they drive (but don't do that!). E-mail is still one of the best ways for people to exchange and share private messages and files with each other. More people than ever are checking their e-mail on mobile devices because people are always on the go. Mobile e-mail is also one of the lowest-cost ways to deliver your message — it's low-cost for you and your customers. You can read about designing and delivering mobile friendly e-mails in Chapter 7.

Mobile Internet Sites

Phones with Internet browsers have the ability to access the Internet so people can interact with Web sites from almost anywhere. People who browse the Internet on phones and other mobile devices are often looking for directions, contact information, reviews and ratings, and other stuff that helps them make fast decisions while they are away from their computers. Because mobile phones aren't as powerful or big as computers, you need to make sure your Web sites are formatted to provide a good experience to your mobile visitors. After you have a handle on the differences between designing Internet pages for computers versus mobile devices, you can build mobile sites for your products, your promotions, and your entire company. Read more about designing mobile Internet sites in Chapter 8.

Mobile Applications

You can provide rich software-like experiences to smartphone owners and people who use mobile devices such as the iPad by developing mobile applications for them to use. Applications are like computer programs that are installed on the device, and they are useful for all kinds of things, from checking account balances to playing games. The benefit of providing mobile applications isn't limited to productivity or entertainment, however. Mobile apps can include your advertising and branding, and you can even sell your mobile applications to make money. You can read more about developing mobile applications in Chapter 9.

Interactive Voice Response (IVR)

Mobile phones can do a lot of cool things, so it's easy to forget that the primary function of a phone is the ability to make and receive voice calls. In fact, voice calls are a lot more convenient while people are on the go in some circumstances. For example, phone numbers in mobile Web sites or text messages can be clicked or touched to automatically dial the number, and placing an order or listening to a voice message is easier to do than staring at a screen or typing while walking down the street or standing in line. Interactive Voice Response (IVR) is a technology that allows you to send and receive voice calls from people and interact with them without involving a live person on your end of the call. We explain how to implement IVR in your mobile strategy in Chapter 11. Of course, you can also use mobile to send and receive live agent calls, so we show you the benefits of doing that in Chapter 11 also.

Mobile Social Media

Why wait until you're in front of a computer to interact with customers and colleagues through a social media site when you can be involved in conversations through a mobile device and never miss a conversation? Social media is one of the main behaviors driving the adoption of smartphones. Your business can be a part of the growing number of real-time conversations when you include social media in your mobile marketing strategy. You can find out how to make your social media marketing strategy more mobile-friendly in Chapter 12.

Mobile Advertising

A mobile device's screen is the focus of attention multiple times per day for everyone who owns one. Wherever there are lots of eyeballs, there are lots of opportunities for advertising to deliver your message. Mobile advertising can be placed on mobile Web sites in much the same way as regular Web sites, but that's not all. You can also advertise in mobile applications, during downloads, in mobile videos, in mobile e-mails, voice and IVR calls, and in text and MMS messages. We show you how to place ads and sell your own mobile advertising space in Chapter 10.

Mobile Commerce and Location-Based Enabled Engagements

Mobile phones and devices can act like order-takers when the goal of your marketing message is an immediate purchase. You can sell your stuff through mobile Internet sites and voice ordering systems, and you can sell downloads and other content by accepting payments by credit card or by charging the purchase to your customer's mobile phone bill. Mobile phones can also act like digital wallets that can pay for things at retail through mobile point-of-sale systems and bar code scanners. You can read more about enabling mobile commerce in Chapter 13.

In addition, marketers have always been concerned with the general geography of prospects and customers when engaging them, but mobile devices are capable of revealing the *precise* present location of those prospects and customers. You can use mobile technology to detect someone's location in order to deliver a location-relevant message, or present a relevant ad or offer. Alternatively, you can place your marketing in relevant locations and allow people to interact with your marketing messages when they are nearby. Marketing based on location isn't limited to one type of technology. Location can be a key factor in almost every type of mobile marketing campaign or engagement offer. We discuss location-based tactics and tips throughout the book when location is relevant to the technology being discussed.

Mobile-Enabled Traditional Media

Marketing, at its core, is about communication and engagement. As a marketer, it's your job to communicate and engage your customer — that is, impart information and news about your products, services, and related activities to your audience (customers, clients, partners, and society at large) so that they can know what your organization does and how to connect with you. Because (as explained in Chapters 1 and 3) the mobile channel requires that you either have permission from a consumer prior to proactively engaging him on his mobile device or that the mobile consumer is aware of your mobile programs so that he reaches out and engages *you*, the best way to do either is to mobile-enable your traditional and digital media by putting mobile call-to-actions in your media and inviting consumers to pull out their mobile devices and contact you. (See Chapters 1 and 2 for more on understanding the approach to mobile marketing and how to build your strategy.)

Chapter 16

Ten Mobile Marketing Resources

Mobile marketing standards and technology are rapidly changing, so it's almost guaranteed that the mobile marketing strategies tactics of today will need to adapt over time. Moreover, more and more people are coming up with new and exciting ways to use all the capabilities with mobile — innovation is occurring on an exponential scale. You can also expect that with all this change, you'll need to keep track of new laws, best practices, and industry regulations.

The following list of ten mobile marketing resources can help you keep up with trends and advancements so you can keep your marketing on track and compliant with the entire mobile marketing ecosystem, now and in the future.

In addition to the list of organizations and players in this chapter that are on the top of their game when it comes to mobile marketing, you can also find a host of other great resources by searching on the Internet.

The Mobile Marketing Association (MMA)

The Mobile Marketing Association (MMA, at www.mmaglobal.com) is a global association with headquarters in New York that focuses on developing and promoting the mobile marketing industry, educating the market players about mobile marketing, measuring the industry, providing best practices in metrics, guiding the industry through the thought-leadership of its members, and publishing industry self-regulatory guidelines and best practices.

dotMobi

dotMobi (www.mtld.mobi) is the main source of .mobi domain names. It provides a number of other valuable mobile technology services and resources to businesses and individuals to ensure that the Web works well on mobile phones. Here are some of the services dotMobi provides:

- ✔ **Instant Mobilizer:** Instant Mobilizer is an automated tool that converts an ordinary Web site into a mobile site. The process is completely automated, so there is no programming or content management required.

- ✔ **mobiThinking:** mobiThinking is a resources Web site with insight, analysis, and opinions from the world's mobi-marketing gurus.

- ✔ **mobiForge:** mobiForge is a developer forum that offers mobile Web developer tools, resources, and support. More than 25,000 developers and designers use the site to compare notes, share tips, upload ideas, and download expertise.

- ✔ **mobiReady:** mobiReady allows you to test your mobile Web site and get a free report and in-depth analysis to determine how well your site performs on a mobile device.

- ✔ **DeviceAtlas:** DeviceAtlas is one of the largest open databases of mobile device profiles. You can use the database to detect a particular mobile phone and then adjust your marketing campaigns automatically based on the features of each device.

- ✔ **site.mobi:** site.mobi enables you to build your own mobile Web site.

The Common Short Code Administration (CSCA)

If you want to register a common short code (CSC) in the United States, you need to go through the Common Short Code Administration (CSCA, at www.usshortcodes.com). The CSCA also has a resource center with whitepapers, tutorials, videos, podcasts, best practices, and case studies. Find more about common short codes in Chapter 4.

Mobile Testing Services

If you can remember only one word before launching a mobile marketing campaign, it should be the word *test*. To test your campaigns, you can go out and buy a few thousand of the most popular devices, or you can use services like Device Anywhere (www.deviceanywhere.com) to provide instant remote access to more than 2,000 real devices across live global networks in seven countries.

Device Anywhere allows you to see how your applications, automations, and certifications are going to function so you can either discover problems or have the confidence to launch your campaigns without fear of technical glitches across multiple devices and networks.

Another great mobile testing and monitoring service is Keynote (www.key note.com). Keynote monitors and tests your messaging (SMS and MMS), mobile Web, and applications. They can do this over short periods of time or you can contract them to continuously monitor your services to ensure that they are performing properly. They can also compare the performance of your services against your competitors.

Another form of testing is test and control benchmarking to compare your customer engagement before and after you add mobile marketing to your marketing programs, or when you make changes to your mobile marketing programs. A number of research firms can help you with this, including Synovate (www.synovate.com), Insight Express (www.insightexpress. com), Dynamic Logic (www.dynamiclogic.com) and Luth Research (www. luthresearch.com).

The Wireless Telecommunications Bureau (WTB)

The Federal Communications Commission has a wireless division known as the Wireless Telecommunications Bureau (WTB). The WTB governs all the wireless telecommunications programs and policies in the U.S. including licensing, enforcement, and regulatory functions.

The WTB publishes resources on its Web site (wireless.fcc.gov) related to new laws and government policies. Be sure to check it out periodically to keep up with changes. See Chapter 3 for more on related resources.

The Federal Communication Commission puts out a great report each year called the FCC Commercial Mobile Radio Services (CMRS) Competition Report. Find it at `http://wireless.fcc.gov/index.htm?job=cmrs_reports`.

Mobile Marketer and Other Reference Sites

Mobile Marketer (`www.mobilemarketer.com`) is the leading news publication covering mobile marketing, media, and commerce. The publication covers topics that are relevant to advertisers, technology partners, publishers, agencies, senior executives, and everyone else who needs to make decisions about mobile marketing. They also include information about successfully combining mobile marketing with other marketing channels.

Mobile Marketer owns other publications and blogs, like Mobile Commerce Daily (`www.mobilecommercedaily.com`). It also delivers Webcasts, events, and other resources with the latest mobile marketing information.

In addition to Mobile Marketer, here are a number of other great blogs and sources that you can check out to find information on mobile marketing:

- Mobile advertising metrics can be found at Smaato (`http://metrics.smaato.com/`), Millennial Media Smart Report (`www.millennialmedia.com/research/`), and AdMob (which was recently purchased by Google, `http://metrics.admob.com/`).

- Marketing Charts, `www.marketingcharts.com`, a really useful Web site that puts out daily report highlights, may of which relate to mobile marketing.

- SlideShare, `www.slideshare.net`, an online community-powered resource of published presentations. Just do a search on mobile marketing to find a ton of great info.

- Pew Internet, `www.pewinternet.com`, a government-funded research program that puts out numerous reports related to consumer mobile usage throughout the year.

- Mobile Marketing Watch, `www.mobilemarketingwatch.com`, a great mobile blog.

- Mobile Industry Review, `www.smstextnews.com/`, a great mobile blog with a focus on Europe.

✔ Mobile Active, www.mobileactive.org, a community focused on applying mobile for social impact work around the world.

✔ Other mobile industry news blogs include MocoNews (www.moconews. net), Fierce Wireless (www.fiercewireless.com), Mobile Crunch (www.mobilecrunch.com), RCR Wireless News (www.rcrwireless. com), Marketing Sherpa (www.marketingsherpa.com), Google Alerts (set up a private Google alerts channel at its Web site (www.google. com/alerts), Google Images, (www.google.com/imghp, search on mobile marketing for a great way to visually see the market), YouTube (www.youtube.com, search on mobile marketing to get videos).

✔ Great industry networking resources include INmobile (www.in mobile.org), LinkedIn, (www.linkedin.com), and Jigsaw (www. jigsaw.com). These are all great resources for finding other executives active in the mobile marketing industry — just do a search on mobile marketing, mobile advertising, mobile commerce, and so on, and you can find someone to help answer your questions or to partner with.

The Direct Marketing Association (DMA)

The Direct Marketing Association (DMA) is the leading global trade association of businesses and non-profit organizations using and supporting multi-channel direct marketing tools and techniques.

Because mobile has a lot of value in the direct marketing space, the DMA works to advocate industry standards and provide cutting-edge research, education, and networking opportunities at its Web site, found at www.the-dma.org/segment/mobile.

Founded in 1917, DMA today represents companies from dozens of vertical industries in the U.S. and 48 other nations, including nearly half of the Fortune 100 companies, as well as non-profit organizations.

CTIA: The Wireless Association

CTIA: The Wireless Association (www.ctia.org) is an international non-profit membership organization that has represented the wireless communications industry since 1984.

The association is an advocate on government policy and provides consumers with a variety of choices and information regarding their wireless products and services. This includes voluntary industry guidelines, programs that promote mobile device recycling and reuse, and wireless accessibility for individuals with disabilities.

CTIA also supports important industry initiatives such as Wireless AMBER Alerts. The association also operates the industry's leading trade shows, as well as equipment testing and certification programs to ensure a high standard of quality for consumers.

Another leading carrier-centric trade association you should be aware of is the GSMA, which can be found at `www.gsmworld.com/`. Whereas the CTIA focuses on U.S. carrier relationships, GSMA has a global focus.

MyWireless.org

MyWireless.org (`www.mywireless.org`) is an advocacy organization promoting government policies that benefit wireless consumers and promote freedom of use and innovation in wireless.

MyWireless.org focuses on unfair and excessive taxes and regulations on wireless that threaten the innovation, value, and choice wireless consumers enjoy, especially for those on fixed budgets, like seniors, working families, and small businesses.

The Netsize Guide

The Netsize Guide (available at `Netsize.com/Ressources_Guide.htm`) is a comprehensive annual industry report documenting the state of the global mobile content and services market. The guide is put together using in-depth research and exclusive interviews with industry executives and opinion-makers.

The guide includes interviews with industry senior executives, survey results, and mobile data from more than 40 countries. The guide can be downloaded as an Adobe Acrobat PDF document from the Web site.

You may also want to check out Clickatel's Web site (`www.clickatel.com`). Like Netsize, Clickatel is a leading mobile aggregator. You can find a lot of useful information on international SMS deployment at its site.

Glossary

3G: The third generation wireless service that provides high data speeds, always-on data access, and greater voice capacity. The high data speeds enable full motion video, high-speed Internet access and video-conferencing, and are measured in Mbps (megabits per second). The data transmission rates range from 144 Kbps to more than 2 Mbps. 1G (the first generation network) and 2G (the second generation network of the 1990 and early 2000s) preceded 3G. The first 4G networks (fourth-generation networks) are launching in 2010.

ad impression: An advertisement impression transpires each time a consumer is exposed to an advertisement (either prepended or appended to an SMS message, on mobile Web or Web page, within a video clip, or related media).

ad unit: Any defined advertising vehicle that can appear in an ad space inside of an application. For example, a rectangular banner is considered to be a common type of ad unit.

advertisement: Any collection of text, graphics, or multimedia content displayed and accessible inside an application for the purposes of promoting a commercial brand, product, or service.

advertisement action: Any activity associated with an advertisement that enables interactivity and communication between the advertiser and the consumer. For example, common actions include clicking on a phone number to call the advertiser, a hyperlink that takes the consumer to an advertiser's mobile Web portal, or a link that adds the advertiser's contact information to the consumer's phone book.

advertiser: Individual or organization that places a paid promotion within media for the purpose of promoting commercial messages, goods, or services, also often referred to as the "buyer."

aggregator: An organization that acts as a middleman between application and content providers and mobile carriers. Provides message traffic throughput to multiple wireless operators or other aggregators; provides mobile initiative campaign oversight, administration, as well as billing services.

alerts: Notifications, typically in the form of a text or multimedia message, containing time-sensitive information (event details, weather, news, services updates) that are pushed to a mobile subscriber who has opted in to receive this information. Note: If the mobile subscriber has not opted in to receive said information, the notification is considered spam.

application: Software solutions that power the business logic for mobile marketing initiative(s), also referred to as "application platform."

application provider: An organization that offers network based applications, or downloadable applications that enable the business logic that supports mobile marketing initiatives.

asynchronous: A type of two-way communication that occurs with a time delay, allowing participants to respond at their own convenience.

banner size: The width and length dimensions (typically presented in pixels) of a banner/image advertisement placed on the mobile Web.

billing aggregator: An organization that provides billing solutions (Premium SMS, direct-to-bill, credit card, PayPal, loyalty points, credits, and so on) to off-portal mobile application solution providers.

Bluetooth: A communication protocol that enables mobile devices equipped with a special chip to send and receive information wirelessly over short ranges using the 2.4 GHz spectrum band.

call to action: A statement or instruction, typically promoted in print, Web, TV, radio, on-portal, or other forms of media (often embedded in advertising), that explains to a mobile subscriber how to respond to an opt-in for a particular promotion or mobile initiative, which is typically followed by a notice. *See also notice.*

carrier: A company that provides wireless telecommunications services.

clear and conspicuous notice: The vehicle by which descriptions, instructions, terms and conditions, and other relevant details pertinent to a specific marketing initiative, are prominently posted. (For guidance on the meaning of "clear and conspicuous" disclosure, please see Section III of the Federal Trade Commission's "Dot Com Disclosures: Information About Online Advertising" document, available at `www.ftc.gov/bcp/edu/pubs/business/ecommerce/bus41.pdf`.)

click: The act of when a mobile subscriber interacts with (highlights and clicks on) an advertisement (banner, text link) or other actionable link that has been served to his screen.

click-through rate (CTR): A way of measuring the success of an online or mobile advertising campaign. A CTR is obtained by dividing the number of users who clicked on an ad on a Web page by the number of times the ad was delivered (impressions).

click-to-call: A service that enables a mobile subscriber to initiate a voice call to a specified phone number by clicking on a link on a mobile Web site. Typically used to enhance and provide a direct response mechanism in an advertisement.

commercial messages: Text or multimedia messages that are sent to a mobile device, usually for commercial purposes.

common short code: Short numeric numbers (typically 4–6 digits) to which text messages can be sent from a mobile phone. Wireless subscribers send text messages to common short codes with relevant keywords to access a wide variety of mobile content.

Common Short Code Administration (CSCA): An organization that administers the common short code registry for a particular country/region. CSCAs are predominantly in Canada, China, the United Kingdom, and the United States. Local mobile carriers and short code aggregators are the administrators of CSC registry in other countries.

confidentiality: The treatment of information that an individual has disclosed in a relationship of trust, with the expectation that it will not be divulged without permission to others, in ways that are inconsistent with the understanding of the original disclosure.

confirmed opt-in: The process used for verifying a mobile subscriber's intention, and for gaining the subscriber's explicit agreement to participate in a mobile program or initiative.

consideration: Although the definition of consideration varies from state to state, generally, consideration means that a willing participant is required to purchase something or pay for access to be eligible to enter a game.

content aggregator: An organization that contracts with an array of content providers and redistributes licensed content.

content provider: A company that creates and offers content, for example, graphic products, ringtones, games, news, information and entertainment services, and so on.

contest: A promotional mechanism that includes a prize and a game of skill. Consideration is allowed, but there cannot be any element of chance.

cost per thousand (CPM): A metric used to price advertising banners. Sites that sell advertising may guarantee and advertise a certain number of impressions (number of times an ad banner is served and presumably seen by visitors) and then set the cost based on the guarantee, multiplied by the CPM (cost per thousand) rate.

coupon: A ticket, message, or document that can be exchanged for a financial discount on a product or service.

data collection: The process by which a marketer collects mobile subscribers' personally identifiable information.

dedicated short code: The process of running only one service on a common short code at any given time.

direct to consumer: Content and services promoted directly by the third-party provider to the phone end user. The promotion of these services does not depend upon listing in (operator) portals; the content provider is responsible for tasks such as pricing and marketing.

double opt-in: The process of confirming a mobile subscriber's wish to participate in a mobile program by requesting the subscriber to opt in twice, prior to engaging the subscriber. A requirement for premium and many other types of mobile services.

end user: A person who accesses and uses a product (for example, a user who watches a video using her mobile device).

global positioning system: A system of satellites, computers, and receivers that can determine the latitude and longitude of a given receiver (within its system) located on Earth. It pinpoints the receiver's location by calculating the time it takes for signals from different satellites (positioned at various locations) to reach the receiver.

handset: Term used in reference to a mobile phone, mobile device, or mobile terminal.

image: A photograph or graphic that may be delivered to the mobile handset as any of several low resolution image formats, including .PNG, .GIF, .JPG, and so on. Images on mobile platform may be classified as mobile content/products (wallpapers, screen savers, and so on), assets for a mobile Web site, or enabled with links to trigger an action.

impressions: A business metric for counting the number of times mobile subscribers have viewed a particular page, mobile advertisement on a mobile Internet site, or ad embedded within a text message or similar mobile medium.

interactive voice response (IVR): A phone technology that allows a computer to detect voice and touch tones using a normal phone call. The IVR system can respond with pre-recorded or dynamically generated audio to further direct callers on how to proceed. IVR systems can be used to control almost any function where the interface can be broken down into a series of simple menu choices.

interstitial ad: A page displaying an advertisement that is displayed in the middle of the MMS message, application, or mobile Web page.

interstitial image ad: An advertising image that is inserted into the middle of a complete MMS message. This image is displayed as the subscriber is viewing the complete MMS message.

keyword: A word or name used to distinguish a targeted message within a Common Short Code-enabled messaging service (for example, SMS and MMS).

landing page: A secondary page to which users are directed when they click on an ad, where they are provided additional information or a mechanism to make a purchase. Users are often driven to a landing page via an ad banner, link, or other offer-related communication.

layered notice: The provisioning of a short-, medium-, and long-form description for a program/service overview, terms and conditions, and related program details.

location information: Information that enables a mobile marketer to identify the specific location of a particular wireless device. Zip codes and area codes typically do not alone provide the specificity to qualify as location information. However, a global positioning system (GPS) is an example of a functionality that provides location information.

location-based services (LBS): A range of services that are provided to mobile subscribers based on the geographical location of their handsets within their cellular network. Handsets have to be equipped with a position-location technology such as GPS to enable the geographical-trigger of service(s) being provided. LBS include driving directions, information about certain resources or destinations within current vicinity, such as restaurants, ATMs, shopping, movie theaters, and so on. LBS may also be used to track the movements and locations of people, as is being done via parent/child monitoring services and mobile devices that target the family market.

messaging: Collectively, SMS and MMS messages sent to mobile phones/devices. This definition does not include advertisements delivered on WAP sites or advertisements delivered into games on mobile devices. *See also WAP (Wireless Application Protocol).*

MMS banner: A transparent advertising screen image that is inserted with text onto an MMS message. This image is displayed as the subscriber is viewing the complete MMS message.

mobile advertising: A form of advertising that is communicated to the consumer/target via a handset. This type of advertising is most commonly seen as a mobile Web banner (top of page), mobile Web poster (bottom of page banner), and full-screen interstitial, which appears while a requested mobile Web page is loading. Other forms of this type of advertising are SMS and MMS ads, mobile gaming ads, and mobile video ads.

mobile content: Entertainment, sports, and news information and games delivered via any wireless media type in a non-advertising format. Location, delivery, and technology of content is irrelevant and can include both on- and off-deck.

mobile marketing: Mobile marketing is a set of practices that enables organizations to communicate and engage with their audience in an interactive and relevant manner through any mobile device or network.

mobile marketing program: Any marketing or advertising program distributed via a handset. This includes, but is not limited to, a mobile messaging program, one or more advertisements delivered on WAP sites, or one or more advertisements delivered via games on mobile devices. *See also WAP (Wireless Application Protocol).*

mobile message: SMS or MMS message sent to a handset but does not include advertisements delivered on WAP sites or advertisements delivered into mobile games. *See also WAP (Wireless Application Protocol).*

mobile originated message: An SMS/MMS message sent from a mobile device.

mobile search: Executing a search via mobile Internet, application, or text messaging.

mobile subscriber: A consumer that enters into an agreement with a carrier. After it's executed, the agreement requires the carrier to provide wireless telecommunications services to the consumer.

mobile terminated message: An SMS/MMS message received by a mobile device.

mobile Web: The mobile Web is a channel for delivery of Web content, which offers and formats content to users in awareness of the mobile context. The mobile context is characterized by the nature of personal user information needs (for example, updating your blog, accessing travel information, receiving news updates), constraints of mobile phones (that is, screen size, keypad input) and special capabilities (for example, location, connection type such as 3G or WLAN).

Multimedia Messaging Service (MMS): Standard for telephony messaging systems that enable the sending of messages that include multimedia objects (images, audio, video, and rich text). May or may not include normal text.

non-personally identifiable information: Information that may correspond to a particular person, account, or profile, but is not sufficient to identify, contact, or locate the person to whom such information pertains.

notice: An easy-to-understand written description of the information and data collection, storage, maintenance, access, security, disclosure, and use policies and practices, as necessary and required, of the entity collecting and using the information and data from the mobile subscriber.

off portal: Point of sale or access on the mobile network, but outside of the carrier's walled garden (also known as portal or deck), where consumers can access and purchase information and mobile products, content, or utilities.

on portal: Point of sale or access within the carrier's walled garden (also known as portal or deck) where mobile customers can access or purchase information and mobile products, content, and utilities.

opt-in: The process where a subscriber provides explicit consent, after receiving notice from the mobile marketer.

opt-out: The process through which a subscriber revokes consent after receiving notice from the mobile marketer. An example of an opt-out process includes, but is not limited to, a subscriber replying to an SMS message with the phrase _stop_.

opt-out mechanism: A process by which a subscriber may exercise his or her right to opt-out.

page view: Unit of measure that tracks the number of times users load a particular Web or WAP site or page. _See also WAP (Wireless Application Protocol)._

payout: The net revenue provided to a marketer after mobile carrier and aggregator allocation.

penetration: The percentage of the total population that owns a mobile phone.

personalization content: Any content that serves to personalize the handset or service for the owner, often based on the owner's personal style and entertainment preferences. Includes all graphics (wallpapers, screen savers, phone themes, and so on) and certain audio (ringtones, ringbacks, alerts, greetings) and video products (video tones, and so on).

personally-identifiable information: Information that can be used to identify or contact a person, including name, address, telephone number, or e-mail address. PII also includes any other data, such as, but not limited to, anonymous identifiers, demographic or behavioral data, when such data are linked to PII and identify a person to the party holding such data. Data that are PII for one party may not constitute PII for another.

placement: The area where an advertisement is displayed within a publisher's mobile content.

post roll: The streaming of a mobile advertising clip after a mobile TV/video clip. The mobile advertisement is usually 10–15 seconds.

potential audience: The total number of unique users/devices that is reached by any site's content (pull advertising), or the number of addressable devices to which the service provider or marketer has the permission and ability to push advertising (push advertising).

premium billing: The ability to bill above standard SMS/text rates.

premium content: Content for which the provider levies a charge separately and in addition to any fixed charges made by the network operator to access that content.

premium rate: Programs or messages that result in charges above and beyond standard text messaging charges normally applied to the subscriber's wireless bill.

premium short message service (PSMS): Billing mechanism by which the mobile subscriber is charged above standard text messaging rates for mobile content and/or subscription.

pre-roll: The streaming of a mobile advertising clip prior to a mobile TV/video clip. The mobile ad is usually 10–15 seconds in length.

privacy: The quality of being secluded from the presence or view of others.

program approval: A specific program presented for approval to an aggregator and carrier for the usage and provisioning of a short code.

publisher: A company that provides space in its mobile media properties (SMS, MMS, e-mail, voice, mobile Web, applications) or facilitates the delivery of advertising via one or more mobile media paths.

pull messaging: Any content sent to the wireless subscriber upon request, shortly thereafter, on a one-time basis. For example, when a customer requests the local weather from a WAP-capable browser, the content of the response, including any related advertising, is pull messaging. *See also WAP (Wireless Application Protocol).*

push messaging: Any content sent by or on behalf of advertisers and marketers to a wireless mobile device at a time other than when the subscriber requests it. Push messaging includes audio, short message service (SMS) messages, e-mail, multimedia messaging, cell broadcast, picture messages, surveys, or any other pushed advertising or content.

random short code: A random number sequence assigned by the administration body to the company leasing the short code.

Really Simple Syndication (RSS): The model for content discovery and purchase that is provided by operators on-deck. This model is increasingly emerging off-deck, and replicates the PC Web experience for sites designed for handsets.

redemption: The number or percentage of consumers that actually take advantage of a particular offer.

redirect: Automatically sending a user to a URL different from the one clicked on. Considered a very negative tactic if used deceptively, it is approved by the engines for the purpose of sending users to content formatted appropriately for their device.

referrer: The Web page that delivered your visitor to your Web site.

relevance: The likelihood that a given Web page will be of interest or useful to a search engine user for a keyword search.

revenue share: Each party behind the mobile marketing initiative splits the revenue derived from the mobile marketing program.

revenue share percentage: The designated percentage share of revenue to which a stakeholder/rights holder is entitled based on revenue sharing agreements and so on. Applies to revenue collected from the sale and distribution of content, programming, services, and other revenue-generating property.

ringtones: The audio or "ring" a handset owner hears when a call is received. Can be a Mastertone, Polytone, or Voicetone and is either a device default or set by the handset owner when personalizing her mobile device. Ringer length is based on carrier requirements.

royalties: A fee paid by a content aggregator or service provider or mobile carrier to the content owner — for example, music publisher or movie distributor — for the right to use or repurpose the content for mobile consumption.

screen characteristic: The pixel size and color of the device screen that can display advertising. This would include text limit for SMS messaging.

screen real estate: Pertaining to the quality and size of the handset screen, the area of which advertisers can utilize for banner placements.

screen size: Amount of display space a particular handset offers. Size usually is measured in pixels, inches, or millimeters.

secondary keyword: Similar to a keyword but used for gathering metrics, repurposing existing keywords, or as a geographic locator.

service provider: A third party that performs or assists in the performance of a function or activity involving the use or disclosure of personally identifiable information or non-personally identifiable information on behalf of a mobile marketer.

shared short code: A short code that is utilized to run multiple mobile services or marketing campaigns simultaneously.

short code: Short for common short code. *See common short code.*

short code program: A marketing campaign that utilizes a short code as the primary means of opt-in.

short message service: A standard for telephony messaging systems that allow sending messages between mobile devices that consist of short messages, normally with text only content.

single opt-in: When a mobile subscriber opts in to a program via a subscriber-initiated message to a service provider as prompted by the terms of the program. For example, when a subscriber texts JOIN HEALTH ALERTS to a short code, that subscriber is opting in to the service.

smartphone: A handheld device that integrates mobile phone capabilities with the more common features of a hand-held computer or PDA. Smartphones allow users to store information, send and receive e-mail, install programs, and make and receive calls in one device.

SMiShing: A security attack in which the mobile subscriber is tricked into downloading a Trojan horse, virus, or other malware onto his handset. SMiShing is short for *SMS phishing.*

SMS message: A message sent via a Short Message Service. Messages are 160 characters max in length and most commonly referred to as a text (or txt).

standard rate: Programs or messages that result in only normal text messaging charges being applied to the mobile subscriber's wireless bill or that result in messages being deducted from a subscriber's messaging plan allowance.

subscriber information: Information that pertains to a mobile subscriber, including personally identifiable information and non-personally identifiable information. Subscriber information includes demographic information (for example, user's age, income range, and education level), or preference information (for example, user visits travel WAP sites).

subscription: Product or services initiated by a mobile subscriber to receive content on an ongoing basis, typically with periodic premium billing events. It is not a one-time usage service.

subscription period: A period of time set for a subscription program, usually no longer than one month.

subscription program: Any program in which the mobile subscriber opts-in to a program which results in the mobile subscriber passively incurring premium or standard charges over time for content delivery.

sweepstakes: A legal game that includes a prize and a game of chance. No consideration is allowed.

synchronous: A type of two-way communication with virtually no time delay, allowing participants to respond in real time.

targeting: Various criteria to make the delivery of a mobile advertisement more precise (age, gender, geographical, time of day, household income, and so on).

text ad: A static prepended or appended text attached to an advertisement.

text link: A creative use for mobile advertisements — represented by highlighted and clickable text(s) with a link embedded within the highlighted text. Usually limited to 16–24 characters.

text message: *See SMS message.*

throughput: The number of messages an application can process within a specified period of time, typically in seconds (for example, 30 messages/sec).

tracking: The ability to assess the performance of a mobile campaign.

triple opt-in: An additional opt-in that is required from the program participant after she has exceeded a defined premium fee threshold.

unsolicited messages: Commercial SMS or MMS messages sent to subscribers without seeking prior approval.

vanity short code: Common short codes that are specifically requested. It usually spells out a content provider's name, brand, an associated word or is an easy to recall number sequence; for example, DISNEY = 347639 or 88888.

viral marketing: The communication via text message or other mobile content including ringtones, games, and wallpaper by a process in which consumer A receives the original message and identifies consumer B who she believes will be interested in the message. Consumer A then initiates a process — such as inputting a phone number — by which consumer B automatically receives the same message.

visibility: How well placed your Web site is for relevant keyword searches in the search engines.

wallpaper: A piece of graphic content that is formatted to fit the screen of handsets.

WAP (Wireless Application Protocol): A format of mobile Web. Relies on WML markup language and special protocols designed for ultra-efficient transmission of content to limited devices over limited connections.

WAP billing: A billing interface that enables third-party content to be charged directly to the subscriber account (that is, not via an intermediate system such as PSMS). WAP billing is usually delivered by the carrier as a wholesale offering of the billing scheme used for on-deck content purchase. The carrier retains a percentage of all transactions as its cost of billing. *See also WAP (Wireless Application Protocol).*

WAP push: A specially encoded message which includes a link to a WAP address that allows WAP content to be pushed to the handset with minimum user intervention. *See also WAP (Wireless Application Protocol).*

wireless advertising: *See mobile advertising.*

Wireless Markup Language (WML): A markup language developed specifically for wireless applications to enable optimum usage of the limited display capabilities of a handset. Based on XML, it is used for tailoring WAP content.

wireless spam: Push messaging that is sent without confirmed opt-in.

Index

• S •

• U •

Apple & Macs

iPad For Dummies
978-0-470-58027-1

iPhone For Dummies,
4th Edition
978-0-470-87870-5

MacBook For Dummies, 3rd
Edition
978-0-470-76918-8

Mac OS X Snow Leopard For
Dummies
978-0-470-43543-4

Business

Bookkeeping For Dummies
978-0-7645-9848-7

Job Interviews
For Dummies,
3rd Edition
978-0-470-17748-8

Resumes For Dummies,
5th Edition
978-0-470-08037-5

Starting an
Online Business
For Dummies,
6th Edition
978-0-470-60210-2

Stock Investing
For Dummies,
3rd Edition
978-0-470-40114-9

Successful
Time Management
For Dummies
978-0-470-29034-7

Computer Hardware

BlackBerry
For Dummies,
4th Edition
978-0-470-60700-8

Computers For Seniors
For Dummies,
2nd Edition
978-0-470-53483-0

PCs For Dummies,
Windows
7 Edition
978-0-470-46542-4

Laptops For Dummies,
4th Edition
978-0-470-57829-2

Cooking & Entertaining

Cooking Basics
For Dummies,
3rd Edition
978-0-7645-7206-7

Wine For Dummies,
4th Edition
978-0-470-04579-4

Diet & Nutrition

Dieting For Dummies,
2nd Edition
978-0-7645-4149-0

Nutrition For Dummies,
4th Edition
978-0-471-79868-2

Weight Training
For Dummies,
3rd Edition
978-0-471-76845-6

Digital Photography

Digital SLR Cameras &
Photography For Dummies,
3rd Edition
978-0-470-46606-3

Photoshop Elements 8
For Dummies
978-0-470-52967-6

Gardening

Gardening Basics
For Dummies
978-0-470-03749-2

Organic Gardening
For Dummies,
2nd Edition
978-0-470-43067-5

Green/Sustainable

Raising Chickens
For Dummies
978-0-470-46544-8

Green Cleaning
For Dummies
978-0-470-39106-8

Health

Diabetes For Dummies,
3rd Edition
978-0-470-27086-8

Food Allergies
For Dummies
978-0-470-09584-3

Living Gluten-Free
For Dummies,
2nd Edition
978-0-470-58589-4

Hobbies/General

Chess For Dummies,
2nd Edition
978-0-7645-8404-6

Drawing
Cartoons & Comics
For Dummies
978-0-470-42683-8

Knitting For Dummies,
2nd Edition
978-0-470-28747-7

Organizing
For Dummies
978-0-7645-5300-4

Su Doku For Dummies
978-0-470-01892-7

Home Improvement

Home Maintenance
For Dummies,
2nd Edition
978-0-470-43063-7

Home Theater
For Dummies,
3rd Edition
978-0-470-41189-6

Living the
Country Lifestyle
All-in-One
For Dummies
978-0-470-43061-3

Solar Power Your Home
For Dummies,
2nd Edition
978-0-470-59678-4

Internet

Blogging For Dummies,
3rd Edition
978-0-470-61996-4

eBay For Dummies,
6th Edition
978-0-470-49741-8

Facebook For Dummies,
3rd Edition
978-0-470-87804-0

Web Marketing
For Dummies,
2nd Edition
978-0-470-37181-7

WordPress
For Dummies,
3rd Edition
978-0-470-59274-8

Language & Foreign Language

French For Dummies
978-0-7645-5193-2

Italian Phrases
For Dummies
978-0-7645-7203-6

Spanish For Dummies,
2nd Edition
978-0-470-87855-2

Spanish
For Dummies,
Audio Set
978-0-470-09585-0

Math & Science

Algebra I
For Dummies,
2nd Edition
978-0-470-55964-2

Biology For Dummies,
2nd Edition
978-0-470-59875-7

Calculus For Dummies
978-0-7645-2498-1

Chemistry For Dummies
978-0-7645-5430-8

Microsoft Office

Excel 2010 For Dummies
978-0-470-48953-6

Office 2010 All-in-One
For Dummies
978-0-470-49748-7

Office 2010 For Dummies,
Book + DVD Bundle
978-0-470-62698-6

Word 2010 For Dummies
978-0-470-48772-3

Music

Guitar For Dummies,
2nd Edition
978-0-7645-9904-0

iPod & iTunes For
Dummies, 8th Edition
978-0-470-87871-2

Piano Exercises
For Dummies
978-0-470-38765-8

Parenting & Education

Parenting For Dummies,
2nd Edition
978-0-7645-5418-6

Type 1 Diabetes
For Dummies
978-0-470-17811-9

Pets

Cats For Dummies,
2nd Edition
978-0-7645-5275-5

Dog Training For Dummies,
3rd Edition
978-0-470-60029-0

Puppies For Dummies,
2nd Edition
978-0-470-03717-1

Religion & Inspiration

The Bible For Dummies
978-0-7645-5296-0

Catholicism For Dummies
978-0-7645-5391-2

Women in the Bible
For Dummies
978-0-7645-8475-6

Self-Help & Relationship

Anger Management
For Dummies
978-0-470-03715-7

Overcoming Anxiety
For Dummies,
2nd Edition
978-0-470-57441-6

Sports

Baseball
For Dummies,
3rd Edition
978-0-7645-7537-2

Basketball
For Dummies,
2nd Edition
978-0-7645-5248-9

Golf For Dummies,
3rd Edition
978-0-471-76871-5

Web Development

Web Design
All-in-One
For Dummies
978-0-470-41796-6

Web Sites
Do-It-Yourself
For Dummies,
2nd Edition
978-0-470-56520-9

Windows 7

Windows 7
For Dummies
978-0-470-49743-2

Windows 7
For Dummies,
Book + DVD Bundle
978-0-470-52398-8

Windows 7 All-in-One
For Dummies
978-0-470-48763-1

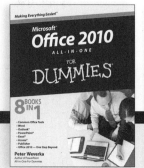

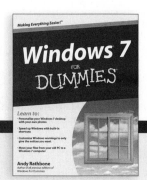

Available wherever books are sold. For more information or to order direct: U.S. customers visit www.dummies.com or call 1-877-762-297
U.K. customers visit www.wileyeurope.com or call (0) 1243 843291. Canadian customers visit www.wiley.ca or call 1-800-567-4797.

From fashion to Facebook®,
wine to Windows®, and everything in between,
Dummies makes it easier.

Visit us at Dummies.com

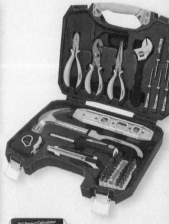